The No-Growth Society

Essays by

Mancur Olson
Kingsley Davis
John P. Holdren
Norman B. Ryder
E. J. Mishan
Kenneth E. Boulding
Richard Zeckhauser
Marc J. Roberts
Harvey Brooks
Lester Brown
Willard R. Johnson
William Alonso
Roland N. McKean
Hans H. Landsberg
Joseph L. Fisher

The No-Growth Society

Edited by MANCUR OLSON *and* HANS H. LANDSBERG

W · W · NORTON & COMPANY · INC · *New York*

Copyright © 1973 by The American Academy of Arts and Sciences
Library of Congress Cataloging in Publication Data
Main entry under title:
The No-growth society.
    Reprint of the Fall 1973 issue of Dædalus.
    1. Population—Addresses, essays, lectures.
2. Birth control—Addresses, essays, lectures.
3. Economic development—Addresses, essays, lectures.
I. Olson, Mancur, ed.   II. Landsberg, Hans J., ed.
III. Dædalus.
HB871.N63   1974   301.32   74–5267
ISBN 0–393–01111–9
ISBN 0–393–09260–7 (pbk.)
All Rights Reserved
Published simultaneously in Canada
by George J. McLeod Limited, Toronto

Printed in the United States of America

    2 3 4 5 6 7 8 9 0

CONTENTS

PREFACE

THIS book is the product of a unique collaboration between *Dædalus,* the Journal of the American Academy of Arts and Sciences, and Resources for the Future. Our thanks are due to both those institutions for recognizing the opportunity provided by this subject, and for affording us the possibility to pursue it in the way that we have. We wish to express our thanks to Joseph Fisher of Resources for the Future and to Stephen R. Graubard of *Dædalus.*

M. O.

H. H. L.

The No-Growth Society

MANCUR OLSON

Introduction

ALL SIDES AGREE that the changes in intellectual attitudes in the last decade have been unusually great.[1] A new generation of intellectuals has grown up not only with a somewhat different ideological coloration, but also, and more significantly, with a focus on a new set of problems and purposes. These new concerns and objectives, like the altered life style that goes with them, are for the most part alien both to the old left and to the old right. Though the new style of thought is more remarkable for the intensity of its social criticism than the specificity of its proposals, it does offer a few fresh proposals and a somewhat different conception of what issues are worth fighting about.

Of the policy proposals that are receiving a new emphasis, two are particularly notable, and perhaps even prototypical. Though not entirely original, they owe nothing to the long-standing and often tiresome controversies between left and right. Rather, they suggest new perceptions of reality and a changing sense of values. They are, moreover, thoroughly radical, and indeed subversive, since they attack two fundamental features of modern society: its tendency to exponential growth and its assumption of continuous progress. The two proposals are zero economic growth and zero population growth.

However original and rapidly growing the no-growth movement may be, it is tempting for those of us who are economists to dismiss opposition to economic growth as unworthy even of serious discussion; surely the desire for a more wholesome environment calls for a change in the composition of output entailing more expenditure on environmental improvement and less use of pollution-intensive goods and productive processes, rather than a ukase against growth itself. Similarly, as demographers are quick to point out, zero population growth *now*, when a particularly large proportion of the population is in the young and reproductive stages of life, would for some time require fewer than two children per family, and would before long bring about a society with the top-heavy age distribution of a Florida retirement community. Is there anything to be gained, many of us may ask, from discussing such ill-conceived proposals as these?

1

II

This essay will argue that there is much to be gained—that even those of us who cannot accept the no-growth proposals literally should take them seriously. At the very least, it is clear that if many people are mistaken, it is important that they should be told why, especially if they are from cohorts that will be around long after most of their critics have passed away. It must be obvious too that the antigrowth arguments should be studied for the clues they offer into the subtle dynamics through which perceptions and values are so rapidly changing.

Less obviously, but more importantly, there is the value of the novel insights that can be discovered amidst some of the no-growth arguments, even some of the more confused of them; there is nothing about valuable insights that makes it impossible for them to lie lost within logically inadequate or seriously unbalanced arguments. This is particularly possible when the insight results from a special experience or opportunity for observation. And some of the opponents of growth have been particularly disturbed by some of the more uncivilized features of modern life which many proponents of growth seem to endure rather too easily. The unsatisfying aspects of modern life behind many no-growth arguments are by no means found only, or perhaps even mainly, in the natural environment. As the Epilogue endeavors to show, no-growth arguments may owe more to the social and psychological stresses of modern life than to the environmental degradation that they normally invoke. Proponents of growth should try to appreciate even some of the less impressive arguments against growth, the way a wise policeman would listen to the testimony of a drunk who was the only witness to an accident.

There is another reason why some no-growth arguments should be taken seriously even by those who cannot now accept them: they will become increasingly attractive the longer modern rates of growth of population and economic growth continue. Even if nothing else about the future is known, we can be certain that current rates of population growth cannot continue on this earth indefinitely, because, to state only one of many reasons, the weight of the human bodies produced would in a few centuries exceed the mass of the earth. So the issue of zero population growth, at least for the world as a whole, is not "whether," but "when and how," and there can be no doubt that this matter needs attention now.

The long-run implications of continued economic growth are far more complicated; nonetheless, it is clear that the problems that have led to the proposal to halt economic growth will ultimately become far more difficult if current economic policies and growth rates continue. Because of the law of the conservation of mass, the weight of materials taken into the economy must equal the weight of materials released as waste minus that of any additional materials recycled. This means that if the exponential growth

in the material output of the economy continues, there must be an enormous increase either in pollution or in recycling, or in both, notwithstanding the fact that changes in the form and distribution of pollutants,
as well as in our adjustments to them, are also important. It may also be the
case that some biological processes have inherent limits which set maximum
levels for biologically degradable residuals. And, as Georgescu-Roegin has
emphasized, entropy could ultimately restrict the human race to a level of
economic activity that could be sustained by power garnered from the
current flow of energy from the sun. Kenneth Boulding has said that anyone who believes exponential growth can go on forever in a finite world is
either a madman or an economist. Even if one does not accept this view,
it is clear that no sensible person can deny the seriousness of the possibility that current rates of economic growth cannot be sustained indefinitely
because of the environmental constraint. And if environmental necessity
did not ultimately limit growth rates, a more general concern about the adverse effects of economic growth on what is loosely called the "quality of
life" still might. Thus the advantages, disadvantages, and other properties
of a society with little or no economic growth demand serious attention,
however one views demands for an immediate halt to economic growth.

III

Any meaningful inquiry into the zero-zero school of thought must first
of all be clear about what ZPG and ZEG mean. In the case of ZPG there
isn't much doubt about what people have in mind. One can raise questions
about whether all of its proponents understand that it does *not* mean an
average of two children per couple, and in general will not until a steady
state is reached. One can also wonder whether the arbitrariness of the
zero level and the practical impossibility of reaching *precisely* that level
have always been appreciated (why not Negative Population Growth,
perhaps combined with a growing level of per capita income?). But certainly it is clear what people mean by the word "population," and obvious
that the proponents of ZPG don't want it to get any larger.

The case of zero economic growth is by no means so straightforward.
Indeed, a significant part (though by no means all) of the disagreement
over ZEG is due to the fact that "economic growth" means different things
to different people. To many, especially in the ZEG camp, it means growth
in the quantity of "material" goods produced for sale in the stores—more
cars, color television sets, and the like. There is no basis on which anyone
can say that one definition is correct and another is incorrect, so this definition must be taken seriously, especially since it is so often taken for
granted outside of the economics profession. Yet it is profoundly arbitrary.
If people buy automobiles or television sets, it is presumably because they
want transportation, entertainment, or some other *service;* in other

words, people buy cars and TV sets for the same reasons they buy bus tokens and theater tickets. Thus it would be totally arbitrary to exclude services from the definition of economic output, and happily the existing statistics normally do not do so. Nor need economic growth be used to satisfy the tastes that we are accustomed to describe as less exalted. If the tastes of modern man were suddenly to change in such a way that he devoted most of the time and money he now devotes to cars and television to cathedrals and art galleries, the change would not reduce economic output or growth: it could, like other changes in the composition of output, be perfectly consistent with an increase in the rate of economic growth. It is also arbitrary to think of economic growth as involving only the goods and services obtained in the marketplace. It makes no sense to say that on the day a nation nationalizes its health services or raises taxes to spend more on schools, its economic output has fallen, and indeed the income statistics do include government expenditures on health, education, and other purposes as part of the national income or product.

Because of the arbitrariness involved in any restrictive definition of what is economic, I have, like other economists of the more single-minded sort, often defined utility or welfare from any source or of any kind as part of income or welfare. With this definition, there is an economic problem whenever people have wants which cannot be entirely satisfied with existing resources, and economic growth whenever existing wants are satisfied to a greater degree than they were in a previous period. Reality, in this view, is not divided into departments like a university; the economic dimension has no logical outer limit. If this definition is accepted, then belief in ZEG comes down simply to saying that people should have no more of anything they want—even a cleaner environment—unless they give up something of equal value that they now have; it comes down to opposing progress of any kind. Perhaps it is the habitual use of this definition in theoretical writings that partly accounts for the "progrowth" tendencies I may reveal in these pages.

Unfortunately, what the economic purists' definition gains by avoiding arbitrariness it loses, at least for general purposes, through its unfairness and unfamiliarity. It is unfair and unhelpful to consider the demand for a halt to economic growth a demand for a halt to general progress. When environmentalists advocate zero economic growth, they do not mean that we should not be better off; on the contrary, they mean that if what they understand to be economic growth were to cease, we would be better off.

Where does this leave us? With agreement, one hopes, that the debate about whether or not there should be an end to economic growth is partly a matter of definition. If this isn't understood, and it usually isn't, there is a great deal of pointless polemic. But what is the meaningful—the necessary—debate about? What definition of economic growth can both sides agree to use for the duration of the debate?

There is, happily, a fairly satisfactory and, I think, more or less generally accepted operational definition of economic growth in the national income statistics. Economic growth, from this pragmatic perspective, is simply what the Department of Commerce and comparable institutions in other countries define it to be: if real (that is, price-deflated) Net National Product per capita has gone up, there has been economic growth, and otherwise there hasn't. Admittedly, official calculations or definitions of national income can vary a little from country to country and from time to time. More seriously, there is some likelihood that if critics of economic growth (or others) show that economic growth as officially defined is a bad thing, the official definitions will, in the interest of more useful statistics, be changed in such a way as to make the critics wrong. But in the short run these problems don't matter much, so it is fortunate that many proponents and opponents of ZEG have focused on the question of whether income, as it is measured in the national accounts, should grow.

IV

If there is agreement to define growth in terms of official income statistics, then the next task is to ask whether growth in this sense is, from some specified perspective, desirable. But this depends on the composition of output—on what specific goods and services are made available in larger quantities. And this depends most notably on what goods and services people in the society want more of. If people want to spend additional income on transistor radios, then growth means essentially more such radios. If, on the other hand, people want to have additional income spent on government projects to clean up the environment, or on individual purchases of recycled products, or on the arts, growth will have a different meaning.

If we leave aside many complications that have little relevance here, the NNP can be defined as the sum of consumer, government, and business expenditures on final goods and services, including investment in new capital, minus an estimate for the depreciation of capital. It follows that an increase in real per capita income means, *approximately*, that the people of a society can do more of whatever they want to do, either as individuals acting separately or as a collectivity through government. From this it would seem that the single-minded welfare economists' definition of growth forms the basis for the design of the national accounts, and that the ZEG school is facing a stacked deck of computer cards.

Not quite. The word "approximately" covers a range of issues on which a number of people (the present writer included) are writing books. There is a need to examine changes in the availability of leisure and in the output of housewives' services, as well as a variety of other developments that are not measured in the national accounts. This is a huge and rather technical task that cannot be handled in a single essay.

But there is one aspect of the problem that is so fundamental to the no-growth debate that it must be discussed. That is what the economist calls "external diseconomies," or roughly speaking the costs firms or individuals impose on others for which they are not charged, such as noise, pollution, crime, and congestion. How do official statistics deal with an increase in output that is accompanied by an increase in external diseconomies?

This by itself is a huge question, and one which some distinguished economists have recently got wrong. In essence, the answer, which I prove elsewhere,[2] is that if the external diseconomies affect only consumers in their role as consumers or nonproducers, then they are left out or mis-construed in the national accounts, whether they directly affect "psychic" income alone or also lead to "defensive" expenditure. If, on the other hand, they raise producer costs, as when air pollution reduces the yields of the truck farmer, they are already properly accounted for in the national accounts.

Basically then, the national accounts offer a fairly comprehensive meas-ure of the extent to which the people in a society are getting what they want, but they do, most notably for present purposes, leave out external diseconomies affecting consumers. On the one hand, they are so compre-hensive that one must doubt whether many of the proponents of ZEG understand the implications of their proposals. On the other hand, the neglect and misconstrual of diseconomies that impinge upon consumers, along with other shortcomings of the accounts, mean that economic growth, as officially measured, definitely can become undesirable, and that it is logically possible that it has already become so. Thus the question of whether, given present tastes and policies and the resulting composition of output, it would be better if we had less economic growth is a valid one. It cannot be answered *a priori* and thus justifies inquiry and reflec-tion. One's answer depends in part on his value judgments about the rel-ative importance of the marketed goods and government activities that are now obtained as compared with the damage growth does to the qual-ity of life. It also depends in part on one's empirical judgments about how much current patterns of economic growth endanger the ecological system. If the composition of the Net National Product were changed to suit the wishes of the critic of growth, it would, to be sure, be far more difficult for him to find a valid reason to oppose growth. Yet, as the Epilogue shows, there are some atypical but probably significant value judgments which could consistently justify opposition to economic growth even when the composition of output is allowed to vary in response to the desires of the opponent of growth. An individual, moreover, may reasonably believe that the particular change in the composition of output that he wants will not occur, so that if he finds existing growth on balance undesirable, he sees no alternative but to oppose growth itself. Finally, even if there were no doubt that economic growth as defined in the official statistics is on balance desirable now, it certainly does not follow that this will always be true in the future.

V

Once growth has been defined, and it is clear that no-growth proposals and predictions do not necessarily result from misunderstandings about definitions or from national income accounting procedures, it is meaningful to ask what a no-growth society might be like. Quite apart from the question of the desirability of a no-growth society, or even the possibility that it may ultimately be a necessity, what properties would it have? How would its social, political, and economic systems function? What would people be like in such a society? What sort of culture or "consciousness" would be appropriate in it? If anything resembling a no-growth society is to come about, whether as a result of social choice or of ecological necessity, what will the path from a growth-oriented to a stability-oriented society be like? These are questions that are very hard to answer—so hard that they are not, in the fullest sense of the word, researchable. Yet they are questions which every advocate of a no-growth society is obliged to answer and which everyone concerned about our planet's future must concede are significant.

The importance of asking questions about a no-growth society becomes evident when we realize that life in such a society would probably have some features that are not immediately obvious. It is, for example, entirely possible that a no-growth society would be torn by conflict over distribution. If there were no growth of income and a constant population, there would be no possibility of anyone having more without someone else having less.[3] It is easy to say that people could strive for nonmaterial and culturally exalted ends, but resources devoted to such highbrow ends tend to be included, not only in the economist's definition of welfare, but for the most part in the national income statistics as well, so that if such ends could always be attained in increasing degree without the sacrifice of others it would not be a no-growth society. If whatever the poor would gain, the nonpoor would lose, could the standard of living of the poor increase? It has occasionally been suggested that the cessation of growth would bring distributional issues to a head, and that in such a charged situation there might, because of the heightened resentments of the poor, be an increased demand for redistribution of income despite the fact that it would cause a drop in the living standard of the nonpoor. The history of traditional, nongrowing societies is not by any means encouraging about the prospects for redistribution in a future steady state economy. Yet it is, perhaps, conceivable that an end to growth in a democracy would change political attitudes in such a way that redistribution of income would become possible, maybe even without introducing more divisiveness than a democratic society can endure. But what about foreign aid, or redistributions to those who don't have a vote in the matter? It strains the imagination to suppose that even the present modest provisions for foreign aid would survive the passage of no-growth proposals.

It is also possible that a no-growth society would require a different psychology or morality. Diverse observers have noted that in traditional societies most people take it for granted that what one gains, others must lose. Though underdeveloped societies are criticized for having this zero-sum attitude, it must be recognized as appropriate to their pregrowth situation, and would be natural also in any future no-growth world. Similarly, in a world where economic growth was ruled out, there would be no need for the pioneering spirit, for there would be no frontiers. Not only would geographical frontiers have been extended about as far as possible, as they already have been, but the frontiers of science and innovation would also be closed off. A society that continues to innovate will not be a no-growth society. Frederick Jackson Turner spoke of the frontier of the American West as a "safety valve" which could draw the energies of the discontented and thereby bring social peace. Since then scholars have rightly pointed out that the prairies were not the only frontier; there were urban and technological frontiers as well. But there would be few if any frontiers or safety valves in a no-growth society. Where then should the discontented and the aggressive and the venturesome go? There would be few, if any, places, for them to go, and so it seems not unreasonable to assume that a culture or consciousness would and should emerge which would minimize the number of people with dynamic and creative personality characteristics.

VI

Another characteristic that no-growth societies have is an extraordinary degree of governmental or other collective action. This would be true whether growth ceased through ZEG and ZPG policies now or because growth had someday proceeded to the point where it was obviously and immediately impossible to grow any further. Whether it became so by choice or by necessity, a no-growth society would presumably have stringent regulations and wide-ranging prohibitions against pollution and other external diseconomies, and thus more government control over individual behavior than is now customary in the Western democracies. Even if effluent fees or other taxes were the only means used to internalize external diseconomies, the scope of government and the degree of its control over citizens would still increase because of the number of such taxes that would be required, the need to change tax levels with changing conditions, and the fact that, since we lack a simple and objective way of calculating the optimal levels for such taxes, administrators or politicians would have to exercise arbitary authority in setting them. It happens that democratic society—and indeed what we call modern civilized society—has emerged in places and periods in which society and politics were pluralistic and private enterprise the major form of economic activity. The *laissez-faire* ideologists may very well be wrong in saying that there was a causal connection, but no one has the evidence to prove them so. Thus there is reason to ask how well democracy as we know it would fare amidst the ubiquitous controls that would be involved either in stopping growth now or in adjusting ultimately to the inescapable environmental constraint. An examination of the attitudes and "consciousness" of the undergraduate generation suggests that there is more resistance to bureaucracies and "establishments," and perhaps more fondness for decentralization and for letting each individual do his own thing than was evident in the fifties. How would the New Left resistance to hierarchy mate with the centralized regulation a halt to economic growth would involve?

Zero population growth might in some cases also involve hazardous or offensive forms of control. If, for example, the desire or need to limit births is sufficiently intense, mightn't there be a special concern to limit the procreative possibilities of the less desirable or fortunate elements of the population? Why not tell the least fit that they are really sweet, but that we don't want anyone like them around in the next generation? How would traditional morality and egalitarian values stand up in such a situation? It might seem that inoffensive monetary incentives would be sufficient to limit the planet's population to an appropriate level, but how can one tax parents who have too many children without damaging the children? The point is that it is possible that the number of births occurring under free and decentralized decision making by families, even in a situation in which birth control prevented all unwanted births, would not give us a world with zero population growth. In that case, new solutions or controls, possibly very offensive to us, might be demanded or required. This is at any event another matter that deserves thought, not only because zero population growth is widely demanded today, but also because it is obvious that if the human race is to survive it will be needed someday.

When we focus on the longer-run possibility that growth will be limited by immediate physical necessity, we can see also the danger that the world of the environmentalist's vision (or nightmare) will be far more interdependent and vulnerable than the one we live in. If the world's population should double or, as is entirely plausible, reach a level of 10 or 15 billion, it would probably be much more dependent upon compact urban services than we are today. What, in such a world, would be the effect of another East Coast blackout, a new variety of wheat rust, or a new contagious disease? What would be the vulnerability to sabotage of a world in which growth of income and population had proceeded to the point where the environmental constraint was the overriding one? If nuclear fission had to be used to obtain energy and thus created vast residues of fissionable waste material that must be *permanently* stored, there would be a need for a responsible organization that would last longer than any government the world has yet seen. We cannot be sure about any aspect of such a world, but it might very well have vulnerabilities and short-comings that have no parallel in present-day societies, and which we may need to think through before too long.

VII

We also need to ask how a society could maintain a constant level of income, assuming it wanted to do so. It is by no means easy to specify acceptable policies that would halt growth at whatever level of income was thought best and then maintain that level. Monetary and fiscal policy could, of course, be used to maintain a more or less constant level of aggregate demand, and thereby to prevent growth, but the firms in the economy would still have some incentive to innovate, so that as time went on less resources would be needed to produce the target level of output and unemployment would continually increase. In order to avoid an ever-increasing level of unemployment, some set of policies or social arrangements would be needed to insure that individual firms had incentives to behave in a way that would prevent growth and at the same time insure that those who wanted jobs could get them. Firms would also have to develop incentives, whether of a monetary or an extra-monetary kind, that would induce employees to provide the appropriate level of output at a cost the firm could afford.

Under the present system, each firm knows that if it can find a more economical way of producing its output, or change its product in such a way that consumers will be willing to buy it even at a higher price, it will be better off. Firms in turn try to offer their employees incentives to be more productive. It might seem that a satisfactory no-growth world could be obtained simply by ending all connection between reward and productivity so that firms and employees would get the same reward no matter how much or what quality they produced. But in fact this wouldn't work, for people would then have no incentive to produce the ideal level of income, if indeed they would produce anything at all.

At this point the critic may say that the answer is obvious: firms must be rewarded for producing the ideal, fixed level of output (taking into account some *post hoc* adjustment for weather and other productive factors beyond each firm's control), but given no reward for producing either more or less than that. This method would indeed make it possible to attain a more or less constant level of output, but it has a serious short-coming that no opponent of economic growth, to my knowledge, has dealt with: it would fix the *composition* as well as the level of output. Consumers' needs and tastes change over time: in a cold year they need more fuel, in a hot one more refrigeration, in one decade they will want cars with fins, in another bicycles. In the world we live in, an extra demand for fuel or bicycles normally raises the price of these products just as the corresponding drop in demand for some other products normally causes their relative prices to fall. These changes in relative price induce firms producing the goods which are in greater demand to produce more and those producing the goods which are in less demand to produce less or even to close down or shift into another line of production. Workers who seek higher wages and owners of other factors of production who seek higher returns face incentives which bring about a shift from the production of goods that are in less demand to those that are in more demand.* In a no-growth world, however, in which firms were not generally given greater rewards for commanding higher prices or for producing and selling more than in the past, there would be no tendency for resources to be reallocated in response to changes in needs and tastes. It might well be possible to design a system that would somehow acquire information on changes in the pattern of consumer demands and then induce firms and resources to shift in ways appropriate to the changing composition of demand, without inducing growth. But it wouldn't be easy.

It won't do simply to say that "planning" is the answer. The planning systems the world has had experience with have been designed to induce growth and, to the extent to which they work ideally, they provide the same maximum output that perfectly competitive markets would. The kind of planning or market system that would be needed is one in which agencies or firms were punished for overproduction as well as for underproduction, and in which the quotas for each enterprise somehow kept changing in response to consumer demands. Presumably such a system could be designed; perhaps it could even be made to work. But a proposal to stop economic growth cannot be taken seriously and literally unless it is accompanied by a plan for such a system.

VIII

If the questions asked here have meaning, surely any adequate effort to answer them would have a considerable impact on our understanding of some of the most important emerging features of modern life. A no-growth society poses in an extreme form problems that already exist to

---

* This analysis of the existing arrangement, it may be well to add, does not depend upon the unreal assumptions of the economist's model of pure competition; useful, though not optimal, reallocations in response to shifts in demand would tend to occur even in a world where all firms had monopoly power; and there is massive empirical evidence that the existing economies in the developed nations of the West do reallocate resources in response to changes in demand.

some degree in all economically developed nations, but which have failed to attract the curiosity of most researchers or to fit into the controversies that until recently have divided left from right, religious from secular. As the Epilogue will attempt to show, a careful examination of the no-growth proposals helps to reveal a number of the most fundamental failings and fears of modern life, some of which have no important relationship to the natural environment. If the arguments in the Epilogue are correct, however, it is also clear that many opponents of growth have not thought through the implications of their own proposals.

But neither have the supporters of growth grasped the ultimate consequences of their position. Surely any extended study of this issue will remind growthmen of the obvious possibility that modern rates of growth cannot continue forever in a world with finite resources and capacity to absorb wastes. Whether or not Boulding was right in saying that it is a sign of madness to suppose that exponential growth can go on forever in a finite world, it is unquestionably true that current world rates of population growth cannot continue very much longer, and that the economy can continue to grow at its current speed only if there are unending advances in recycling and, in addition, since recycling is out of the question for materials from which energy is drawn, the development of clean and continuously expandable forms of energy. Only a transcendent faith in the idea of permanent progress could persuade anyone that recycling and the development of sufficient nonpolluting energy sources will always advance fast enough to prevent an increase in residuals in an economy with permanent rapid growth.

Though it is utopian to assume that the output of clean energy and recycling can increase forever without increasing costs, it is also unrealistic to suppose that technological advance in energy conversion must at some point permanently cease, or that the potential for recycling must necessarily reach a permanent limit short of 100 percent (in fact, complete recycling would be consistent with continuous growth, albeit at a cost of ever-expanding inventories). As long as man and society retain a capacity to innovate, a more plausible possibility is that there will be at least occasional increases in output, however severe the environmental constraint becomes, because of advances in energy conversion, increases in recycling, or improvements in the efficiency with which nonpolluting services are provided. In other words, there is an assumption about the future that falls in between the extreme visions of the growthman who sees a world in which continuous breakthroughs in recycling permit high rates of exponential growth to go on forever, and the antigrowthman who sees a world in which the environmental constraint prevents emission of more pollutants and yet man is permanently unable to think of any ways to increase the ratio of output to pollutants. This in-between assumption ultimately suggests, of course, a world of slower, presumably far slower, rates of growth of income.

This probability—that growth will slow down for environmental reasons—and the extra-environmental grounds for opposition to economic
growth set forth later in this issue remind us that a few of the proponents
of no-growth might speak differently if they expected to be believed. Perhaps some of the advocates of the zero-zero slogans don't mean to be
taken quite literally. Conceivably, they are pushing their arguments to the
zero extreme and relying exclusively on the nearly universal desire for a
habitable natural environment in the hope that in this way they may attain
a marginal change in the direction they favor. Indeed we must, notwithstanding any distaste we may have for hyperbolic argument, wonder
whether it is all that unfortunate that the zero-zero proposals have taken
such an extreme and slogan-oriented form. Perhaps it takes new slogans
and even a new generation to tell us that, as growing incomes bring increasingly ambiguous luxuries associated with an imperiled environment,
strident social protest, and unabated examples of personal despair, it is
time to do some new thinking.

REFERENCES

1. The author particularly thanks Jack Cumberland, Joseph L. Fisher, Hans Landsberg, Talbot Page, and Fred Singer for contributing ideas to this draft, and the
   National Science Foundation and Resources for the Future for support of his writing
   and research. He alone is responsible for the views expressed.

2. See my "National Income and the Level of Welfare," *Proceedings of the American
   Statistical Association,* 1971, pp. 198-207, and a forthcoming book on the subject.

3. Incomes could, of course, increase over the life cycle with old or middle-aged people
   receiving a large part of the total than young people. I am thankful to Martin
   McGuire for calling this point to my attention.

KINGSLEY DAVIS

Zero Population Growth: The Goal and the Means

WHEN IN 1967 "zero population growth" was first mentioned as a goal of population policy,[1] it was not itself defended or discussed; only the means of reaching it were considered. Since that time, with ZPG becoming the name for a movement, a lively debate has ensued over the goal as well as the means. In what follows, I shall first consider some of the main developments in the debate, then search for what lies behind the debate, hoping to illuminate the nature of population policy.

I

The question at issue when ZPG was introduced was whether the population policies then current were effective or ineffective. To answer that question, one obviously needed to know what goal the policies were trying to achieve. A search of the literature of the population movement revealed no clear statement of the goal. "Population control" could not be considered a goal, because it did not specify "control to what end." However, since population control was frequently justified in the policy literature by graphic accounts of the dangers of population increase—dangers seldom specific for given rates of increase but ascribed to any continued exponential rate—I drew the conclusion that the implied aim was no population growth at all. I therefore undertook to determine whether the population measures being pursued or advocated in official circles were likely to achieve ZPG. Although a prominent fellow demographer described me as having "vigorously endorsed" the goal of ZPG,[2] the question was simply, *if* ZPG is the goal, will the measures being adopted succeed or fail? The answer was independent of whether I or anyone else actually held that aim, but, as subsequent debate proved, ZPG or even NPG (negative population growth) was indeed a common aspiration among people concerned about population growth.

My conclusion was that measures then current did not provide population control for any collective purpose, least of all for population stability. Limited to "family planning" and hence to couple control, about all they

15

could accomplish would be to help countries approaching a modern condition reach *an industrial level* of fertility, a level they would soon reach anyway. An industrial level, however, is far above ZPG. Between 1960 and 1970, for example, the fifty industrial countries of the world increased their population by 14 percent, a rate that would double it in less than fifty years. As a class these countries had a more rapid increase after World War II than the underdeveloped countries ever had before that.

For ZPG as a goal, it was unfortunate that the concept first arose in the context of a critique of family planning as the exclusive approach to population policy. The powerful interests vested in this approach reacted by attacking not only the idea that other means than family planning might be necessary, but also the goal of ZPG itself. Spokesmen for the population programs of foundations, international agencies, and government bureaus— all committed to the assumption that the population problem is due to unwanted births (unwanted, that is, by the people who have them) and that therefore the solution is to provide massive contraceptive services—felt that their leadership had been challenged. Accused either of not pursuing a goal that many of their ardent supporters had assumed they were pursuing and which their own arguments seemed to imply, or else of using means incapable of reaching that goal, they had either to deny the goal or to affirm the adequacy of the means. Actually, they began by doing both but later yielded ground, especially with reference to the goal. Let us examine the arguments and counterarguments.

ZPG as a Goal

To declare that ZPG was not the goal of existing population programs was dangerous. Yet soon after the ZPG concept appeared, three leaders of the population movement not only made this declaration but went further to say that the family-planning program, at least in the United States, is not for population limitation at all. "The federal program [of family planning] has been advanced," they said, "not for population control, but to improve health and reduce the impact of poverty and deprivation."[3] Others were less hasty. They did not directly repudiate ZPG as a goal but painted its advocates as naive, unrealistic, or authoritarian. For instance, the uncertain *timing* of ZPG was used as a basis for criticism. By interpreting ZPG advocates as demanding ZPG immediately, critics could accuse them of being enthusiasts ignorant of the science of demography who were unwittingly threatening Americans with a child embargo. On the other hand, by interpreting them as wanting ZPG only sometime in the indefinite future, critics could say that they were merely recommending the inevitable. These points are worth examining.

Immediate ZPG would certainly require a drastic reduction in fertility. Since existing societies have had more births than deaths, their age structure is younger and more favorable to future births than it would otherwise be. To compensate for this fact, if instant ZPG were to be attained, each current young woman would have to reduce her fertility, on the average, below her own replacement. This prospect was described in frightening terms:

Dr. Frejka warns that to achieve zero population growth immediately, it would be necessary for each family to limit itself to one child only for the next 20 years or so, with two-child families not permissible until after the year 2000.[4]

The U.S. Population Commission said that the sudden drop in reproduction would create a regrettable cyclical fluctuation in fertility.[5]

This [ZPG] would not be possible without considerable disruption to society. . . . In a few years, there would be only half as many children as there are now. This would have disruptive effects on the school system and subsequently on the number of persons entering the labor force. . . . The overall effect would be that of an accordion-like continuous expansion and contraction.

Actually, Frejka found that, with migration excluded, a U.S. population fixed from 1965 would require age-specific birth rates during the next twenty years which, if experienced by each woman during her reproductive life, would yield an average of 1.2 children per woman. However, not all women bear children. Among white women aged 35 to 39 in the U.S. in 1960, some 15.5 percent had either never married or never borne a child. So, in Frejka's fixed population, each woman who *did* have a child could bear, on the average, 1.4 children—a mean that could be reached if 60 percent had one child and 40 percent had two. Put in these terms, instantaneous ZPG does not sound so frightening. As for "disruption to society," the resulting fluctuation in school-age children would be less than that actually experienced in the past. During the twenty years from 1950 to 1970 the number of children aged 5 to 19 in continental United States shot up from 34.9 million to 59.5 million, a 70 percent increase. In Frejka's hypothetical calculations of ZPG beginning in 1965, the most drastic change in children of this age would be that of the twenty-five-year period from 1965 to 1990, when the number would fall by 41.5 percent.

In trying to discredit immediate ZPG, the Population Establishment was arguing against a straw man, because ZPGers, scarcely so literal-minded, would have been happy to see ZPG achieved within their lifetime. But not content with hitting them over the head for presumably wanting ZPG instantaneously, the Establishment buffeted them for the opposite as well, for supposedly wanting it in the indefinite future. "Zero growth," said Notestein, "is . . . not simply a desirable goal; it is the only possibility in a finite world. One cannot object to people who favor the inevitable."[6] The answer to this was given by Judith Blake:[7]

By this reasoning, the human effort to control the time and manner of all sorts of inevitabilities—the effort expended on postponing death, maintaining houses, saving money—is all pointless. The spokesmen for ZPG do not argue that a stationary world population will never come about without ZPG policy, but rather that, without directed effort, zero growth will occur only after human numbers have greatly increased over present levels, and perhaps then by the mechanism of high mortality instead of fertility control.

A related question was whether ZPG advocates had in mind an "actual" or a "stable" zero rate. In demography the term "stable population" refers to the population that would eventually result if age-specific fertility and mortality rates remained constant long enough (usually three or more generations) to produce a fixed age structure, at which time the birth and death rates (called "stable" or "intrinsic" rates) would be different from the current ones. The "stable population" is an abstract concept used, among other things, to measure the import of current age-specific rates independently of the current age structure. Thus a population that is actually growing at the moment is sometimes described as "failing to replace itself," because *with the age structure that would eventually be produced by the current age-specific birth and death rates,* the population *would* decline. This usage, however, is misleading; the stable population concept has no relevance to the actual future for it rests on the assumption of constant age-specific rates, a situation which never comes about in reality. It is useful to calculate the attributes of a nongrowing stable population (called a "stationary population") together with the demographic changes required to reach it in given lengths of time, and this has often been done,[8] but this is different from calculating an actual nongrowing population and the age-specific birth and death rates required to reach it in some given length of time from the present. In any case, the question of which kind of ZPG they meant was at first confusing to those ZPGers who were not acquainted with technical demography. Soon, however, they overcame that hurdle.

Apart from cavils about the timing of ZPG, there were two objections to a nongrowing population regardless of when it came about: that it would interfere with economic development and that it would produce a high proportion of aged persons. These arguments, both old, are worth examining.

The economic argument holds that some population growth is a good thing because it provides economies of scale, promotes a bullish investment psychology, and provides openings for the young; but, as the economist Stephen Enke pointed out, "the more slowly population grows the more capital can be accumulated per member of the labor force," and "only those who own something valuable and scarce can count on larger real incomes as a result of population growth."[9] His simulation models for the United States show that a net reproduction rate of unity from 1975 on would yield a higher per capita GNP than either of two higher growth trends.

One has only to look at history to see that slow population growth does not mean economic stagnation nor does fast growth mean prosperity. Between 1890 and 1940 Ireland's population *declined* by 16 percent, yet during that period, according to figures compiled by Colin Clark,[10] the real product per manhour rose by 99 percent, whereas in Great Britain, whose population grew by 42 percent, the improvement in product was only 62 percent. France, whose population rose more slowly than Britain's, had a rate of rise in real product nearly three times that of Britain. Sweden had such a low fertility that its cohorts born after 1885 were not replacing themselves,[11] yet after that time it had what is probably the most rapid economic rise and is now the richest country in Europe. If human productivity is a function of resources and technology, and if resources are limited (as they indubitably are), the way to get a higher product—once population has gone beyond the point of providing adequate specialization—is to advance technology and decrease population. As Enke points out, the entire world is involved in a system of specialization and trade; there is no economy of scale to be gained from further population increase. In comparison to India, Sweden is not impoverished by virtue of the fact that India's population is 68 times greater and its average density 9 times greater. Probably Japan's technology is now the equal of Sweden's, so, if Sweden's per capita income is more than twice that of Japan, as the United Nations data for 1970 show, one reason may be that Japan's population density is sixteen times as great.

The other objection—that ZPG means an aged population—was voiced as follows in 1968:

A stationary population with an expectation of life of 70 years has as many people over 60 as under 15. . . . A society with such an age structure is not likely to be receptive to change, and indeed would have a strong tendency towards nostalgia and conservatism.[12]

Actually, there are three questions involved here. First, since "life expectancy" is an average, can the age distribution vary independently of that average? The answer is yes, because it is affected by the skew in deaths by age. Suppose, for example, that in a stationary population everybody died at exactly age 70. The proportion of the population under age 15 would be 21.4 percent, and over 60, 14.3 percent. Even assuming a probable distribution of deaths by age, would the age structure of a ZPG population be highly abnormal? Table 1 shows the age structure of the U.S. population under two assumptions—that ZPG starts immediately, and that it is reached sometime between 1995 and 2000. In either case, not only is the proportion aged 65+ considerably less than that found in West Berlin now and close to that found in Sweden, but the distribution is especially favorable to economic production because of the high proportion of people in the productive ages. Third, would the age distribution of a ZPG population "disrupt the normal workings of the society"? Again no. There seems to be no correlation between the age structure and political outlook. The age distribution of the USSR is very similar to that of the USA; socialist Sweden has an older age structure than Falangist Spain. Some of the wildest political schemes ever known have been advocated by lobbies of the elderly and some of the most atavistic movements (such as the Nazi movement in Germany) were manned by dogmatic youth. As Table 1 shows, the South African white population is much younger than that of Sweden or West Berlin, but we do not associate South Africans with progressive liberalism.

Table 1

The Age Structure of ZPG and Actual Populations
(Females Only)

Population		Percentage in Each Age Group		
	Date	0–19	20–64	65+
U. S. ZPG (*Starting in 1965*)[13]				
	1990	20.2	64.4	15.5
	2015	23.2	57.3	19.5
	2040	30.5	59.7	19.6
	2065	23.3	61.3	15.7
Transitional (*ZPG U. S. Reached by 1995–2000*)[14]				
	1980	30.9	75.2	12.0
	2000	23.0	63.2	13.9
Actual Populations[15]				
U. S. White	1970	35.2	53.1	11.7
Sweden	1970	26.9	57.9	15.2
West Berlin	1969	17.1	57.3	25.6
S. Africa White	1965	40.0	52.4	7.6
Honduras	1970	57.6	40.0	2.5

The big difference in age structure is not between one industrial country and another, with or without ZPG, but between industrial and nonindustrial countries. This is demonstrated in Table 1 by comparing Honduras with the other countries. In Honduras only 40 percent of the population is in the productive ages compared to 58 percent in Sweden and 57 percent in West Berlin. ZPG would place the highest proportion in the productive ages.

What has happened, then, to ZPG as a goal? In the end the Establishment, in the form of the U.S. Population Commission, professed ZPG as its goal, but without using the term or endorsing its immediate attainment:

Recognizing that our population cannot grow indefinitely, and appreciating the advantages of moving now toward the stabilization of population, the Commission recommends that the nation welcome and plan for a stabilized population.[16]

This was a remarkable victory for the ZPG movement in six years, but of course it did not mean benign consensus. Much goal conflict remained hidden, to emerge only when means were considered.

The Means to ZPG

If ZPG were the supreme aim, *any* means would be justified. By common consent, however, raising the death rate is excluded; also, reducing immigration is played down. This leaves fertility reduction as the main avenue. (In the past, had population growth been feared above all else, deaths would never have been reduced below births.) If then, the means is birth limitation, why not take measures to reduce births? Why not simply limit each couple to two births, with sufficient penalties to discourage three?

The response of the Population Establishment is that this would be "compulsion." Although plenty of compulsion has been used to lower death rates, it is not to be used to lower birth rates. On the contrary, the right of couples to have the number of children they want has been declared by policy leaders to be "a fundamental human right."[17]

What lies behind this response? When the aim is game protection, the conservationists do not proclaim each hunter's right to shoot as much game as he wants. When the goal is clean air, the authorities do not assert each person's right to put as many pollutants into the air as he pleases. Why, to achieve birth limitation, is it efficient to give each woman the right to have as many children as she wants?

The answer is that the problem is wrongly diagnosed—like attributing anemia to excess blood and prescribing blood-letting as the remedy. The assumption behind the "freedom-to-choose" emphasis in population policy is that the population problem is a function of unwanted births and therefore, if women have the means to limit births, the population problem will be solved.

But why make such a dubious assumption? The key lies in our unstated background. Our mores were formed when societies could survive only with a birth rate thrice that required by a modern death rate. Built into the social order, therefore, are values, norms, and incentives that motivate people to bear and rear children. These cultural and institutional inheritances form the premises of our thinking. Respected leaders of society are not about to disavow them, nor is the general public likely to do so. Accordingly, what is strategically required, if one wants to be a population policy leader, is a formula that appears to reduce reproduction without offending the mores that support it. The formula is to interpret the social problem as an individual one and the solution as a technological matter. Thus "fertility control" becomes control by the woman, not by society; and the means becomes a medically approved contraceptive. By this formula, population policy embraces research on the physiology of reproduction (to find better contraceptives), diffusion of contraceptive services (to get the devices to the women), and propaganda about the use of contraceptives and about the right of each woman to have as many children as she wants. The only traditional attitude affronted by this formula is the belief that

God forbids birth control, as indeed he did in most religions, for good reasons. This belief, however, is not directly attacked by the family planners, but rather flanked by an ingenious concretizing of God's will. Each woman, say the family planners, should be free to choose a method "consonant with her religious beliefs." Since God did not specifically forbid the contraceptive pill or the plastic IUD, these should be acceptable; but if they are not, some other method must be.

The respectability of this approach to population policy is reinforced not only by its appeal to health and medical authority and its link with science (reproductive physiology) but also by its preoccupation with parenthood and children. "Family planning" and "planned parenthood" implicitly feature the family. Nearly every family-planning booklet depicts on the front two radiantly happy offspring, and on the inside implies that every woman's main concern is her children, a concern that alone justifies her limiting their number.

Any other means than family planning tends to be characterized as "unacceptable" and/or "compulsory." The Committee on Population of the Academy, for example, declared in *Science* (February 1968) that "Many of his [Davis'] arguments are unlikely to be approved. . . ." This objection is unassailable. Virtually all proposed social changes are initially unacceptable, or else they would not need to be proposed. If ZPG is the goal, "existing values" are not a help but a hindrance, for they are pronatalist in character, and measures entirely conforming to them will not bring ZPG. For that reason measures to stop population growth cannot be found which can be guaranteed in advance to be acceptable. They have to *win* acceptance, and this can be done only if the benefits of ZPG are demonstrated and the encouragements to reproduction in the old system exposed. In that case the public will accept modification of the received incentive system, although it will never tolerate throwing away the entire institutional order insofar as family and children are concerned. In calling for approval in advance, the family-planning movement confuses the issues. The question of whether a policy, *if adopted,* would succeed is different from the question of whether, *if proposed,* it would be accepted. Clarity requires that the two questions be kept analytically distinct; in practice, demonstration that a policy would or would not be effective may influence its acceptability. My judgment is that, in the absence of clear analysis, family planning was acceptable as population policy precisely because it conformed to social sentiments and had not been challenged.

Ironically, the "voluntarism" so much emphasized by the Population Establishment,[18] if consistently advocated, would be unacceptable. A regime of complete freedom in reproduction would be anarchy. It would dissolve social mechanisms ensuring parental responsibility, eliminate rules against incest, rape, child abuse, and desertion, and wipe out obligations based on kinship and marriage, thus making a mockery of "family planning." The tenet of the family-planning approach—"to extend to women and men the freedom and means to determine the number of children. . . ."[19]—is not a prescription for any social control, much less population control.

Interestingly, the anarchy of pure voluntarism·has recently tricked the Population Establishment into its most dangerous brushes with unacceptability. Pressed by critics that its stand against abortion and its preoccupation with married women violated its principle of freedom, the movement switched to an endorsement of legal abortion and teenage contraception. With respect to abortion, a majority of the Population Commission affirmed

that women should be free to determine their own fertility, [and] that the matter of abortion should be left to the conscience of the individual concerned, in consultation with her physician. . . .[20]

The only authority figure mentioned is the physician; the woman's husband is ignored. This undermining of marriage is doubtless one factor in the unexpected strength of the public reaction against liberalized abortion laws. With respect to unmarried teenage girls, the Commission recommended that they receive contraceptive information and services (and presumably abortion) without regard to parents.

It is paradoxical to expect to attain social control over one thing by abandoning it with respect to all else. Abolishing all previous social controls over sexual behavior, abortion, and pregnancy without putting any new ones in their place will not give the nation or the world population control. It may reduce the birth rate through venereal disease and sterility, or through distaste for pregnancy, or through increased mortality by violence and neglect, but it will not, except by accident, lead to a socially desirable population target. Although the public may be bamboozled for a while, in the long run it is likely to conclude that, if anarchy is the price of population control, the price is too high.

A social goal is not attained by making the members of a society irresponsible, but by making them responsible. The fact that in many ways the old social order encouraged reproduction does not make social order per se the enemy. The European social order exercised considerable restraint on childbearing, but it did so by affirming rather than denying obligations. If a new order capable of providing population control under conditions of low mortality is to be forged, it will come in no other way than by social regulation of rights and obligations with respect to childbearing.

II

If it is true that the Population Establishment has espoused ZPG but has clung to family planning (broadened to include abortion, sterilization, and teenage services and sex education) as the means for reaching it, there are two questions: Have demographic events proved the Establishment to be right? If they have not, what additional means may be necessary?

Recent Population Trends and Population Policy

In the last few years spectacular declines in birth rates have given heart to the leaders of the population movement. In the United States, for example, the births per 1000 women aged 15 to 44 reached a peak in 1957, then fell until, in 1972, the rate was only 60 percent of the 1957 figure. This has led to widespread elation that our fertility has reached, or fallen slightly below, a replacement rate. "Couples are now averaging 2.04 children per family," said the Population Crisis Committee in March, 1973, "which is below the 2.11 child replacement rate." However, the Committee knew that this meant zero growth only in the "stable population," not in the actual, sense, for it added: "If this rate continues for some 70 years, U.S. population would stabilize or even decline slightly." There is no likelihood whatever that a fertility rate found in one year will continue for 70 years, and there is no way to find out what it will in fact do. To know how many children "couples are averaging," one would have to follow couples to the end of their reproductive period, which would take too long. A way to get some indication in advance is to ask young people how many children they intend to have. This was done most recently by the Census Bureau in June, 1972. The expectations, the lowest on record, led the Bureau to the conclusion that women 18 to 24 years old in 1972 might "complete their childbearing with an average of about 2.1 births per woman [which] approximates 'replacement level fertility.' "[21] The only trouble is that since expectations have changed in the past, they may change in the future. Indeed, the current cohorts of young people may have been unduly influenced by the nihilistic mood of the period from 1964 to 1972; the new ones coming along may be more favorable to the family. This possibility is suggested by actual fertility trends.

In the decline of fertility in the United States after 1957, the lowest *monthly* rate was reached in July of 1972, when the seasonally adjusted general fertility rate (births per 1000 women aged 15 to 44) was 68.2. In the nine later months for which data are available, the rate has been slightly higher. Such a change of direction is what one would expect, because in all industrial countries the birth rate since 1920 has exhibited a strongly cyclical character. Also, in the twenty-one of these countries for which recent data are available, the trend in the crude birth rate between 1970 and 1971 was, on the average, upward.

The drop in the American birth rate was particularly sharp between 1970 and 1972, when the new state abortion laws came into effect. Liberal abortion laws permit women who become pregnant through carelessness, unwillingness to offend a boyfriend, or desire to get married an opportunity to remedy their mistake. This effect is limited, however, and of itself cannot keep exerting a downward pressure on fertility. The main effect of the new abortion laws was probably to postpone by two or three years the cyclical rise in American fertility.

Not only are industrial countries at present far from a zero rate of natural increase, but they are receiving large numbers of migrants from the less developed countries. Thus in the United States in 1972, when the birth rate was at its lowest ebb, the population increased by 1,628,000 people, of whom 1,290,000 derived from more births than deaths and 338,000 from net migration. As long as the less developed two-thirds of the world continues to increase its population at a rapid rate, the pressure on the developed third to receive massive immigration will be enormous. Are official policies likely to bring ZPG in the latter countries?

The spectacular decline of birth rates in many less developed countries is frequently taken as evidence of successful population policy. For example, in eight countries (Ceylon, Chile, Costa Rica, Egypt, Fiji, Jamaica, Taiwan, and Trinidad), between 1960 and 1970, the crude birth rate fell, on the average, by 27 percent. However, as is usual in citing such statistics, these countries were selected because in general their data are reasonably reliable, which means that on the whole they are more advanced than most under-developed countries. It is precisely in such countries—those on the verge of becoming urban-industrial—that the fastest declines in fertility have oc-curred. This suggests that the declines are being caused by changing social and economic conditions rather than by family-planning policy. In fact, it seems to make little difference whether the country has a major family-planning program or not, or, if it does have one, when it began. In Taiwan, where there is a much publicized quasi-official family-planning program, the birth rate dropped by 29 percent between 1960 and 1970, but in Trinidad, where there is no such program, the birth rate fell from almost exactly the same level by 38 percent. Furthermore, in Taiwan the family-planning program did not get started until 1964, before which time the drop in fertility was already rapid. It is hard to escape the conclusion that official programs of the sort being adopted around the world have little to do with the trend of birth rates. To be sure, most of the decline is due to the use of contraception, abortion, and sterilization, but the public, if it wishes to limit births, will find a way to get the means; if it does not wish to limit births, no official program for providing services will lead it to do so.

If family-planning policies, even when broadened somewhat as they have been in the last few years, are not likely to bring about ZPG, then additional and more drastic measures may be required. Before hastening to imagine such measures, however, we might first make an attempt to rethink the problem.

The Nature of Population Policy

The hypothesis must be entertained that the goal of population policy is too weak—that if the goal were strong enough, the means would be found. If this is so, the reason may be that population growth does not have serious consequences, or that people are ignorant of those consequences, or that to eliminate population growth would require too much sacrifice of other things. My hunch is that the last two explanations are the most likely.

From the standpoint of being solved, the population problem has three strikes against it. First, it refers to a condition of the community at large. It is not a personal disaster like drug addiction or bankruptcy; on the contrary, it is an outgrowth of personal satisfaction. Second, it is a problem that evolves slowly and therefore never reaches a sudden crisis. Unlike war, famine, fuel shortage, or political scandal, it does not appear at a particular moment and demand instant action. Third, it is not a problem "out there" in the external world, like crop disease or soil deficiency, to be dealt with by science and technology. The overabundant population is composed of people. When people themselves are the problem, the solution is always difficult, because subject and object are one and the same.

If the population problem were easily soluble, it would have been solved a century ago. By 1850 anyone could see that the revolution in productive technology enabled fewer people to manage more resources. Instead of utilizing this fact and limiting population growth, thereby providing themselves with a utopian level of living with little effort, the Europeans used it overwhelmingly to support more people. Europe became the world's most densely settled continent and, in turn, sent out migrants to overrun whole new continents. As other peoples came into contact with modern technology, they too eventually multiplied instead of decreasing their numbers. As a result, the human species is now in the preposterous situation of using an extremely advanced technology to maintain nearly four billion people at a low average level of living while stripping the world of its resources, contaminating its water, soil, and air, and driving most other species into extinction, parasitism, or domestication.

It is now too late to "solve" the world's population problem. Much that has been destroyed or wasted can never be restored. To reach without mass slaughter the small population compatible with a scientific technology will require centuries of negative population growth. What is being discussed now is not a solution but an amelioration. Standing in the way even of amelioration, however, are the same myths, interests, and conflicts that prevented a solution in the first place. Man has been shrewd enough to figure out the process of evolution but not wise enough to master it. The process has two principles: first, the world belongs to whatever animal can breed faster than it dies; and second, the world never belongs very long to one animal. The human race could escape being a victim of evolution if it were willing to forego being its darling, but this it has not done, at least up to the present.

Recent history suggests, however, that ZPG is gaining strength as a goal. If so, what are the reasons? Whatever they are, they are to a large extent feedbacks from the unplanned and undesired human multiplication since World War II—1.5 billion people added to the population in twenty-eight years. This has led to disenchantment with growth in general and with economic growth in particular as a goal of human endeavor, because the double multiplier—more people times more goods per person—is obviously stripping the world of its metals and fossil fuels faster than either multiplier alone would do, and also making the world more unpleasant and inconvenient as a place to live. As normally measured, per capita income is simply an index of activity entering the exchange system. Up to a point, it bears some relation to satisfaction, but as population density and technological complexity increase, an ever larger proportion of human exchange activity is devoted simply to escaping the consequences of a high level of exchange activity. Sensing this, people are coming to view population growth as a problem, not because it restrains economic activity but because it makes its effects worse. If there were only 25 million Americans, they would not have to put antismog devices on their cars. Their "level of living" would therefore be lower, because this "economic activity" (making and installing antismog devices) would not be added to the economy.

The onus of proof is shifting from those who want ZPG or NPG to those who do not. Formerly, population stability had to be justified by citing *future* calamities that would result from continued population growth. Now, with a more sophisticated view, it is taken for granted that the calamities are not distant but here and now. Also, it was once considered inhuman to object to people; now the sheer frustration of dealing with people is readily acknowledged. The effort to escape the crush—to escape the city in the suburbs, to escape the suburbs in a second home in the country, to escape vacationers in the countryside—all attest the desire of people to escape from people. Formerly, too, a nongrowing population was regarded as abnormal; now, with wider knowledge of demographic history, it is realized that ZPG is normal and that the growth in the last two centuries is abnormal. The only thing abnormal about ZPG as now proposed is that it would be achieved with low rather than with high birth and death rates, which is why its detractors stress the small families, the older age structure, and the alleged social and economic difficulties that would result from those features.

How to Attain ZPG

The unconscious assumption that solving the population problem is a technological matter has a curious consequence for the demographer. He is constantly told, "Tell us what can be done about population," with the implication that if he cannot come up with a satisfactory answer, he is a failure. It is of no importance that the demographer has already made suggestions. These are brushed aside as not being practical. The demand is for "a solution that will work." What is being demanded is some mysterious "key" to population limitation, which can unlock the door painlessly and quickly. If only enough money is put into research, the thinking goes, if only the right disciplines are brought to bear, the solution will be "discovered."

The truth is that there is no mystery about population control. There is no special "technique" required, because the technological part is simple. If people want to control population, it can be done with knowledge already available. As with other social problems, the solution is easy as long as one pays no attention to what must be given up. For instance, a nation seeking ZPG could shut off immigration and permit each couple a maximum of two children, with possible state license for a third. Accidental pregnancies beyond the limit would be interrupted by abortion. If a third child were born without license, or a fourth, the mother would be sterilized and the child given to a sterile couple. But anyone enticed into making such a suggestion risks being ostracized as a political or moral leper, a danger to society. He is accused of wanting to take people's freedom away from them and institute a Draconian dictatorship over private lives. Obviously, then, reproductive freedom still takes priority over population control. This makes a solution of the population problem impossible because, by definition, population control and reproductive freedom are incompatible.

Why, however, are people so concerned with freedom in connection with reproduction? Freedom has always been denied to murderers, rapists, and armed thieves. If having too many children were considered as great a crime against humanity as murder, rape, and thievery, we would have no qualms about "taking freedom away." Indeed, it would be defined the other way around: a person having four or more children would be regarded as violating the freedom of those other citizens who must help pay for rearing, educating, and feeding the excess children. The reason why reproductive freedom is still regarded as "a basic human right" regardless of circumstances is of course that it accords with traditional sentiments and established institutions. These, it will be recalled, are pronatalist. Reproductive freedom can be construed as antinatalist only to the degree that it undermines the built-in profertility compulsions of the old system, which, however, as I have noted, are not ordinarily felt to be compulsions until attention is called to them.

Thus the "population problem" is not a technological problem. It is not something the definition of which is universally agreed upon and the solution to which awaits only the discovery of an effective means. It is not like yellow fever or wheat rust. It is a social problem in the sense that it involves a conflict of wants. People want families and children. If they did not want families and children, it would be technologically easy to satisfy them. But they do want families and children. That being the case, they are not whole hearted about population control. They do not want runaway population growth either, but they want to avoid it painlessly.

They want a solution that leaves them their freedom to have five children if they wish. In short, they want a miracle.

REFERENCES

1. Kingsley Davis, "Population Policy: Will Current Programs Succeed?" *Science*, 158, November 10, 1967, pp. 730-739.

2. Ansley J. Coale, "Should the United States Start a Campaign for Fewer Births?" *Population Index*, 34 (October-December 1968), 467. This was Coale's presidential address to the Population Association of America, the organization of professional demographers in the United States.

3. Oscar Harkavy, Frederick S. Jaffe, and Samuel M. Wishik, "Family Planning and Public Policy: Who is Misleading Whom?" *Science*, 165, July 25, 1969, p. 367.

4. Robin Elliott, Lynn C. Landman, Richard Lincoln, and Theodore Tsuoroka, "U.S. Population Growth and Family Planning: A Review of the Literature," *Family Planning Perspectives* (the magazine of the Planned Parenthood Federation of America), 2 (October 1970), v. The reference is to Tomas Frejka, "Reflections on the Demographic Conditions Needed to Establish a U.S. Stationary Population Growth," *Population Studies*, 22 (November 1968).

5. *Population and the American Future*, Report of the Commission on Population Growth and the American Future (Washington, D.C.: Government Printing Office, 1972), p. 110.

6. Frank W. Notestein, "Zero Population Growth," *Population Index*, 36 (October-December 1970), 444.

7. Judith Blake, "Reply to Notestein," *ibid.*, p. 456.

8. See Frejka, "Reflections on the Demographic Conditions Needed to Establish a U.S. Stationary Population Growth"; Stephen Enke, "Zero U.S. Population Growth— When, How and Why?" *Socio-Economic Planning Science*, 5 (1971), 263; U.S. Census Bureau, "Illustrative Population Projections for the United States: The Demographic Effects of Alternate Paths to Zero Growth," *Current Population Reports*, Series P-25, No. 480 (April 1972).

9. Stephen Enke, "Zero U.S. Population Growth," p. 263.

10. Colin Clark, *The Conditions of Economic Progress*, 3d ed. (London: Macmillan, 1960), Ch. 3.

11. "Cohorts of Swedish women born after 1885 have not reproduced themselves." Eva Bernhardt, *Trends and Variations in Swedish Fertility: A Cohort Study* (Stockholm: Statistiska Centralbyran, 1971), p. 159.

12. Coale, "Should the United States Start a Campaign for Fewer Births?" p. 471. This statement was paraphrased in *Population and the American Future*, p. 62.

13. Frejka, "Reflections on the Demographic Conditions Needed to Establish a U.S. Stationary Population Growth," p. 379.

14. Calculated in *International Population and Urban Research* by Sarah Tsai.

15. United Nations, *Demographic Yearbook*, 1970 and 1971.

16. *Population and the American Future,* p. 143; see also p. 75.

17. On Human Rights Day, December, 1966, Secretary-General U Thant welcomed on behalf of the United Nations a statement on population circulated by John D. Rockefeller 3rd and signed by the heads of state of twelve countries (later, in 1967, signed by thirty heads of state). It stressed that "the opportunity to decide the number and spacing of children is a basic human right." U Thant's welcoming message added, "We must accord the right of parents to determine the number and spacing of children is a basic human right."

18. This emphasis is seen in the following statement in *Population and the American Future,* p. 78: "In regard to childbearing . . . the goals of our recommendations are to (1) maximize information and knowledge about human reproduction and its implications for the family; (2) improve the quality of the setting in which children are raised; (3) neutralize insofar as it is practicable and consistent with other values those legal, social, and institutional pressures that historically have been mainly pronatalist in character; and (4) enable individuals to avoid unwanted childbearing, thereby enhancing their ability to realize their preference."

19. Office of the Foreign Secretary, National Academy of Sciences, *Rapid Population Growth* (Baltimore: Johns Hopkins Press, 1971), p. 93.

20. *Population and the American Future,* p. 103. For an analysis of abortion in the context of current discussion and legal decisions, see Judith Blake, "Elective Abortion and Our Reluctant Citizenry: Research on Public Opinion in the United States," eds. Howard and Joy Osovsky, *Abortion Experience in the United States* (New York: Harper and Row, forthcoming).

21. "Birth Expectations and Fertility: June 1972," *Current Population Reports,* Series P-20, No. 248 (April 1973), 5-6.

JOHN P. HOLDREN

Population and the American Predicament: The Case Against Complacency

THAT THE United States should and probably can achieve a condition of zero population growth at some time in the next hundred years is no longer a matter of much dispute. Most students of contemporary American problems seem to have agreed, at least, that the costs of long-continued population growth would considerably outweigh the benefits; and the achievement in 1972 of a total fertility rate slightly below replacement has convinced many that a spontaneous and fortuitous approach to a stationary population is already underway. Since the factors that have led to the decline in fertility have not been disentangled, however, it is difficult to be sure yet whether the recent experience represents a fluctuation or a trend. Against this backdrop of loose consensus on the long-term desirability of ZPG and uncertainty about the origins and persistence of recent levels of fertility, serious and controversial questions remain to be settled. Do the potential consequences of continued population growth in the United States justify systematic measures to hold fertility at replacement level if it should show any tendency to rise again? Should such measures be used to push fertility well *below* replacement, if it does not drop that far without them, in order to bring the attainment of ZPG closer than seventy years hence and to render the intervening population increment smaller than some 70 million? Is even the present U.S. population of 210 million too large? Should there be zero economic growth as well as zero population growth?

Obviously, one's degree of concern about, say, a 30 percent increase in the U.S. population—the increase that would result if fertility remained at the replacement level in the absence of immigration—depends on the way one perceives two basic relations: the role of population size in contributing to existing problems, and the role of population growth in aggravating these problems and impeding the success of attempted nondemographic remedies. I believe that those who are unconcerned by the prospect of 280 million Americans have seriously underestimated the importance of population in both roles. I will argue here that 210 million now is too many and 280 million in 2040 is likely to be much too many; that, accordingly, a continued decline in fertility to well below replacement should be encouraged, with

31

the aim of achieving ZPG before the year 2000 and a gradually declining population for some time thereafter; and that redirecting economic growth and technological change (*not* stopping either) is an essential concomitant to but not a substitute for these demographic goals.

The Moderate Position

For the purposes of developing this argument, it is useful to begin with the more moderate position taken by the National Commission on Population Growth and the American Future. One can then focus on the specific issues that justify, I believe, a greater sense of urgency than the Commission's recommendations convey.

The Commission's March 1972 final report[1] concluded that "no substantial benefits would result from continued growth of the nation's population," and, more positively, recommended that "the nation welcome and plan for a stabilized population." Of the possible specific justifications for its recommendation, the Commission chose, perhaps wisely, to emphasize those that are relatively easily demonstrated and unlikely to be controversial: it said that coping with continued population growth would divert money, materials and talent from urgent domestic tasks; that, although solutions can be found to the problems of meeting the physical needs of an expanded population, these may include a good many measures we do not like; and that many policies desirable on their own merits (such as equality for women and universal access to contraceptives) will move us automatically in the direction of population stabilization.

With respect to the effects of American population growth on problems of resources and environment, the Commission's report held population stabilization to be desirable if not urgent. The report noted that population size, while far from being the sole cause of environmental damage, is a multiplier of other causes of such damage. Thus, argued the Commission, even in cases where reduction of emissions per person represents the easiest short-term approach to reducing environmental disruption, unabated population growth could wipe out the long-term gains from such measures. As for mineral and energy resources, the Commission anticipated few problems of absolute supply in the next several decades that could not be alleviated by moderate increases in price. Such increases, the Commission concluded, would stimulate the use of lower grade domestic ores, or increased imports, or technological substitutes. Their basic verdict about resource adequacy held even under the assumption of rather rapid population growth in the U.S. and substantially increased demands elsewhere. The most serious resource-related difficulties facing this country in the next fifty years were deemed to be regional water shortages, increased pressure on scarce recreational land, and substantially higher food prices owing to shortage of good agricultural land.

The Commission's position, then, was hardly one of unrestrained optimism concerning the consequences of further population growth in the United States, but neither was it a flat statement that this country is overpopulated now or a clear call for early stabilization. What are the grounds for holding a stronger view? They emerge, I think, from a closer look at five sets of issues: the character of the environmental problems related to population, and their potential impact on well-being; the international ramifications of U.S. resource consumption; the specific mechanisms through which demographic variables contribute to problems of resources and environment; the liabilities and limitations of "direct," nondemographic attacks on problems with demographic components; and the meaning of "optimum" population size.

Environment and Well-Being

The Population Commission divided environmental pollutants into two classes. The first class included most products of combustion and several conventional measures of water pollution. The apparent ease with which technological improvements could reduce emissions of these pollutants to levels below those posing acute threats to health formed the basis for the Commission's main conclusions concerning the environment. The second class of pollutants, including long-lived general poisons such as pesticides, radioisotopes and heavy metals, was not considered in detail, owing to the Commission's belief that insufficient information was available on these subjects. Neither were the effects on human well-being of ecological disruption in forms other than direct poisoning of people considered in any depth, presumably also on grounds of insufficient evidence. And yet, ignoring for a moment the practical difficulties of implementing controls on even the common pollutants in the first class, it seems likely that the most serious environmental threats lie in precisely the categories that the Commission did not explore.

The long-term human consequences of chronic exposure to low levels of persistent environmental contaminants, for example, may be more serious—and the causes less amenable to removal—than those of acute pollution as it is perceived today. Much remains to be learned about this subject, including especially the potential for induction of cancer or genetic damage by contaminants present at low concentrations and in combination—pesticide and fertilizer residues, heavy metals, plasticizers, food additives, prescription and nonprescription drugs, and so on.

Still more threatening, in all probability, is civilization's interference in the smooth functioning of biological processes that provide us with services we do not know how to replace. Most potential crop pests are controlled by their natural enemies or by other environmental conditions, not by technology.[2] Similarly, many agents of human disease are controlled not principally by medical technology but by environmental conditions, and some carriers of such agents are controlled by a combination of environmental conditions and natural enemies.[3] The cycling of essential plant nutrients such as nitrogen, phosphorus and sulfur is contingent at various stages on biological processes, and these same cycles play an important role in the disposal of civilization's wastes. The environmental concentrations of ammonia, carbon monoxide, and hydrogen sulfide—all poisonous—are biologically controlled. These "public service" functions of the biological environment cannot be replaced by technology now or in the next century. This is so not so much for lack of scientific knowledge or technical skill (although such limitations are important in many cases), but rather, for the most part, because the sheer size of the tasks simply dwarfs civilization's capacity to produce and deploy new technology.

The specific mechanisms by which civilization's activities are disrupting the performance of indispensable natural services have been described at length in the technical literature.[4] They include selective poisoning of vulnerable organisms and the corresponding disruption of terrestrial and oceanic food webs, alteration of chemical balances in the environment, overexploitation of commercial species, and the destruction of natural communities serving as ecological buffers and reservoirs of species diversity. Virtually all of the natural services are influenced in some degree by climate, especially those related to food production and the regulation of disease. Civilization's activities have the potential to disrupt climate in a variety of ways: the effects of carbon dioxide and particulate matter on the global radiation balance; large-scale modification of the reflectivity and heat- and moisture-transfer properties of the earth's surface by agriculture, urbanization, and oil films on the ocean; the influence of the heat release that attends all use of energy by mankind.[5] Much uncertainty exists concerning the precise possibilities of inadvertent modification of climate by these various factors. Global warming or cooling is possible in principle, but a more complicated alteration of climatic patterns seems a more probable and more imminent consequence of the very unevenly distributed impacts of civilization.

This, then, is the central issue that is missed by those who view environmental concerns as a matter of nuisances, damage to scenery, and dirty air and water: with industrial nations in the forefront, mankind is systematically diminishing the capacity of the environment to perform its essential functions of pest control, nutrient cycling, waste management, and climate regulation, at the same time that growing population and rising consumption per person are creating ever larger demands for these services. Evidently, the inadequacy of present scientific knowledge to predict the time and character of the ultimate breakdown in this process is often taken to be grounds for complacency, but our ignorance here should be alarming, not reassuring.

International Ramifications

In its examination of the impact of the U.S. population on resources, as in its treatment of environmental problems, the Commission on Population Growth and the American Future may have left the most important stones unturned. For the Commission assumed, in concluding that the resource needs of an expanding U.S. population can be met without great difficulty, that we would continue to have access to rich foreign deposits of fuels and minerals. Whether this actually will (or even should) be so hinges on deep and unresolved questions. How serious will the tensions be between the U.S. and increasingly prosperous but resource-poor Japan and Europe, as we compete for the world's remaining rich ores? Will the U.S. balance of payments be able to bear the bill? Does the rate at which the U.S. extracts high grade raw materials from less developed countries today compromise the ability of those countries to develop tomorrow, when only low grade ores remain? Can the prosperity gap between the rich and poor nations of the world be narrowed at a meaningful rate without drastic modification of present patterns of resource consumption?

It is well known that the United States accounts for roughly one third of the world's annual consumption of energy, and a similar fraction of the consumption of most industrial metals. The combination of the U.S., the Soviet Union, Europe, Japan and Australia accounts for 85 percent or more of the world's consumption of energy, steel, and tin.[6] The U.S. in 1970 was importing 100 percent of its chromium, 94 percent of its manganese, almost 70 percent of its nickel and tin, and 22 percent of its petroleum.[7] It has also been calculated, as a measure of the prosperity gap, that to supply the present world population with the average per capita "standing crop" of industrial metals characteristic of the ten richest nations would require more than sixty years' world production of these metals at the 1970 rate.[8] (Of course, the world population is growing, and, under existing patterns, the vast bulk of the extracted materials will go not to establish the underpinnings of prosperity in the poor countries but to support wasteful practices and further industrial growth in the rich ones.) Such figures need little elaboration. They suggest that even moderate population growth in rich countries exerts a disproportionate pressure on global resource flows, all else being equal, and that rapid progress toward developing the poor countries may be possible only if resource consumption is stabilized in the rich ones. Stabilized consumption, of course, is unlikely unless population size has also been stabilized.

That the United States is in for a period of relative resource scarcity and balance-of-payment problems is hard to doubt, regardless of how one views the likelihood of a major diversion of resource consumption from rich countries to poor ones. The present worsening petroleum situation is illustrating this problem all too vividly. So far, it is also leaving room for question as to whether the price mechanism can handle such difficulties smoothly (although, in fairness, it may be argued that mismanagement and inept regulation have not given the price mechanism a chance). In any case, the growing "energy crisis" has led to a predictable clamor for relaxation of environmental standards that have impeded development of new supplies. Curiously, the role that continued population growth will play in pushing up demand in an already precarious situation has not received as much attention.

The Role of Population

The reason for the widespread neglect of the population factor in the energy situation—and most other problems related to resources and environment—is that many observers regard such problems as primarily the result of faulty technologies and high rates of growth of consumption per capita rather than of population size or growth rate.[9] This view can only arise from a failure to comprehend the implications of the multiplicative relationships that actually prevail. Essentially, total consumption equals population times consumption per capita; total pollution equals total consumption times pollution per unit of consumption. Perhaps the basic point is that it is not meaningful to try to divide the "responsibility" for a given level of total consumption (or pollution) between population size and consumption (or pollution) per person. Such a procedure is analogous to trying to apportion the responsibility for the area of a rectangle between the lengths of the two sides. The property of interest, whether geometric area or population pressure, resides inextricably in the combined action of the contributing factors.

One can, on the other hand, distinguish among the relative contributions made by the rates of change of the various contributing factors to the rate of change of the total. Even in this strictly arithmetical exercise, however, it is easy to be misled, particularly when percentages are used. Consider the true statement, "Total energy consumption in the United States increased 1100 percent (12-fold) between 1880 and 1966, while population increased 300 percent (4-fold)."[10] On a quick reading, one might infer from this statement that population growth was not the major contributing factor. Actually, the increase in energy consumption per capita in this period was only 200 percent (3-fold); the 12-fold increase in total energy use is the product, not the sum, of the 4-fold increase in population and the 3-fold increase in use per person.

That simultaneously growing multiplicative factors yield a disproportionately growing product leads to even more startling numbers when three factors are considered rather than two. For example, an observed increase of 415 percent in emissions of automotive lead in the U.S. between 1946 and 1967 proves to have been generated by a 41 percent increase in population, a 100 percent increase in vehicle-miles per person, and an 83 percent increase in emissions per vehicle mile ($1.41 \times 2.00 \times 1.83 = 5.15$).[11] The dramatic increase in total impact arose from rather moderate but simultaneous increases in the contributing factors; no factor was unimportant. Performing the same kinds of calculations on a variety of statistics shows, for the post-World War II period in the United States, that in strictly numerical terms the role of population growth in contributing to pressures on resources and environment has been substantial but not dominant.[12] Neither, however, has either of the other major contributors to these pressures—rising affluence and technological change—been consistently dominant.

Does the conclusion that population is a significant factor in the United States still hold in the 1970's, with population growing at 1 percent per year while per capita consumption of many kinds grows at 4 percent? In a word, yes. It should be obvious that the impact of rapid growth of consumption per capita is greater in a large population than in a small one, and, correspondingly, that the *absolute* impact of an increment in population is increased by rapid growth of the per capita consumption factor that the population multiplies.[13] (That the *relative* importance of population growth compared to growth of per capita consumption decreases in this situation is small consolation.) It is equally clear that the absolute significance of a fixed percentage increment of population goes up with the size of the base to which that increment is added—1 percent of the U.S. population now is 2.1 million people; in 1933 it was 1.25 million.

The foregoing observations on the role of population have been strictly arithmetical ones, with no attention to the possible cause-and-effect relations between population and the other factors contributing to pressures on resources and environment, and no consideration of possible differences in the response of the environment and the society to successive increments of impact. It is in these possibilities, however, that the greatest potential for harm in further population growth resides. Consider some of the ways in which changes in demographic variables can cause changes in consumption per capita and in pollution per unit of consumption. The present spatial pattern of population growth—suburbanization—leads to increased use of the automobile (more vehicle miles per person). This effect, together with that of population density itself, leads in turn to increased traffic congestion, hence more gallons of gasoline and harmful emissions per vehicle mile, and longer periods that the drivers are exposed to elevated concentrations of pollutants. The demand of each new increment of population for food is met by means of disproportionate increases in the use of fertilizer and pesticides on existing land;[14] a 1 percent increase in output now requires increases in inputs much greater than 1 percent—an example of diminishing returns. Growing demand for materials and fuels—the combined result of population growth and rising affluence—accelerates the application of more energy-intensive and environmentally disruptive techniques needed to exploit lower grade ores. In all these cases, population growth is generating pressures, directly and indirectly, that grow faster than the population itself.

A further 30 percent increase in the population of the United States, then, is likely to cause an increase in pressure on resources and environment that considerably exceeds 30 percent. The threat is compounded by the fact that the response of any system, environmental or social, may change dramatically with rather small changes in pressure as its capacity is approached. That is, the next 5 percent may cause a very different response than the previous 5 percent. Such thresholds are not uncommon in everyday experience—the difference between a freeway carrying a capacity load at 60 miles per hour and a massive traffic jam is a few extra cars; and they are not uncommon in nature—fish that tolerate a ten degree rise in temperature without difficulty may turn belly up when the temperature goes up five degrees more. Neither the thresholds of the environmental systems discussed earlier nor those of our social systems have yet been identified, but symptoms of stress in both areas are abundant enough that it seems imprudent, to say the least, to regard *any* further increase in population-related pressures with complacency.

Liabilities of "Direct" Approaches

No one has seriously suggested that stabilizing or reducing the size of the American population would, by itself, solve the problems of environment, physical resources, poverty, and urban deterioration that threaten us or that already exist. Attacks on the symptoms of these problems and on their causes other than population should be imaginatively formulated and vigorously pursued. There is evidence that the growth of energy consumption per person can be significantly slowed, by reducing waste and inefficiency, without adverse effects on the economy.[15] Economic growth itself can be channeled into sectors in which resource consumption and environmental impact per dollar of GNP are minimized.[16] Practical mechanisms to alleviate the maldistribution of prosperity must be devised and put to use. But those who advocate the pursuit of these "direct" approaches to the exclusion of population limitation are opting for a handicap they should not want and cannot afford.

For the trouble is that the "direct" approaches are imperfect and incomplete. They are usually expensive and slow, and often they move the problem rather than remove it. How quickly and at what cost can mass transit relieve the congestion in our cities? Redesigning the entire urban community is a possibility, of course, but an even slower one. If substantially more economical cars are designed, how fast will their share of the market grow, and how much of the gain will be wiped out by an increased total number of cars? If residences and commercial buildings that use energy more efficiently are developed, how long will it be until the tens of millions of inefficient buildings that now exist have been replaced? Fossil-fueled power plants can, in time, be replaced by nuclear reactors—trading the burden of the noxious routine emissions of the former for the uncertain risks of serious accident, sabotage, nuclear terrorism, and management in perpetuity of radioactive wastes. We could back away from energy-intensive and nonbiodegradable nylon and rayon and plastics in favor of a return to cotton and wool and wood, thereby increasing the use of pesticides, the rate of erosion due to overgrazing and overlogging, and the fraction of our land under intensive exploitation. It is evident, in short, that there are difficult trade-offs to be made, and that fast and comfortable solutions are in short supply.

It has sometimes been suggested that such population-related pressures as exist in the United States are due mainly to spatial maldistribution of people, and that, accordingly, the "direct" solution is redistribution rather than halting or reversing growth. It is true that congestion and some forms of acute pollution of air and water could be relieved by redistributing people. But many of the most serious pressures on resources and environment—for example, those associated with energy production, agriculture, and ocean fisheries—depend mainly on how many people there are and what they consume, not on how they are distributed. Some problems, of course, would be aggravated rather than alleviated by redistribution: providing services and physical necessities to a highly dispersed population would in many instances be economically and ecologically more costly than doing the same for a concentrated population. In the end, though, the redistribution question may be largely an academic one. People live where they do for relatively sound reasons of economics, topography and taste. Moving them in great numbers is difficult. Therefore, even those kinds of population pressure that might in principle be alleviated by redistribution are likely in practice to remain closely linked to overall size.

I point out these shortcomings of "direct" approaches not to suggest that intelligent choices are impossible or that pathways through the pitfalls cannot be found, but rather to emphasize that the problems would be tough enough even without population growth. Why, then, should we compound our plight by permitting population growth to continue? Is it logical to disparage the importance of population growth, which is a significant contributor to a wide variety of predicaments, only because it is not the sole cause of any of them?

How Much Is Too Much?

Those who advocate the early attainment of zero population growth, or a return to a smaller population by way of a period of negative growth, are often challenged to name an "optimum" population figure and defend it. What, after all, is the point of stopping or turning around if we don't know what the optimum is? Perhaps it is actually larger than the present population. The question of the optimum is not an easy one, but I think one can make some sensible observations about it.

First, we can probably agree that the optimum and the maximum are not the same thing. The maximum population, or carrying capacity, is determined by such factors as usable land area, fertility of soils, availability of mineral resources and water, and the ability of biological systems to absorb civilization's wastes without breakdowns that deprive us of essential services. No one knows just what the maximum is or which limiting factor will determine it,[17] and, in any case, the answer will almost certainly vary with time as technology changes. But in no event is a population size that is at or near the maximum likely to be optimum: if availability of resources defines the limit, the maximum implies bare subsistence for all; if environmental constraints define it, the maximum is likely to represent a precariously unstable situation. By the same token, it is easy to imagine a population size smaller than the optimum—one, for example, too small to enjoy the benefits of specialization, economies of scale, and cultural diversity.

A general, and perhaps innocent, definition of the optimum population size is the size that permits the maximum average well-being per person. It is the definition of "well-being" that gets us into trouble, for this term clearly must include physical necessities such as food, water, shelter, and a livable environment; social essentials such as employment and economic security, education, and means for conflict resolution and the administration of justice; and amenities such as recreation and cultural pursuits. Not all of these values can be adequately reflected in the economic marketplace, and there are considerable differences in the relative importance that different groups and individuals would assign to the various ingredients. What is important to me—say, proximity to a great museum—may be unimportant to you compared to some other value—say, proximity to wilderness. Yet without consensus on what well-being consists of, how can we say anything useful about optimum population?

I believe that from these fundamental differences in human values an operationally useful conclusion does emerge: the concept of the optimum population hinges on the need for social, cultural and environmental diversity, for only thus can a wide variety of preferences be satisfied. At very low population sizes, the raw material for sufficient cultural and social diversity does not exist; near the physical maximum, on the other hand, diversity must be sacrificed in order to maximize efficiency.[18] From the individual's perspective, of course, diversity in the social and physical environments is related to personal options—access to a variety of employment possibilities, living accommodations, educational and recreational opportunities, degrees of privacy, and so forth. With respect to this criterion, then, one can say that the optimum population size is that beyond which further growth closes more options than it opens. The reader may wish to ponder what this definition implies in the case of the United States. For myself, I am unable to think of many options being opened by further population growth (greater variety in airline schedules?), but I can think of a good many that are being closed (the opportunity to escape congestion, to survive without an automobile, to live anywhere but in a city).

Of course the optimum population size and the maximum size are dynamic quantities, not static ones. "Optimum" should mean "optimum under existing social and technological conditions." To argue that a region is not overpopulated by pointing out that certain technical and social changes could, in time, relieve the population-related pressures there is to miss the point. Technological innovation and cultural evolution will no doubt lead to changes in the population size regarded as optimum, and perhaps will push up the maximum. But a prudent society will let its actual population conform to such changes as they occur, rather than hope blindly, as most do today, that technology and social change will render acceptable whatever degree of population growth happens to materialize.

My own suspicion is that the United States, with about 210 million people, has considerably exceeded the optimum population size under existing conditions. It seems clear to me that we have already paid a high price in diversity to achieve our present size, and that our ability to elevate the average per capita level of well-being would be substantially greater if the population were smaller. I am also uneasy about the possibility that 280 million Americans, under conditions likely to include per capita consumption of energy and materials substantially higher than today's, will prove to be beyond the environmentally sustainable maximum population size.

That many people will disagree with these conclusions should not be surprising, given the value judgments and uncertainties that are involved. In a practical sense, however, disagreements at this point about the hypothetical optimum and maximum population sizes are relatively unimportant. What is surprising, and more important, is that there is not more agreement concerning what the rate of change of population size should be. For given the uncertain, but possibly grave, risks associated with substantially increasing our impact on the environment, and given that population growth aggravates or impedes the solution of a wide variety of other problems (including the land-use predicament, pressure on water and energy resources, and the imbalance of international resource flows), it should be obvious that the optimum *rate* of population growth is zero or negative until such time as the uncertainties have been removed and the problems solved.

It is also obvious that this "optimum" condition cannot be achieved instantly. Unfortunately, the importance of achieving it sooner rather than later has been widely underestimated. In this connection, the recent rapid decline of fertility in the United States is cause for gratitude but not for complacency. Efforts to understand the origins and mechanisms of the decline should be continued and intensified, so that the trend can be reinforced with policy if it falters.

REFERENCES

1. *Population and the American Future,* Report of the Commission on Population Growth and the American Future (Washington, D.C.: U.S. Government Printing Office, 1972).

2. *Man's Impact on the Global Environment,* Report of the Study of Critical Environmental Problems (Cambridge, Mass.: M.I.T. Press, 1970).

3. Jacques M. May, "Influence of Environmental Transformation in Changing the Map of Disease," *The Careless Technology,* ed. M. Taghi Farvar and John P. Milton (Garden City, N.Y.: The Natural History Press, 1972).

4. For synopses and extensive bibliographies, see, for example, *Man in the Living Environment,* Report of the Workshop on Global Ecological Problems (Madison, Wisconsin: University of Wisconsin Press, 1972); and *Man's Impact on the Global Environment.*

5. *Inadvertent Climate Modification,* Report of the Study of Man's Impact on Climate (Cambridge, Mass.: M.I.T. Press, 1971).

6. United Nations, *Statistical Yearbook, 1972* (New York: United Nations Publications Office, 1973).

7. National Commission on Materials Policy, "Towards a National Materials Policy: Basic Data and Issues, An Interim Report" (Washington, D.C.: U.S. Government Printing Office, April 1972).

8. Harrison Brown, "Human Materials Production as a Process in the Biosphere," *Scientific American* (September 1970).

9. For an exposition of this viewpoint, see, for example, Ansley Coale, "Man and His Environment," *Science,* 170, October 9, 1970, 132-136.

10. U.S. Bureau of the Census, *Historical Statistics of the United States: Colonial Times to 1957* (Washington, D.C.: U.S. Government Printing Office, 1960); *Statistical Abstract of the United States, 1972* (Washington, D.C.: U.S. Government Printing Office, 1972).

11. Barry Commoner, "The Environmental Cost of Economic Growth," *Population, Resources, and the Environment,* Research Reports of the Commission on Population Growth and the American Future, 3, ed. Ronald G. Ridker (Washington, D.C.: U.S. Government Printing Office, 1972), p. 343.

12. Paul R. Ehrlich and John P. Holdren, "Impact of Population Growth," *Population, Resources, and the Environment,* p. 365; Paul R. Ehrlich, Anne H. Ehrlich and John P. Holdren, *Human Ecology: Problems and Solutions* (San Francisco: W. H. Freeman and Co., 1973), Ch. 7.

13. As an example, consider the potential effect of population growth on total energy consumption. Most forecasts show energy consumption per capita increasing at 3 percent per year in the United States during the remainder of this century. Although I think this estimate is too high for a variety of reasons, it is instructive in the present context to explore the effect of two differnt scenarios for population growth under the assumption that the per capita energy forecast is correct. My "high" population possibility assumes a total fertility rate corresponding to replacement (2.1 children per family average) through the year 2000, with immigration remaining at 400,000

per year. This gives 265 million Americans in the year 2000. The "low" possibility assumes a fertility rate corresponding to 1.4 children per family through the year 2000, with the same immigration rate, which gives 238 million in 2000. The lower population scenario cuts *in half* the increase in total energy consumption between 1973 and 2000, assuming 3 percent per year growth in per capita energy consumption in each case. The savings in the year 2000 over the high population result amounts to 20 quadrillion BTU, which happens to be equal to *total* U.S. domestic petroleum production in 1971.

14. David Pimentel, L. E. Hurd, A. C. Bellotti, M. J. Forster, I. N. Oka, O. D. Sholes, and R. J. Whitman, "Corn, Food, and the Energy Crisis," *Report 73-1*, Department of Entomology and Section of Ecology and Systematics (Ithaca, N.Y.: Cornell University, March 1973).

15. Office of Emergency Preparedness, Executive Office of the President, *The Potential for Energy Conservation* (Washington, D.C.: U.S. Government Printing Office, October 1972).

16. It is not economic growth per se that puts pressure on resources and environment but rather the physical components of economic activity—specifically, flows of materials and energy. Stabilization of these flows, which is necessary, need not entail stabilization of the level of economic activity for a long time thereafter. What is needed, in part, is a major effort to devote the sort of technical skills and ingenuity that have been applied so enthusiastically to space and weapons to the task of increasing the economic good that can be extracted from each pound of metal and gallon of fuel.

17. It is clear, however, that the limit for the United States will not be land area. To argue that we have plenty of room is to be correct but irrelevant. The pressure of population in this country is not on land area as a whole, but on some specific kinds of land (coastlines, good farmland), on environment, on resources, on institutions, and on values.

18. The statement that diversity must be sacrificed if one wishes to maximize efficiency appears to be true of ecosystems as well as for human society, if by efficiency we mean high net production per unit of input of energy or other resources. The trade-off between diversity and efficiency may prove to be a fundamental dilemma for civilization; efficiency is essential in a world of limited resources and growing demands, but diversity is the best (perhaps the only) insurance against uncertainty about what the future will be like. The dilemma is already being experienced in global agriculture: the need to increase production encourages reliance on a few high-yielding strains of wheat and rice, but the loss of diversity as the new grains replace traditional types increases the threat of widespread crop failure from pests or disease.

NORMAN B. RYDER

Two Cheers for ZPG

THERE IS A substantial probability that the United States is approaching the end of its era of population growth. Furthermore, an important sector of professional and public opinion is advocating that federal and state governments take actions designed to ensure or hasten that process. This article is concerned with the demographic characteristics of zero population growth (ZPG) in the United States, and with their economic and social implications. Although no explicit attention is devoted to the question of zero economic growth, there are various evident analogies between the economic and the demographic systems of variables. Perhaps an examination of the simpler properties of the demographic system can suggest fruitful ways of considering the more complex properties of the economic system.

Like so many terms employed in discussion of social problems and policies, ZPG has a penumbra of meanings which inhibit clarity of thought. Of these, the simplest and most simple-minded is the literal interpretation: immediate cessation of population growth and stabilization of population size at its current level (209 million in mid-1972). Frejka has prepared a computer simulation of the future this would create; his results provide us with a useful beginning for our discussion.[1] (For the time being, the role of net migration in population growth is excluded from consideration.)

The demographic arithmetic behind the conditions for immediate literal ZPG is as follows. In 1971 our population experienced 3.562 million births and 1.924 million deaths. Assuming that ZPG is not to be achieved by purposeful elevation of the number of deaths, in order to terminate population growth under current conditions we must reduce the number of births to the number of deaths, a reduction by 46 percent. This is a heroic prescription indeed, considering that, barring the grossest of departures from our traditions of freedom, we have confident knowledge of no policy weapon which can nudge fertility down (or up) more than a trace. But let us suppose for the moment that a massive propaganda campaign were successful in reorienting the reproductive part of the populace to accept something like one-half of the family size currently produced. Gradually, over the decades to come, our population would age as a consequence of the advancing age of those large cohorts (a cohort being the aggregate of persons born in a particular year) already in existence before the Procrustean policy was instituted. But, since an older population means an increase in deaths, and since ZPG could be maintained only by a concomitant and equal increase in births, we would find it necessary to relax our previous posture of reproductive discouragement. Indeed, after some sixty years had passed, we would find that we were encouraging a level of fertility for the average couple substantially in excess of the current level. Then the process would begin again, because the small post-Procrustean cohorts would move into the ages of death. Yet again the signals from Reproductive Control Headquarters would have to point sharply downward, and we would be embarked on a repetition of previous history. Over long reaches of time, the necessary modifications of reproductive posture up and then down would gradually become muted, but even a thousand years hence the elusive goal of constant population size would still require some alternation of encouragement and discouragement of childbearing.

Fixity of population size at its present level implies carefully synchronized oscillations of substantial amplitude in reproductive behavior, and continual alteration of the directions of normative pressure. Frankly, the scenario is bizarre. Moreover, concealed within the outcome is a massive irony. The obsession with total population size it reflects would by no means eliminate those changes in population size which are of the most immediate consequence. The oscillation in the numbers of births, first abruptly down, and then up, and then down, and so on, implies that one-half of our future cohorts would be experiencing the penalties of declining population size, from the standpoint of their birth cohorts, and one-half would be experiencing the penalties of increasing population size. The major institutions of the society and the economy are highly age specific in their structure: for the twenty-one-year-old looking for his first job it matters a lot how many other twenty-one-year-olds there are, and not at all how many ten-year-olds or sixty-year-olds there are. The relevant population size in many activities throughout the life cycle is that of the birth cohort, and to use fixity of population size as the overriding demographic principle guarantees that the size of the birth cohort will forever change. To be specific, in order to keep population size steady as a rock at its initial level, the size of the birth cohort must double during the next seventy years, and then be cut by 40 percent over the subsequent twenty years, such alternations of size continuing on into the future. It would be difficult to convince the representatives of these cohorts that ZPG had been achieved.

We see from this exercise of the imagination that three components of the demographic puzzle are locked in algebraic embrace: total population size, the level of reproductivity, and the sizes of successive cohorts. To insist on fixity of population size is to require incredible modifications both upward and downward in reproductive levels and to suffer the consequences of well-nigh eternal fluctuation of cohort size. Surely we can design a more reasonable future than that.

One of the basic propositions of demography is that if a regime of fertility is instituted (in a closed population) which is just sufficient to provide one female in the child generation for each female in the child-bearing generation (technically called a net reproduction rate of one), the size of that population will eventually become stationary. Note that this way of posing the problem begins with reproductive behavior and ends with its consequences for other aspects of population rather than, in the peculiar projection we were looking at before, starting with the outcome, population size, and working back to the necessary reproductive input. It can be shown by simple mathematics that if a net reproduction rate of one were to be established immediately in the United States on the basis of the current age pattern of reproduction, our population size (barring net migration) would eventually become 272 million. For those who are concerned about the absolute size of our population, this is most disconcerting. The cause of this increase by more than one-third is that, like any population which has been growing in the past, we have acquired a large amount of demographic momentum manifest in the considerable numbers of women below the highest age of childbearing. They are, in a sense, the launching platform for our future population. Each of those childbearing cohorts has an initial size of about 3.78 million, and each cohort member will live about seventy-two years. The size of the hypothesized stationary population produced by continual repetition of that experience is simply the product of those two numbers, or 272 million.

The virtue of this approach, from the standpoint of the three interdependent demographic components identified above, is that only one change in reproductive behavior is required and thenceforth the same normative signals could be maintained. Its first obvious drawback is the penalty of growing to what many regard as an unacceptable total population size of 272 million. But it has other problematic features. In the first place, although the net reproduction rate for 1972 has been reported to be at the replacement level, that estimate fails to consider discrepancies between the statistics for a particular year, and the potential lifetime fertility of the responsible parties. Such discrepancies often occur as a consequence of the way in which women choose to distribute their childbearing through time. A more realistic evaluation is that the cohorts now in the mainstream of childbearing will end up with a total which may exceed replacement by 10 percent or even more.

Accordingly, a policy oriented toward a replacement level for the net reproduction rate must take into account the fact that some time will be required to modify current behavior down toward that level, and time is costly in terms of population size. Calculations which allow a reasonable time for that modification to take place show an ultimate population size of 292 million rather than 272 million, the additional 20 million being the price paid for introducing considerations of feasibility as well as desirability into the population model.

The final negative aspect of this projection concerns its implications for the sizes of successive cohorts. If the net reproduction rate is locked at unity (if not immediately, then shortly), the numbers of births year by year will directly reflect the numbers of potential parents. During the period from the late 1940's through the early 1960's, this country experienced a baby boom; one generation hence (approximately from now through the 1980's) we would, with a fixed pattern of reproduction age by age, be destined to experience yet another baby boom, and, a generation later, still another. These successive echoes of our demographic past would dampen with time because each successive generation would reproduce over a wide period of time. Although the magnitude of the oscillations is nowhere near as substantial as those in the projection cued to fixity of population size, this approach still yields an undesirable pattern of successive increase and decrease in the size of successive cohorts.

My own preference is a third approach which is largely absent from discussions of ZPG. I propose that we attempt to achieve fixity in the size of successive birth cohorts at the lowest plausible levels. I have recently developed a projection based on this concept, and will use some of the results in my subsequent discussion.[2] In terms of the criterion of constancy of successive birth cohort size the outcome is by definition optimal; in terms of population size the total increase would be 68 million rather than 83 million as in the projection just discussed; and the modifications of reproductive behavior required are not too great to be feasible.

How is it possible to reduce the ultimate population size by 15 million below the previous projection, and also avoid the fluctuations of cohort size which seem to be implicit in the wake of the baby boom? The key to this procedure is the mathematical fact that, for any fixed level of cohort fertility, the numbers of births year by year will be higher when the successive cohorts of women are having children at successively younger ages, and lower when they are having children at successively older ages (because, in effect, there will be fewer parental cohorts bearing children each year). Accordingly, we can counterbalance what would otherwise be an increase in the annual birth crop over the next decade or so (attributable to larger numbers of potential parents) by inducing a progressively later childbearing pattern (without any decline in the total number of children any cohort eventually produces). Indeed our current birth crops are depressed below what they would otherwise have been precisely because such a change in the age pattern of childbearing is now occurring.

What is the likelihood that childbearing will occur at appreciably older ages over the next decade? The principal determinants of the age pattern are the age at which a woman has her first birth, and the length of the interval between births. Currently both are increasing. Should there be a continuing improvement in fertility regulation (including abortion) among the young, and should there be an increase not only in the ability to terminate childbearing at the wanted level but also in the efficacy with which the next birth can be delayed, then the average age of fertility will advance from cohort to cohort. This will provide a downward pressure on the birth output period by period as a counterweight to the upward pressure caused by the large size of the cohorts now moving into parenthood.

Obviously the development of a reproductive pattern in which the average age of childbearing is a few years higher than it is now would proceed more assuredly with some legislative and judicial assistance, but the important point is that all of the relevant indices are now pointing in the requisite directions. Without considering matters from a demographic standpoint at all, without, in other words, specific policies to modify the future of our population, a demographically desirable outcome is in prospect merely as a result of current social changes desirable in their own right, particularly freedom from unwanted fertility, and sexual equality in the spheres of education and employment.

Before presenting the results of an illustrative projection, it is essential to bring into the account two other components of population growth which have consequences for ultimate population size and for the concept of ZPG. The first of these is net external migration, currently a little less than 400,000 per annum, a level at which the Bureau of the Census assumes it will continue for the indefinite future. My own opinion is that this is too high a figure and that, as fertility approaches a replacement level and population growth approaches zero, there will be legislative action to reduce the migratory flow substantially. Otherwise, the native-born population would increase by some 40 percent while the foreign-born population increased by some 100 percent. In my projection, I have assumed a permanent net inflow of only 200,000 per annum. The implications for the future population are two: First, since the average age of immigrants is twenty-five, each migrant will spend approximately fifty years as a member of the United States population. Accordingly, the population contributed by migration will be 200,000 times fifty years, or 10 million. Secondly, migrants will bear children. In order to prevent them from pushing reproductive levels above replacement, it is necessary to achieve a net reproduction rate of 0.97 rather than 1.00.

The second component of population growth which has been neglected is the force of mortality. We have followed the lead of the official projections of the Bureau of the Census in assuming that the overall expectation of life at birth will rise between now and the end of the century to about seventy-two years, and thenceforth remain fixed. It is difficult to know whether this is a reasonable assumption. However, two points can be made unequivocally. In the first place, large improvements in our control over mortality can result in only small improvements in our average length of life. For example, a 20 percent decline in the mortality rate at every age would result in an increase in life expectancy of less than 5 percent. The reason the increase is proportionately so small is that in a low-mortality population like ours, those who would be spared death are mostly so old that the additional years of life they can expect are, in any event, few. The second point is a theoretical one and, for the reason just given, of minor empirical importance. Population growth occurs not simply because more people are born into the child generation, but also because the number of person-years of life in the younger generation exceeds that in the earlier generation. Thus a couple with one child would replace themselves if they died at forty, but their child lived to eighty. As long as the life expectancy of children is greater than that of their parents, population replacement can be achieved only by a net reproduction rate which is lower than unity by an appropriate proportion. This, then, is the final definition of ZPG which is worth considering—a population replacement ratio of unity. It is, of course, difficult to see how one would devise an anticipatory policy to achieve such an objective.

However, taking into account the assumptions specified above, we have determined the ultimate shape and size of the population which would result. Because of the inclusion of a migratory component, the ultimate size which we would reach within approximately sixty years is 288 million, or some 38 percent larger than our mid-1972 size. Of greater interest from a number of standpoints than the total size is the distribution of growth by age (see Figure 1). Two points are immediately evident: growth would be confined to ages above twenty, and the extraordinary current irregularity would be eliminated. To understand the implications of change in the age distribution of the population, two indices are helpful. The first is the so-called dependency ratio. The population can be divided into three parts: young dependents, productive members, and old dependents. The age boundaries are somewhat arbitrary, but a plausible case can be made for age twenty and age seventy as identified in the diagram. The current ratio of young and old dependents to the rest of the population is 0.79; the ratio in the ultimate projected population is 0.60, a 24 percent decline. This is a major point in favor of a stationary population, whatever its size, provided the level of mortality is low. The second index indicates that the current mean age of the producing population, that between the ages of twenty and seventy, is 42.0, while the mean age in the ultimate population would be 43.9. This is a much smaller change in the mean age of the

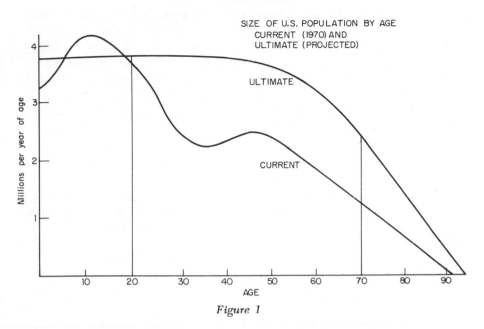

Figure 1

producing population than we experienced in the past as we moved from rapid to moderate growth. In fact, the mean age of the producing population will decline before it rises, as the baby boom cohorts (the modal ages in the current distribution) move into productive ages.

Economic Consequences of the Population Growth Rate

Within the range of plausible futures for a population like that of the United States, the lower the growth rate (including negative values), the lower the ratio of net consumers (below age twenty and above age seventy) to net producers (between ages twenty and seventy), and the higher the mean age of the net producer population. Provided human and non-human resources are effectively utilized, a lower dependency ratio makes feasible more savings and investment, more formation of human and non-human capital, and accordingly higher productivity and per capita income.[3] Provided the source of lower growth in one population than in another is lower fertility, it will begin with a smaller proportion of young net consumers, and later develop a lower "birth rate" for the net producer population. The first development in this sequence reduces the proportion of earnings which must be directed into consumption, while the second reduces the amount of capital required to match demographic expansion in order to prevent productivity per worker from declining.[4] In subsequent decades, the low growth pattern leads first to an aging of the net producer part of the population and then to a larger proportion of old people. Although economic advantages in the early phases are thus counter-balanced by economic disadvantages in the late phases, the fact that the advantages precede the disadvantages in time is itself an asset, because of the growth potential for capital formation.

In evaluating the relative advantages and disadvantages of a lower as against a higher growth rate, the common practice of analysts has been to contrast a stationary population with a stable population growing at a positive rate (or occasionally at a negative rate). Neither contrast, however, seems fruitful in the long run because each involves a contrast between the consequences of one particular difference in age distribution, on the one hand, with an ever-growing difference in population size, on the other. Either a positive or a negative growth rate, maintained over the long run, is intolerable. Accordingly, it seems more realistic to compare two populations both of which achieve stationarity: one earlier, with a lower ultimate population size and an older interim age distribution, and the other later, with a higher ultimate population size and a younger interim age distribution. (In the ultimate stationary state, the age distributions, provided there is no discrepancy in mortality, will be identical.)

The argument that a slower rate of population growth is preferable to a more rapid rate because a decreased ratio of net consumers to net producers makes possible a higher rate of capital formation rests on the implicit assumption that the opportunity for investment will be seized. This question was highly visible and much discussed during the late 1930's in a context of general unemployment and low fertility. Three types of propositions were advanced against a slower rate of population growth. In the first place, since a family must provide all of its children with certain necessities, a rapidly growing population increases demand for the same types of goods, so that openings for capital outlay are automatic and obvious and there is constant encouragement to invest. On the other hand, since a family with fewer children can afford more luxuries, a more slowly growing population implies increasing demand for different types of goods, and is therefore a more problematic context for the potential investor. In the second place, the risks of misinvestment and maladjustment and overde-velopment in particular industries are greater in a situation in which there may be an absolute decline in demand for some commodities than in a population which is growing so fast that a relative decline in demand may be an absolute increase. In the third place, the level of investment will depend more, in a more slowly growing population, on the confidence of investors, and on their willingness to take risks, on exactly those psychological dispositions less likely to be present among the older investors and entrepreneurs found in such a population. Thus, the rate of investment may actually decline, and with it the volume of employment and income, resulting in persistent unemployment and still further shrinkage of investment.[5]

Little is heard currently of the stagnation thesis, probably because we have had a moderately high growth rate for a long time, and we have acquired some confidence in the efficacy of contracyclical fiscal and monetary mechanisms to check persistent large-scale unemployment.[6] The literature is difficult to evaluate because so much of it hinges on propositions for which there is little evidence, in particular those concerning the behavior of consumers and investors and entrepreneurs. Three general propositions do seem safe, however. In the first place, one underpinning of the entire stagnation thesis is a variant of the growth ethic—that people lose their confidence if the population is not growing rapidly or if it is somewhat older. This may be no more than speculation and myth. In the second place, it is easy to confuse the interests of the investors with the interests of the population as a whole; it is perverse to enlarge the population merely in order to increase the supply of well-nigh risk-free investment opportunities. In the third place, purely demographic characteristics are probably of relatively small importance as determinants of the development of capital equipment, employment levels, and the pace of social change, and therefore of the economic efficiency of a society.

Implications of the Growth Rate for the Labor Force

One characteristic of the more slowly growing or the declining population which is regarded with dismay is the older average age of its labor force. Myths persist in the analysis of this factor because there is little hard evidence to refute them. Younger workers are considered to be superior in strength, speed and energy; older workers are considered to be superior in skill, dependability, and wisdom.[7] Little can be said with confidence about the meaning of age for individual behavior because of two confounding circumstances. First, most of the research on the subject has confused the significance of age as a stage in a person's life cycle, and age as an identifier of his location in historical time. The behavior of those now over seventy-three reflects mainly the fact that they were born in the nineteenth century. In the second place, behavior in an age is only partly the consequence of the characteristics an individual brings into that role. Every society has age norms specifying the kinds of behavior it expects of a person of a specified age, and it is generally successful in securing performance in line with those expectations.

Although they will hardly settle the issue, four considerations are at least relevant to the comparison of a somewhat older with a somewhat younger labor force. (1) Technological advance reduces the productive significance of the merely physical attributes which clearly characterize the young. (2) Technological advance, however, increases the importance of education; thus, to the extent that secular education increases, a younger labor force will be better educated and, in that sense, more productive than an older labor force. (3) A work force with a youthful age distribution must pay the penalty of devoting a large proportion of its organizational resources to recruitment, selection and training. (4) Finally, arithmetic age cannot be regarded as a constant in its significance for behavior: the sixty-year-old today may be in as good shape as the fifty-year-old of a century ago. It would be strange if there were no correlates, prior to death, of the rising length of life.

Considerable attention is paid, and deservedly so, to the implications of the fact that older men are less willing to change jobs, particularly if doing so implies migrating. Thus, the adaptability of the nation's labor force varies inversely with its age. Although older men are no more likely than younger men to become unemployed, they have greater difficulty securing new posts. The older employee becomes adjusted to his work, gravitates toward tasks that are congenial to him, and learns enough about them to exploit their positive and minimize their negative features. He establishes a network of spatial arrangements around his job, linking the places where he lives, shops, visits and plays. He has a vested interest in his work and his residence; he has more to lose from moving than the younger man. Finally, he may be able to resist a move which would be in the collective interests of the economy and of the firm by exercising the prerogatives of seniority.

From the standpoint of the individual and his career within a system characterized by an older rather than a younger age structure, the verdict at first blush would seem unfavorable. In two organizations with the same hierarchical structure (the same distribution by rank) and the same size, the one with the younger mean age will have the more rapid growth rate. Accordingly, younger people will tend to have higher ranks in the younger organization. Thus, from a dynamic standpoint, it would take longer in the older organization for a young person to achieve a responsible position. This fact may reduce his productivity because discouragement and loss of interest in his work may follow from the frustration of his desire to advance. On the other hand, the young will be at a premium in a society with an older average age because they will be fewer in relative number, their education will probably be superior and, perhaps most important, they will be more receptive to movement between jobs, firms, and regions as a pathway to rapid advance. In short, some of the same characteristics which make the occupational structure of an older society as a whole less adaptable make it possible for the young to avoid the penalty of remaining within an organization which is top-heavy with senior workers reluctant to share their power and responsibility with younger colleagues.

In my judgment, an older work force has a much more convincingly negative effect on the productivity and flexibility of the system as a whole than on the career chances of the individual. Changes in the aggregate demand for labor which require changes in the role-specific distribution of training of the existing labor force can be accommodated either by what I term *mutation* (the changes in occupation made by particular individuals during their active lives, perhaps through retraining) and by *metabolism* (the movement into it by new members and out of it by old members). Industrial shifts in the U. S. have been accomplished mainly through metabolism. Older as well as younger age structures experience metabolism ("fertility" and "mortality") but its effect is greater and much more significant for a growing than for a stationary organization because the metabolic force of mortality is much less selective than that of fertility. In general, the lower rate of metabolism of the older labor force is a serious disadvantage unless it is counterbalanced by institutional changes promoting the adaptability of those already within the system, unless, in other words, the mutation rate is increased.

The problems of structural adaptability associated with the smaller magnitude of demographic metabolism in an older society apply not only to the labor force but to any role structure within the society.[8] Indeed all of the propositions that have been advanced above concerning the meaning of age for occupational behavior have been applied to other spheres of social performance. For example, it is frequently asserted, with a minimum of unimpeachable evidence, that youth is linked with liberalism and age with conservatism, so that a growing population, because it has a more youthful age structure, will be more liberal. More broadly, it has been suggested that the dynamism of the society would be threatened by the conservatism of older leadership to the detriment of cultural and political as well as economic progress. The spectacle is raised of a lobby of the aged, pressuring the state to provide them with security to the disadvantage of younger generations and the future. Clearly the distribution of political power, to the extent that it reflects the characteristics of the citizenry, will be different in a stationary population from what it is in a younger growing population, but the relative thrust of the society, whether toward security or progress, seems much more dependent upon institutional arrangements like the seniority system within Congress, than on the age distribution of the population. There is, however, one other problem posed by an aging population which cannot be gainsaid: the family may be a moderately effective institution for the care of dependent children, but it is unsuccessful as an agency for the maintenance of aged dependents.

In concluding this section on the meaning of an older labor force, it is important first to recall that no realistic projection suggests that there will be any more than a small change upward in the average age of the labor force; certainly there will be less change than has occurred during the past century and even that change has had insufficient impact to attract social or economic commentary. Secondly, the demographic changes that will occur are probably of less significance numerically than future changes in the ages at which people enter into and exit from the labor force. Of even more importance than either of these may be the relative magnitude and age distribution of participation in the labor force by women, particularly in light of the likelihood that their fertility will be substantially lower than in the past, and will begin at a markedly higher age.

More broadly, in discussions of problems associated with demographic change, one is impressed with the overriding importance of available institutional devices for compensating whatever problems of structural adaptability arise. Thus we have spoken above of the rigidity associated with the decline of demographic metabolism and the difficulty of mutation, of the proposition, in short, that training is easier than retraining. However, to compensate for the numerical reduction of metabolism, the process itself could be made more efficient by the nature of the education provided the young, and by associated vocational guidance and placement services. Similarly, it may be much less difficult to teach an old dog new tricks if we regard retraining as a feasible and worthwhile activity, if the initial education of the worker is sufficiently general to permit his acquiring in later years whatever new skills may be demanded by technological change, and if we abandon the idea that education is something which can only precede labor force experience. The pace of social and economic change makes it sensible to extend education throughout a person's life span as an adjunct to his work week or as a routinized sabbatical renovation. As for the hardening of organizational arteries which might occur with the increase in average age, the most meaningful index of the age of an organization is the age of those in authority. If, as I posit above, younger people are at a premium because of their greater education and adaptability and their smaller numbers, it will be in the interest of firms to provide opportunities for young people to obtain leadership experience and to promote them more rapidly, rather than to lose them to greener pastures. This need not imply earlier retirement (and therefore an enlargement of the older net consumers) if we can find institutional innovations to provide older members of the work force with roles which exploit their skills and experience but do not permit them to continue in positions of power.

The Meaning of Population Size

Perhaps the best way to begin this section is by confessing to an apparent demographic heresy: I doubt that within plausible bounds the absolute size of the population of the United States is of substantial importance for any socio-economic concern. For example, I do not know how to evaluate as better or worse a population size of 150 million or of 300 million, partly because I cannot divorce the question from the other demographic consequences of the paths by which these objectives might be achieved, but mainly because I know of no quantitative magnitudes with which it would be appropriate to compare either of these numbers. The quality of the logic and evidence usually presented concerning the consequences for welfare or productivity or whatever of the absolute population size of this nation seems to me tenuous, impressionistic, and quite unquantified.

Various propositions have been advanced concerning the relative economic merits of a smaller as against a larger population size, and each has its qualifications. Thus it is pointed out that the division of labor, and thus productivity, varies with the size of the market, but the counter is that the size of the market is a function of total income rather than of total population, and is also dependent on the strength of economic nationalism since free trade is a much more effective way of enlarging the size of the market than population growth. Secondly, it is suggested that in a larger population more people share the cost of social overhead like transportation and communication and that therefore the per capita burden is smaller. Against this, however, one can say that the smaller the population, the larger each person's stock of capital and therefore the higher his level of consumption and productivity. Thirdly, a population which declines in size is sometimes said to have a burden of redundant capacity with respect to houses, railways, and so forth, but this would be no burden whatsoever from the standpoint of the community at large, although it might reduce the returns to the owners of those particular forms of capital.

The key argument against a larger population size hinges on the concept of a nonrenewable resource which would either be used up at a more rapid rate or have to be shared among more people. It is difficult to come to grips with this proposition because of the slipperiness of the notion of nonrenewability. For example, clean air and water cannot be regarded as nonrenewable, despite the current decline in their availability. There is obviously a price tag on these goods which heretofore we have more or less treated as free; our ability to pay that price, however, depends on our productivity (although our willingness to do so is, up to this point, a matter of some doubt).[9]

In the search for something in our environment which cannot be increased, and the use of which must therefore be reduced on a per capita basis in a larger population, the new Malthusians have emphasized space itself, for privacy, solitude, and recreational purposes. Several aspects of this argument make it difficult to discuss. First, the resources of recreational space are not limited to the confines of the United States, nor are the potential users of the space within the United States limited to members of our population. Second, it seems to me that the principal reason that these limited resources are now being shared among more people is that more people now have the incomes necessary to claim their share. I would find it ethically unacceptable for those who have already achieved access to rare public goods to engage in a conspiracy to inhibit economic growth or to establish barriers in order that they not be forced to share those goods with others. Third, it does not seem to be technically correct that space is limited—it too can be created. Finally, as far as privacy and solitude are concerned, these are much less matters of spatial distance between people than of the social norms governing individual rights and of the material means by which privacy can be produced and purchased.

With relation to the economic consequences of the rate of population growth, my net conclusion is that a lower rate of population growth is preferable to a higher one.[10] I know of no realistic projection that leads to an immediate decline of the population; on the contrary, the prospect is for continued growth at least for the next several decades, even with subreplacement fertility. While I can see no advantages to a larger population size, there seem to be no clear and substantial bases for heroic measures to prevent demographic momentum from enlarging our present population by 30 or 40 percent.[11] My own preference is for a policy which would tolerate subreplacement fertility for a long time to come, accepting the eventual decline in population size which would result, and anticipating that, some time in the distant future, long after we are all gone, subsidization of parenthood will be instituted in order to achieve replacement. On the one hand, I doubt that population size is a sufficiently important variable in the social scheme to justify the major social and economic readjustments necessary to reduce it; on the other hand, I find unconvincing the arguments that it is worth substantial expenditure to avoid an older population. On balance, my message is that we are overplaying the importance of the population variables in our future.

Notes on Population Policy

The key question which underlies the issue of population policy is the extent to which the aggregate consequences of individual reproductive behavior may be unfavorable and yet fail to stimulate appropriate responses by individuals. Can equilibrium be achieved by leaving decisions up to individuals or must the collectivity actively seek it? Assume for the time being that the latter is the case, that we need a population policy to redirect the course of population growth. Three categories of government action are available:

1. *Education and exhortation.* We can communicate to the citizenry what is known about the aggregate consequences of their reproductive decisions, and urge that, in their future decisions, they give more prominent weight to those consequences. In my judgment, such an approach would be marginally influential at best, and virtually impossible to calibrate.

2. *Economic incentives and disincentives*. Various proposals have been advanced, based on the principle of redistributing income away from the more prolific toward the less prolific. In theory they fulfill the requirement of quantitative modifiability to check excesses in either direction, although the lead-time for demographic processes is long indeed. There are three flaws to this approach. First, the relationship between income and fertility is very weak and probably nonmonotonic; the approach, in other words, probably will not work, at least not to reduce fertility. Second, even if it did work, the outcome would be undesirable because the penalties would fall not only on the miscreant parents but on their children as well. Any policy which is regressive with respect to the new generation is, to my way of thinking, a bad policy. And third, there is no guarantee that the necessary magnitude of disincentives needed to achieve the desired demographic result would be tolerated by the individual taxpayer, given the distance between his concerns and those of the aggregate.

3. *Compulsion*. Some writers with impressive academic credentials have concluded that the pursuit of individual interests is ineluctably detrimental to the commonweal, and that authoritarian procedures must be initiated, such as compulsory abortion or sterilization after the second child has been born. Entirely apart from the moral repugnance which such a proposal provokes, it poses a problem in arithmetic which enlarges its ethical disrepute. Some couples are incapable of having two children, either because they fail to survive to the age of reproduction, or because one of them is sterile. Others prefer to have no child or one child. Couples are not permanently paired: some women with fewer than two children will marry husbands who already have two. In short, no general rule specifying an integral number of children would satisfy the replacement requirement, a fact which necessitates a system for granting permission to some parents to have a third child. By what principles can such aggregate discrimination be pursued? Presumably any policy involving such compulsion would be advocated only if it seemed the sole pathway to survival. But this is a classic argument based on the principle that the end justifies the means. And the issue here is not one of survival willy-nilly, but of survival because a way of life is regarded as deserving of preservation.

Consider now the possibility that demographic equilibrium is achievable at the individual level, without collective intervention. There can be no unequivocal judgment on this at present, because we have no relevant experience. Our fertility has always occurred in the context of massive collective intervention of a pronatalist type; at the level of means, we have inhibited individual access to the knowledge, agents and services required for effective fertility regulation, and at the level of ends we have encouraged parenthood and discouraged nonparenthood using virtually the entire spectrum of available pressures to induce conformity. Throughout the population, we continue to support unequal treatment for women which, among other things, prejudices their role choices very strongly in the direction of motherhood. Finally, many of our subcultures have been blocked from complete participation in the national trend toward modernization, a trend which has everywhere been accompanied by a lowering of fertility.

Despite all of the pressures upward on reproductive intentions, and despite all of the barriers the collectivity has placed in the way of access to effective fertility regulation, the current level of fertility is certainly no more than 20 percent and may be no more than 10 percent above replacement, and the direction of change is indisputably downward. (Interpreting current behavior is admittedly problematic because the cohorts of women on which we most need a reproductive reading are far from having completed their fertility cycle, but the above estimates rely on the best available techniques of measurement.) And once that component of current fertility attributed by parents to failures in fertility regulation is removed, the outcome of intended behavior ranges from replacement to somewhat below replacement.[12]

From this perspective, to eliminate population growth the government need not institute procedures for supplanting individual determination about reproduction by some collective goal, but only abandon current pronatalist policies. In other words, the elimination of population growth is a likely consequence of policies which enlarge the scope of individual freedom—policies eminently worthy of adoption whatever their demographic side-effects.[13] In particular, the government should encourage completely free and open access to the knowledge, supplies and services requisite to contraception; abortion and sterilization without restriction by marital status or implicit restriction by economy; equality of opportunity for education and employment without restriction by sex; and openings to modern life for the depressed subcultures in the population.

In my judgment the demographic consequence of accomplishing these objectives would be a subreplacement level of fertility. Population size would first become appreciably larger than at present, as we exhaust our demographic momentum, and then begin to decline. If this assessment of the future is correct (and it must be admitted that demographic projections have almost always been wrong), government action to change the natural course of the growth rate will eventually have a positive rather than negative goal. Re-examination of possible government actions with this in mind puts economic incentives and disincentives in a different light. If the goal is to induce couples to have more children than they otherwise would have, the direction of redistribution of income will be toward rather than away from the children as well as the parents, and thus progressive with respect to the next generation.

Given the disparity of perspective between the individuals who make reproductive decisions and the social aggregate which is exposed to the consequences of those decisions, it is most improbable that equilibrium would be achievable without representation of collective interests in those decisions. On the assumption that the problem we face is the approach to equilibrium from a superreplacement position, analysts have to date focused their attentions on policies which would depress fertility and have generally put forward the stark alternatives of regressive disincentives to childbearing on the one hand, or authoritarian intervention on the other. In my view, the approach to equilibrium, and this would certainly be many decades hence, is more likely to be from the subreplacement position, and accordingly can take a progressive form within the traditions of freedom and justice that we are presumably interested in maintaining along with our demographic survival.

We would be remiss in this presentation if we were to sidestep an ominous possibility which lurks within the context of a stationary or declining population size. Our attention in this paper has been devoted entirely to the population of the United States, without consideration for the implications of its size relative to those of other nation-states. Although our power and prestige and influence in international affairs obviously have something to do with our population size, it seems to me that, in a military sense and in other respects, they have more to do with the size of our gross national product. On the other hand, within the United States there are various distinct subcultures, identifiable ethnic groups with their own patterns of natural increase. Since numbers contribute to the relative political power of domestic groups, especially under a representative government, conflicts between ethnic groups, like conflicts between nations, may be pursued by means of policies seeking demographic advantage. Just as it is implausible to expect national demographic equilibrium as the fortuitous outcome of individual decisions, so too it is implausible to expect each constituent ethnic group within the population to achieve equilibrium. In brief, a population with a zero rate of natural increase is likely to contain some subpopulations which are growing and some which are declining. There is less likelihood of ethnic conflict when all groups are growing than when some are growing and others declining; this is the political analogue to the economic proposition that growth simplifies problems of accommodation and change. As with so many other problems that have been raised in this essay, the solutions that seem plausible and effective and acceptable are nondemographic in character.

Finally, if we grant that the worth of survival is intrinsic to the concept of a society, the question remains, although essentially unbroached in discussion, of what we want to see survive, and by what means. A collective commitment to population replacement is a defensible posture only if we assume that whatever it is that we are proud of must be transmitted biologically. If, on the other hand, we think of ourselves from a sociocultural standpoint, might not our thrust toward immortality be satisfied by efforts to ensure that future generations share our values, whether or not they share our genes? In this sense the rate of population growth is irrelevant to the issue of sociocultural survival.

REFERENCES

1. Tomas Frejka, "Reflections on the Demographic Conditions Needed to Establish a U. S. Stationary Population Growth," *Population Studies*, 22, No. 3 (November 1968), 379-397.

2. Norman B. Ryder, "A Demographic Optimum Projection of the U.S. Population," Commission on Population Growth and the American Future Reports, *Social and Demographic Aspects of Population Growth*, 1, eds. C. F. Westoff and R. Parke, Jr. (Washington, D.C.: U.S. Government Printing Office, 1973).

3. Stephen Enke, "Zero U. S. Population Growth—When, How and Why?" *Socio-Economic Planning Sciences*, 5 (1971), 263-273.

4. Ansley J. Coale, "Population and Economic Development," *The Population Dilemma*, 2nd ed., ed. Philip M. Hauser (Englewood Cliffs, N.J.: Prentice-Hall, 1969), pp. 59-84.

5. W. B. Reddaway, *The Economics of a Declining Population* (London: George Allen & Unwin, 1939).

6. Paul Demeny, "The Economics of Population Control," *Rapid Population Growth: Consequences and Policy Implications*, Study Committee of the Office of the Foreign Secretary, National Academy of Sciences (Baltimore: Johns Hopkins Press, 1971).

7. United Nations, Department of Social Affairs, Population Division, *The Determinants and Consequences of Population Trends*, Population Studies, No. 17 (New York: United Nations, 1953), esp. Ch. 14, "Implications of Population Trends in Highly Industrialized Countries."

8. Alfred Sauvy, *General Theory of Population* (New York: Basic Books, 1969).

9. Ansley J. Coale, "Man and His Environment," *Science*, 170 (October 9, 1970), 132-136.

10. U. S. National Academy of Sciences Study Committee, "The Consequences of Rapid Population Growth," *Rapid Population Growth: Consequences and Policy Implications* (Baltimore: Johns Hopkins Press, 1971), pp. 16-69.

11. Commission on Population Growth and the American Future, *Population and the American Future* (Washington, D.C.: U. S. Government Printing Office, 1972).

12. Norman B. Ryder and Charles F. Westoff, "Wanted and Unwanted Fertility in the United States: 1965 and 1970," *Social and Demographic Aspects of Population Growth*.

13. Ansley J. Coale, "Should the United States Start a Campaign for Fewer Births," *Population Index*, 34, No. 4 (October-December 1968), 467-474.

E. J. MISHAN

Ills, Bads, and Disamenities: The Wages of Growth

Do People Have What They Want?

"I BELIEVE simply in giving people what they want." This expression of democratic largesse has come from a business tycoon[1] and, I regret to say, from a well-known economist as well. The idea has, of course, a superficial appeal, so it is as well to point out at the start that people can have "what they want" only in a limited sense, before going on to consider the problems involved in the attempt to give them more of "what they want" in years to come.

If I want to be as strong as Hercules, as wise as Solomon, as talented as Michaelangelo, I shall want in vain. One need not be so innocently ambitious, however, to experience frustrations. A great many people ardently wish that they were taller, handsomer, and more gifted than nature ever intended them to become. And there may be moments in their lives when all the tea in China—assuming it could be sold at a reasonable price—would not compensate for their unfulfillment. Clearly, then, people get what they want, even in a liberal democracy, only in the narrow sense that policies are enacted by the party voted into power, and that the flow of market goods is adapted over time to the changing pattern of demand.

Confined as is the area of choice for society, it is yet further restricted for the individual. As far as government policies are concerned, he has to accept much that goes against the grain of his political convictions. As for the market, it may be that he wants all he buys, but he certainly does not buy all he wants. He has to accept as unalterable data, at least in the short run, the physical features of the environment in which he lives. The law permits him to go wherever he pleases, provided he does not trespass on private property, and to buy whatever he pleases, subject, however, to the constraints of his income, the time at his disposal, and the range of goods available at market prices. Again, he can choose any job he wants, provided he is qualified to hold it, and provided it is offered to him.

63

In addition to these obvious limitations, each person's choice of purchases is subject to innumerable laws and regulations. The manufacture,
sale and consumption of any product may be regulated or prohibited.
Restrictions abound with respect to location of property, to hours of
business, to manufacturing processes, and to the employment of labor. In
addition, a prolific variety of taxes and subsidies, though resented less
than direct controls, nonetheless act to delimit and shift the area of each
person's choice.[2]

We may conclude that, whatever the general level of consumption, a
person obtains "what he wants"—or rather "what he chooses" (which is not
the same thing)—only in a limited sense, and that his choices among
the man-made goods on the market alter with changes in prices, taxes,
advertising, and availabilities.

Having placed in a more sober light these much-touted privileges
conferred by political democracy and the competitive private enterprise
system on the citizen of a "free society," we may reconsider the urgency and
perhaps question the wisdom of attempting to maintain the present pace of
economic growth into the indefinite future. Two related questions are
raised here. First, is sustained economic growth physically possible? Second,
is it desirable for the West? These are related questions inasmuch as economists are prone to invoke the concept of a "trade-off" wherever the
attainment of one good entails the loss of some other. In particular, they
tend to set against the presumed benefits of further economic growth the
ecological risks arising from the attempt to maintain pressure on the
growth pedal. But if people can be persuaded that the benefits of further
economc growth (exclusive of ecological risk) are slight or dubious or
negative, the "trade-off" concept becomes inappropriate. For there would
be naught to resolve: the issue would then be simply that of deciding
whether to embark on a joyless voyage, fraught with increasing risk, and
bound for an unattractive destination. And if I may be allowed to
anticipate my conclusions, that is just how I view the prospect of further
economic growth in the West.

Whether Continued Economic Growth Is Physically Possible

Though I pose the question, whether continued economic growth is
physically possible, it could be rephrased more sensibly as follows: under
what conditions, and for what length of time, is an x percent rate of
growth possible for a particular area? Put more generally yet, what time-
paths of economic growth, as conventionally measured, are physically
possible for an economy having particular economic endowments and
institutions?

Alas, we have no methods as yet by which we can produce convincing
answers to such questions. Indeed, it is entirely possible that we shall be

unable, even in the future, to ascertain the physical limits to economic growth until we experience some manifest deterioration of living standards or incur some ecological catastrophe. The best we can do today is to infer tentatively, from highly simplified global models using controversial assumptions about future technological progress and about world reserves of materials, that growth at present rates, either of population or of industrial output, cannot continue for much more than a century.

Whether or not they believe these conclusions realistic, all the people debating this issue recognize that we inhabit all too tiny a planet. Most of them are alarmed at current population trends; the prospect of some fifteen billion human beings swarming over the planet in fifty or sixty years' time is not an inviting one. With the existing population of about four billion souls, we are already getting in each other's way and stepping on each other's toes. Assuming the mobility indices continue to rise—car ownership in Western Europe increasing at about 8 percent per annum, air travel at about 10 percent—the mounting frustrations of travelers and the resentments of indigenous populations may break out in civil disturbances.

Apart from population growth, though aggravated by it, there are the familiar problems of pollution, food supplies, and the depletion of natural resources. Although there have been some local improvements over the last quarter of a century—there is, for example, less sulphur dioxide (though much more carbon dioxide) in the air of London than there was twenty years ago, and some (possibly mutant) species of fish have recently been discovered in the murky waters of the Thames—nobody seriously challenges the fact that air and water pollution exist on a larger scale today than ever before in man's history. The global scale of pollution not only destroys flora and fauna but spoils the food we eat. Chemical pesticides enter our bloodstream either directly through our consumption of chemically sprayed plants or indirectly through our consumption of cattle that ingest them. The poisoning of rivers destroys fish in estuaries and renders the flesh of the survivors increasingly toxic to humans.

Turning to material resources, in particular fossil fuels and metals, a common estimate is that, if present consumption trends persist, we shall run out of oil by about the end of the century even allowing for the discovery of new reserves, and of all but a few of today's "essential" metals within about fifty years. Indeed, at current rates of usage, all known reserves of silver, gold, copper, lead, platinum, tin, and zinc will have been used up within a couple of decades.

The conventional economic response to the threat of depleting resources is twofold: to quote history in illustration of the principle of resource substitution and to affirm faith in the future of technology and "the wit of man." Concerning the first, economists will point out that the shortage of a resource leads to a rise in its price which induces manufacturers to replace it by other materials that, though less suitable, are now less expensive. The less successful the search for suitable substitutes, however, the higher the resulting costs of the finished goods in question, and the smaller the amounts bought by consumers.

But all this takes place in the world of theoretical constructs. The real world may turn out to be less accommodating. Historical examples, such as those given by Barnett and Morse,[3] cover about a hundred years of recent history and contain few examples apart from the apparent success story of fuels: wood to coal, coal to oil, and oil (hopefully) to nuclear power. I say the *apparent* success story since it may not prove feasible to maintain, much less increase, per capita consumption of energy much further unless we discover economical means of disposing safely of the vast amounts of heat and radioactive wastes generated by nuclear power stations. Neither can one be very optimistic about the impending exhaustion, simultaneously, of a large number of widely used metals. Only in theoretical models are substitutes always available. It is entirely possible that some of these metals will rise steeply in price thus drastically reducing their use and the output of products that depend upon them, without any tolerable substitute being discovered. There will be no comfort to be had from traditional doctrines when we are brought up sharply against the unalterable facts of the physical universe.

Two Reasons for Skepticism about Technology

Over the future of technology a great question mark hangs, and for much the same reason. Two hundred years of scientific discovery and innovation have imbued us with a faith that man will eventually conquer. Thus, whenever some of the less happy consequences of modern technology and its products are brought to our attention—140,000 automobile deaths a year, the ecological disasters of DDT, the genetic effects of Thalidomide—or whenever account is taken of the increasing risks to which humanity is now exposed, the habitual response of technocrats is to transmute the risk into a "challenge" or to quote some historical piece of "doomsdayism." Yet if, as philosophers are agreed, there are no laws of historical development, the proposition must be extended also to the development of science and technology. We cannot be sure of technological progress either. Man may, then, become engaged endlessly in some kinds of research that, in the nature of things, cannot come to fruition.

Apart from these real possibilities, there are at least two reasons for feeling less than sanguine about the future of technology. First, the unprecedented scale of the current exploitation of the earth's finite resources makes virtually a qualitative difference between the situation today and that of yesterday. For this reason alone, deriding yesterday's Jeremiahs affords little consolation. Time works vast changes, and the alarums of today should not go unheeded simply because those of yesterday were premature. The apprehensions of an octogenarian about his impending demise are not to be soothed by reminding him that he thought he was going to die when he was twenty.

To pursue the same analogy, the discovery that some poet was lamenting the disappearance of the English countryside at about the time of Chaucer is, in itself, no answer to those who lament today for the same reason. The English countryside can indeed disappear. It is, in fact, being irreparably destroyed. Again, from the observation that the fears of Malthus and others were premature at the turn of the nineteenth century, it does not follow that the earth can comfortably support any size of population. And however abundant the earth's reserves of fossil fuels and minerals, their continued mining must eventually exhaust them, and faster than we are prone to imagine. Sustained rates of growth build up to incredible magnitudes. If, for example, actual oil reserves turn out to be four times as great as we estimate today, the current growth of consumption could be maintained for only fifteen years longer than it could according to current estimates. To take another example, if the growth of air travel in Western Europe maintains its pace, there will be about fifteen times as much air travel at the end of the century as there is today, and more than sixty times as much in another fifteen years. I need hardly remark that the trend is unlikely to continue at such rates for many years—though not because governments are far-sighted enough to take measures to discourage the trend. Owing to limitations of air and ground space, commercial attempts to maintain the expansion of air travel will run into difficulties long before air travel has multiplied fifteenfold.

In sum, we of this generation are already being pressed against the inescapable limitations of a finite planet. Whether or not we succeed in stabilizing population in time, we cannot continue much longer to use up space, to ransack the earth's resources and to fill its air and waters with effluent with the reckless abandon that has characterized our activity since the industrial revolution. The implications of this new situation can be crucial for technology, for its development over the last 200 years has been based on physical conditions that no longer obtain: virtually unlimited resources and a virtually unlimited assimilative capacity of the biosphere. It remains to be seen how technology will cope when abundance in these respects gives way to constriction.

The second reason for feeling less than sanguine about the contribution of technology in maintaining the existing growth rates is that we are moving into an area of increasing uncertainty. In order of diminishing tractability we can list four types of global risk, none of which existed before the industrial revolution.

(1) Insofar as the chief effluents poured into the air, lakes, rivers,

and coastal waters are known and their toxic effects understood, they can be effectively curbed in a number of ways, of which enforcing minimal standards of purity may well be the most economic. The success of this method depends upon the efficacy and frequency of monitoring, and on the severity of the penalties exacted for failing to comply. What economists do not sufficiently allow for, however, are the limits to our present knowledge. There cannot be many effluents whose full range of toxic effects are known to us. Moreover, in consequence of rapid chemical innovation, new gases and fluids are being produced whose effects on the ambient environment and on our health may not be discernible for many years, and possibly only after substantial and irreversible damage has been done.

(2) To these risks that we run from pushing on in a state of semi-ignorance, we may add (a) those arising from the indiscriminate use of chemical pesticides such as DDT, from the gradual dissipation of the protective ozone mantle by the gases emitted in supersonic flight, and from the accumulating deposits of synthetic material that resist absorption into the ecological cycle, and (b) those arising out of the growing assortment of chemical compounds appearing each year on the market, about whose ultimate biological and genetical effects, taken singly or in combination, we know next to nothing. Nor can we reasonably expect to detect the dangers in time. Luckily, the mutilative potential of the medically recommended sedative, Thalidomide, was discovered before it became a genetic calamity—and then, not by doctors or scientists, but by a private citizen working on a hunch. We may not be so lucky with a number of other common drugs on the market. If, after a number of years, the death or sickness of a small proportion of the human population can be traced to some new substance or to some new combination of substances, it will be likely that the disease is latent in a much larger proportion of the population. What is more, it may not be possible to find an adequate antidote in time, and even if one is found in time, its side effects may eventually prove to be more dangerous than the disease it is intended to cure.

(3) The third category of risk arises from our diminishing immunity to contagious diseases—a consequence, ironically, of the apparent success of modern medicine. Just as many insect pests have, over the last three decades, successfully adapted themselves to withstand, or even to thrive on, once powerful pesticides, so too, are micro-organisms, with their faster rate of reproduction, and therefore of mutation, becoming resistant to the action of penicillin, antibiotics, etc. The ultimate effect of "miracle drugs," it appears, is, through the irrepressible mechanism of natural selection, to breed "miracle microbes." But this powerful adaptive mechanism of the micro-organisms that are man's most ruthless foe does not take us "back to square one." The situation is in reality worse. For under

favorable conditions, the human body, aided perhaps by older methods of treatment, could often enough cope with the old strain of germs. Once new strains have appeared in response to the initial efficacy of new drugs, the human body may no longer be able to cope alone even under favorable conditions. Perforce it may have to depend entirely on new and "more powerful" drugs, but drugs yet to be discovered. And there is no assurance that they will be discovered in time, and no assurance that, if discovered, they will not again be rendered useless within a short period by new strains of microbes. It may transpire, then, that the much lauded achievements of medical science will have succeeded only in starting a race for survival between man and microbe in which the advantages seem to lie with the microbe.

(4) The fourth and the greatest immediate risk in the foreseeable future is that humanity will perish as a result of the great scientific discoveries of the last thirty years inasmuch as they have presented man with the means of illimitable thermonuclear destruction and biochemical warfare. Within the next decade the power of instant annihilation of all life over vast areas will be within the destructive capacity of the governments of some thirty nations, including many of the smaller nations that are led by unstable regimes which may continue to include adventurers and fanatics. Introduce into this already inflammable situation the possibility of accident, military bungling, or bluff carried too far, and the chances of humanity surviving the end of the century do not look particularly strong.

The Desirability of Continued Economic Growth

Let us now turn to the second large question, whether further economic growth is socially desirable or, for that matter, whether the current pattern of overall expenditure is socially desirable. There are, however, some preliminary and perhaps trivial objections to be dealt with first.

The answer to the popular gambit of the demagogue—What right have I, Mishan, to "dictate" to others what they should want?—is simple. I do not question people's right to spend as they please or to vote as they please.[4] What I do question is whether their welfare will increase as a result of their increasing expenditures—a judgment of fact, not of ethics. My judgment of the consequences of the pursuit of economic growth may, for the present, be a minority view. But a voice urging a minority view is neither absurd for that reason nor is it, as yet, inconsistent with the operation of a liberal democracy.

And the answer to those who would place against my skepticism of the value for the West of further economic growth the mere fact that people appear to want more to spend, or that they vote for parties apparently committed to economic growth,[5] is no less simple. Such observations constitute evidence neither for the thesis that people prefer continued economic growth to alternative economic policies nor for the thesis that continued economic growth will enhance their welfare. Since I shall be devoting the remainder of the paper to an examination of the latter thesis, let me first say a few words about the former.

One may not infer from the economic state of affairs resulting from the actual economic and political behavior of people that they prefer such a state of affairs to any other for the straightforward reason that a large number of technically feasible alternatives, which might well be preferred by majorities if their implications were understood, are just not understood. Even if their implications are understood, such alternatives are not offered to the public in the form of coherent programs by existing political institutions or by the working of existing markets. For what has been said of the constraints on individual choice can be extended to society at large, at least in the short run.

First, concerning economic behavior, one cannot infer from each person's desire for more money for himself in existing circumstances that he also wants more economic growth for society. His selfish preference for himself under the existing dispensation is quite consistent with an aspiration for a zero or negative rate of growth for society as a whole. Moreover, my earlier comments about the constraints on individual choice apply also to the choices made by society; these also are the result of prices that do not reflect the social costs of "distortions" in availabilities arising from the absence of property or "amenity" rights, of commercial advertising, of economic institutions, and of financial journalism and the resulting belief system that keeps the multitude ever jostling for more.

As for political behavior, in a two-party system at least, the choice available at any moment of time is limited. Democratic parties are obsessed with returning to power or with retaining power. They are of necessity conservative. They address themselves to safe bread-and-butter issues—to a large extent to the current economic issues of employment, industrial conflict, prices, balance of payments, and, since the war, of overall economic growth performance. Of necessity, then, they are myopic and think largely of the electoral effect of their actions over the next one, two, or three years. Moreover, where both parties adopt the same policy on an important issue—say both are concerned primarily with economic growth and only secondarily with environmental problems— then the electorate has virtually no choice for the time being. Even where a majority of the populace has begun to doubt the conventional economic wisdom, the launching of a third political party is a Herculean task requiring time, patience, and vast financial and political resources. And to alter the attitudes and convictions of the party stalwarts on a major issue also takes time, patience, and financial and political resources. So much for preliminary objections to the legitimacy of raising the question of whether further economic growth is socially desirable.

Assuming that per capita growth could be maintained indefinitely at the current rate, the question of its social desirability is still a bit vague and lends itself to a number of interpretations. We might, for example, be asking the question: Are we getting our money's worth from the rising tide of affluence, or is the overall pattern of expenditure socially desirable? The answer is surely no. Even the most conservative economist would agree that a little political initiative would rid us of a lot of unnecessary ill effects. Eighteenth-century believers in progress would be astounded at our technological capabilities, and they would be dismayed at what we have done with them. How could we justify the sheer ugliness and abandon of our cities; their endless clamor, litter, stench, tawdriness and desolation? Let us concede that we could have used our enormous wealth to create more sensible ways of living, and pass on to other possible interpretations of the question.

We might want to compare the quality or wholesomeness of life today with that of bygone ages. And growthmen are ever quick to make such comparisons. Yet the comparisons they make are unfair in several ways. First, they use what little history they know to select the bleaker periods of the past: "the dark satanic mills" and other grim features of the earlier part of the industrial revolution being a much favored point of reference, or the ancient slave economies of the East, or the imaginary life of an early caveman: "nasty, brutish, and short."

Secondly, they accent those aspects of life which, just because of rising affluence and indiscriminate consumerism, absorb our attention—hygiene, longevity, youthfulness, mobility, instant entertainment, self-indulgence, effort-avoidance. Inadvertently, they omit to stress the features that were common to all preindustrial ages, the (by our standards) inordinate number of holidays and holy days, the lack of clear distinction between work and living, and a vaster sense of time and space owing to slow travel, slow news, and few timepieces. Again, they tend to overlook the great myths that gave hope of life beyond the grave, a more settled way of life, a greater joy in nature, and easy access to the countryside—to clean air, to lakes, rivers, quiet fields, and woodlands.*

---

* In pre-industrial civilizations, according to Jacques Ellul, the time given to the use of techniques was short compared with the leisure time devoted to sleep, conversation, games, and meditation.

For primitive man and historical man, work as such was *not* a virtue. It was considered better not to consume than to work hard. Thus man worked as little as possible and was content with restricted consumption.

Today comfort means easy chairs, foam rubber mattresses, bathrooms, air-conditioning, washing machines, etc. Our chief concern is to avoid physical effort, and therefore we become more dependent upon the machine.

According to Giedion (quoted by Ellul) men of the Middle Ages were also con-

Thirdly, in comparing the quality of life at different periods of history, the notion of some average sort of life has to be abandoned. In all ages, including our own, there are rich and poor, fortunate and unfortunate, and the proportions vary from place to place and from one age to another. A historian may be able to pick out certain periods over the last 5,000 years when for certain groups in particular parts of the world life appears to have been good and wholesome while for a fair proportion of the remainder, it was not burdensome.* Such comparisons are to some extent subjective and inconclusive, though there is more agreement among historians on some periods and places than on others. I doubt, however, whether many historians would agree to use GNP as a historical yardstick of well-being, and to conclude, on the basis of it, that life today is transparently happier than it has ever been before.

Finally, we might more reasonably be asking if life is becoming more enjoyable or if we are becoming better or more contented people in consequence of economic growth. Bearing in mind the facts of human nature, we could reflect on current economic and social developments in particular areas and endeavor to obtain clues about the extent to which the modes of living they give rise to accord with, or conflict with, men's biological and psychic needs. And by speculating about technological and economic developments over the foreseeable future, we can debate whether, on balance, we are likely to be better people, or more contented people, over the next few decades. This seems to me the more promising area of inquiry, and the one to which I suggest we direct our attention.

Obviously we cannot *prove* propositions about the decline in social welfare as one can prove, for example, that a significant rise in the price of beef, *ceteris paribus*, will cause a drop in the maximum amount of beef that people are willing to buy. In debating social welfare, subjective judgments are required—judgments of fact, and possibly also judgments of value.

Let us move now toward the hub of the problem by asking an apparently naive question: Why cannot a rise in GNP, or rather in real per capita income, be accepted as an index of an increase in society's welfare? The theoretical economist's short answer is that the sufficient conditions that would allow a translation from GNP to social welfare are not met.

First, the identical population would have to remain in being during a period over which GNP rises. If the period extends to two generations,

---

cerned with comfort. But for them comfort represented a moral and aesthetic order. Space was the primary element. Men sought open spaces and large rooms. They did not care if the chairs were hard or the rooms ill-heated. What mattered was proportion and the materials used.

* For the recent history of England, I should be inclined to pick out the time of Chaucer, the Elizabethan age, the mid-eighteenth century, possibly the Edwardian age.

and each person in the second generation has more goods than some corresponding person in the first, the economist can only report that fact. Since he eschews interpersonal comparisons, he is unable to declare that persons in the second generation experience more welfare than those in the first. Secondly, and for the same reason, the economist cannot state that a person whose real income has grown over time is better off unless it is also known that his tastes and his capacity for enjoyment have remained unchanged.

These conditions do look rather austere, and in his practical recommendations the economist has a tendency to overlook them. Provided that people are not working harder and that the distribution of the aggregate product among the population is no less satisfactory, a rise in real per capita income is commonly regarded as conferring benefits on society, even though its size and age composition are changing. I could be persuaded to go along with this, were it not for the fact that quite a useful proportion of our national resources is devoted expressly to persuading people to change their tastes—not always for the better—and were it not for another proviso.

In order to translate from increments of GNP to increments of welfare there is another condition that has to be met: namely, that all changes in benefits and "disbenefits" arising from economic activity be properly priced. People would then be able to choose the amounts of benefits they would pay for and the amounts of the "disbenefits" they would be paid to endure. But this crucial condition is not met in the dynamic economic systems of the West for two reasons. One, because the pattern of produced outputs and the methods of production are continually being altered in response *not* to the wants of the workers but, instead, to changes in consumers' demand and in technology. Two, because the operation of many consumer goods and the processes by which they are produced generate a range of injurious effects that escape the pricing system and spill over into the population at large.[6] Some of these spillover effects are evident to everybody, being quite visible, audible, or otherwise obtrusive. Some are directly attributable to the output or use of particular goods. Others, however, are more complex and intangible, and are virtually impossible to attribute to any particular good. Let us elaborate these propositions since reflection on their implications for welfare will go far to dissipate any habitual presumption that a rise in GNP entails an increase in social welfare.

The Welfare Significance of the Consumer Bias of the Market

By some accident in the development of economic thought, the choices made by persons *qua* consumers became pivotal in the economic theory of resource allocation. In contrast, their choices *qua* workers, though sometimes treated symmetrically and integrated into formal models, tend to be overlooked in more casual argument. Simplifications about workers' choice—such as the idea of their being indifferent as between occupations —are popular enough in economic analysis. Inadvertently, the worker comes to be regarded as a sort of mobile atom, ready to combine with other resource-atoms according to changes in the pattern of resource prices, and ready also to move from declining to expanding sectors of the economy, or from one region to another, so as to meet the quickening changes in consumers' expenditures. In consequence, plant and equipment in some sectors become useless all too soon, and skilled workers become redundant in the painful adjustments necessary to meet continuing shifts in consumers' demands that, in an affluent society, are often impulsive, fickle, and of doubtful welfare significance. Although economists seek to justify the apparent wastes generated by alternating and wayward currents of demand by affecting to remain neutral with respect to consumers' taste—or rather to the lack of it—and though they readily estimate the social worth of an additional transistor or other inane gadget by a person's willingness to pay for it, there is no corresponding calculation of the really significant losses of welfare suffered by workers who are made redundant, even temporarily, by persistent switches in consumer expenditure. The costs of movement to another industry or area, especially if a worker has a family to support, can be prohibitive. In many cases he has little choice but to remain in his old neighborhood and suffer anxiety and a loss of earnings and status for an indefinite period.

The worker's security in a wealthy and progessive economy is subject, however, not only to the vagaries of demand but also to the stream of technological innovation in goods and in methods of production. New machinery and factory organization may ease his physical labor. They may make his job more interesting, or less so. They may bring him closer to or take him further from his workmates in terms of space or communication. But whatever the outcome, the worker ultimately has no real choice but to adapt to the changing shape of technology. The potential increase in well-being that would come about as a result of providing work that is more creative, more communal, and generally more enjoyable might be worth more than the actual increase in well-being that is provided today by yet more goods.

In any event, these considerations weaken the presumption favoring economic growth and consumerism. For if it is believed that over the last two centuries, during which workers were transformed from artisans and craftsmen to machine hands and dial-watchers, a decline has taken place in the satisfactions that men once derived from their daily tasks, who is to say that the loss has been fully compensated by the consequent proliferation of goods and gadgetry and the transformation to a mechanized environment?

Looking into the future, the time cannot be far off when, for factory production at least, there is little left for the workers to do but to make the complex machinery that will be required for wholly automated factories. The possibility has to be faced that a large proportion of the labor force may be congenitally incapable of performing the tasks that will by then be too complex to be performed by machines. Unless such industrially unemployable labor can be absorbed into the service industries, it will remain unemployable.

For the higher echelons, also, the future does not look very much brighter. Economic growth depends, among other things, on extreme specialization that dulls the spirit, narrows the sympathies, and cuts one off from the largeness of life. In contrast to the hopes of yesterday's enlightened reformers, who conceived of higher education as an emancipating experience, broadening the mind and enhancing the personality, the sad fact today is that higher education is unabashedly vocational. In some fields a man may have to be thirty years of age or more before he reaches the frontiers of his specialization. And if he is an academic or professional he will spend the remainder of this working years striving to keep abreast of the expanding body of technical literature, and striving also to add his mite to it. The price paid by professionals for their status and privileges may indeed be a heavy one.

The New Universe of Spillovers

Let us now turn our attention to the more topical question of spillover effects. The fact that the economic behavior of other people has direct effects on our own welfare—effects, that is, which escape the pricing mechanism and are, in consequence, beyond the control of the persons who suffer them[7]—is no longer a novelty. Before the war, this possibility was treated in textbooks as a minor qualification, one to be revealed when illustrating the virtues of perfect competition. In any realistic appraisal of the economics of an affluent society this judgment would have to be reversed. Indeed, it is hard to think of any broad class of economic activity that does not generate spillover effects that are worth thinking about. For the more wealthy, competitive, mobile and media-bound the citizens of a society, the more vulnerable their welfare to the direct activities of others. Even what a person eats and drinks is in some measure affected by fashions in food and drink—that is, by what he thinks others are eating and drinking.

Two related implications follow. First, inasmuch as a person's welfare now depends not only on his own choices from the range of opportunities offered by the market but, increasingly, on the choices made by others over which he (acting as an individual) has virtually no control, the allocative rationale of the market is diminished. For though regulating or taxing some of the traceable effluents is feasible enough, the more important and more complex and intangible spillovers call for collective action that necessarily interferes with and reduces the scope of the free market. Secondly, as long as the social significance of the major spillovers is not fully recognized, and as long as no effective measures are taken to deal with them, their growth over time in response to the spread of technology weakens the traditional presumption that economic growth promotes welfare.

Keeping this latter implication in mind, consider first the simpler and more tangible spillovers arising directly from the production or use of industrial products. The prevalence of air and water pollution is too familiar to be worth dwelling upon, as also is the growing incidence of engine noise and fume in both urban and rural areas. Yet the measurement of their total damage to society's welfare raises economic and statistical problems that have not yet been solved. If, for example, the quiet of a residential area is shattered by a new airline service, the assumption of a highly competitive housing market might be thought sufficient to imply a tendency for house prices to fall. Such a drop in house prices might then be taken as an index of the loss of welfare caused by the increase in noise. But where the level of traffic noise is everywhere increasing, there will be no tendency for house prices to fall; nevertheless all households afflicted by increasing noise are worse off.

Similar remarks apply to the enjoyment of recreational activities, nearly all of which now involve travel, sometimes travel of many hours. Economists have not yet calculated the loss of welfare that arises when roads, highways, villages, parks, beaches, lakes, and resorts become so crowded as to cause discomfort and irritation to holiday-makers and sportsmen. People would take other routes or travel to other places if other routes and places were made available. As things are, many people incur heavy costs and spend more time traveling further afield, though with diminishing hope of really being able to get away, a fact which obviously reduces the value of their leisure activity. But it is a fact that has so far been ignored in estimating the value of recreation as a growing proportion of GNP.

The Inadequacy of Purely Economic Solutions

Apart from the problems that arise in the attempt to measure the growth of welfare losses that accompany the growth of GNP, there are also the allocative problems of adjusting spillover-producing activities so as "to make the best of a bad job"—what the economist, in these instances, would refer to as *optimizing*.

Well-known economic devices, such as excise taxes on polluting activity, the enforcement of purification standards, or the installation of preventive technology, are all rather limited. For even in the simpler cases, say stream pollution, the economist is apt to take for granted existing laws about property rights. He may then value the direct damage incurred as the sum of money the victims will pay in order to reduce it rather than the sum of money they would require in order to persuade themselves to endure it. No less important, the economist accepts as a part of the cost of reducing pollution all those expenses incidental to the calculation and administration of the taxes or controls, or all the expenses involved in reaching mutual agreement. Since such expenses can be very large, the type of property rights which determine who is to compensate whom can make quite a difference to the economic feasibility of a scheme. If, say, the law were altered so as to prohibit all pollution-producing outputs, at least in the first instance until an economic case could be made for the introduction of optimal amounts of them, all such incidental costs (sometimes known as *transactions costs*) would militate against the introduction of polluting activities. The economist's optimal solution under the existing spillover-permissive law may allow a great deal more pollution than would the optimal solution under a spillover-repressive law.[8] Indeed, if these incidental costs were heavy enough, the optimal pollution-producing output under the latter law would be nil. If, for instance, the law had originally required that every automobile owner had to ascertain the disamenity inflicted on others, and to compensate them for it, the world would have been spared the greatest of all man-made plagues.

The economist's prescriptions in this context are vulnerable for another reason, one touched on earlier. Although a manufacturing process, or its product, is suspect, the extent of its damage cannot be ascertained, indeed may never be ascertained. The common response to such un-certainty is to recommend more research into the suspect process or pro-duct. As soon as anything definite is discovered, the economist, it is stated, is ready to act. But in the meantime what? Apparently such method-ological scruples will allow all processes to continue, and their products to be consumed, until clear proof emerges, if ever, of injurious effects. But knowledge can be bought at too dear a price. By the time researchers claim to have observed a significant relation between some synthetic compounds and some forms of sickness, the damage may be substantial and possibly irreversible. In an economy that produces hundreds of new compounds each year, and each year withdraws a score or two, the difficulties of discovering the range of side effects of any group of them increases, and the risks we run are accordingly greater.

It may be thought that the risk of really serious consequences arising from the genetic or ecological side effects of any one synthetic substance is small. But as the numbers of such substances multiply from one decade to the next, the aggregate risk of some calamity grows until it approaches virtual certainty—the only mitigating circumstance being that prior oc-currence of a lesser calamity might be heeded as a warning. Ordinary regard to self-preservation would then suggest a change in the burden of proof. Rather than requiring evidence that a new synthetic or chemical is dangerous before withdrawing it from the market, the law should require stronger proof of its safety before it is allowed to appear in the shops.[9] Such an innovation would indeed slow down the pace of "progress," but this is a price we should be willing to pay to increase the chances of human survival.

Finally, the economist finds difficulty in prescribing remedies for some of the more egregious and pervasive spillovers because of their intangible nature and because they are jointly produced by goods and by processes. Bronchial diseases, coronary diseases, nervous diseases, and various forms of cancer are each attributable to a large number of factors associated with modern living, factors that range from fume and dust to noise and stress. I cannot see such favored concepts as optimal taxes, or even an extension of property rights, making much headway in these circumstances. No less troublesome is the fact that a single technological innovation, such as the private automobile, the airplane, or television, is responsible for far-reaching repercussions that do not lend themselves easily to measure-ment. The transport economist, for instance, confines his study of spill-overs largely to traffic congestion. But the mutual frustration of traffic looks small compared with the combined effect on society's welfare of such spillovers as noise, stench, fume and the annual toll of those killed and maimed on the roads.

And these are not all. In response to the private car, a physical en-vironment has evolved that is unconscionably expensive, wasteful of land, lavish of time, and destructive of communal intimacy. Not only have the products of the automobile industry destroyed the peace, quiet, and beauty of practically every village and health resort in the West, they have crammed every city with endless lanes of roaring traffic that, like a horde of insatiable locusts, carve it up, wheel around it, over it and under it, forcing every artery, devouring its very heart. The effect of the automobile on our eyes, lungs, nervous system, on our health, humor, and national character has been uniformly bad. Its influence on our architecture, our sense of citizenship, our uses of leisure, and our way of life has been deplorable.

Why do we tolerate it? Worse, why do we subsidize it? The simple fact is that we could not foresee the range of untoward consequences that would follow from its adoption. We have lived with it so long, and, over time, have so adapted our habits, our schedules, and our environment to it, that we have difficulty visualizing how daily life could be arranged without the automobile. What is more, even the sensitive citizen who is appalled by what has emerged cannot by himself opt out. Given the creation of an environment about him that is fit only for automobiles, he would be at a grave disadvantage without one. Only a political decision to create viable nonmotorized communities could do anything to relieve him. Such an initiative would, however, face opposition by powerful automobile and highway interests.

Chief runner-up in environmental destruction is the airliner. Its gift to humanity in opening up a world of beauty to a generation of charter flights and packaged tours cannot, alas, be repeated for future generations. Aided by the ubiquitous automobile, and by the estate agent and developer, every one of the once-famed island and coastal resorts of the Mediterranean has by now been transmogrified into a neon-lit jungle of cement blocks, reeking with gasoline fumes and crawling with transistorized traffic.

How did we come into this inheritance? As I wrote in 1965:

Geographical space, the choicest parts of it anyway, form one of the strictly limited resources of this now tiny planet. And, as in so many other things, what a few may enjoy in freedom the crowd necessarily destroys for itself. Notwithstanding which, under present institutional arrangements (since there is certainly a lot more money to be gained in promoting this process of rapid erosion) unless international agreement can be reached to control further tourist damage, our children will inherit a world almost wholly bereft of places of unmarred natural beauty.

The loss to ourselves, to our children, and to our children's children, arising from the destruction of a heritage of natural beauty that had else endured the passage of centuries, is perhaps incalculable. In the circumstances, what can the economist propose? A belated tax on air travel? If so, how calculated? Again, I believe a political solution to be more practicable: that of international agreement to save some choice areas from what little remains by prohibiting air travel to them and automobile travel within them.

Some Objections of Growthmen

Let me pause in passing to consider some misunderstandings of the environmental issue. Of late, it has been asserted that the new surge of concern about the environment is no more than a cover under which the middle classes are trying to hang onto their privileges, that it has nothing to offer to the working classes or the poor.[10] Strangely enough, the same person may also be found arguing[11] that in order to make *desirable* environmental improvements it is necessary to maintain and, if possible, to increase the rate of economic growth.*

* In this connection, Beckerman and Crosland are not alone in objecting to my proposal to make inaccessible to the automobile and airplane a number of beauty spots all

One can indeed think up environmental improvements that would benefit largely higher income groups, but for the most part these are undertaken by such groups at their own expense and initiative. Insofar as the improvements entail cleaner air, quiet, and purer water, there is no reason to suppose that the schemes proposed do not extend such benefits also to the poorer members of society. In fact it is plausible to believe that the poorer citizens benefit more than the richer ones who can always move with far less inconvenience than the poor from any district that is sinking in the scale of amenity. If, on the other hand, the revenues raised for environmental benefits happen to involve a greater proportional reduction of the income or purchasing power of the poor than of the rich there need be no difficulty in altering the tax structure in order to restore equity. This should present no financial difficulty inasmuch as the strict economic case for reducing pollution requires that aggregate benefits exceed costs—a condition that has to be met, incidentally, quite irrespective of the distribution of incomes.

As for the alleged need for more of this GNP stuff, as a condition for performing good works—removing the accumulated filth in the environment, reducing poverty in the cities, healing the sick, comforting the aged, educating the young—we find that the same arguments were used in the fifties; indeed, similar arguments have been used in justification of growing richer, individually or socially, as far back as Adam Smith. Since we can count on the poor always being among us—the relatively poor, that is*— we shall never lack for an excuse to push onward with GNP.

The obvious weakness of this line of defense is simply that we would not need to grow in order to do good works if we were just a little less reluctant than we happen to be to share what we have more equally with the less fortunate in the community. Had we stronger moral principles, or more patriotic virtue, neither of which, however, find much encouragement in the ethos of an affluent society, the bulk of the population would recognize at once that already it had enough to spare for good works.

---

over the world on the grounds that the rich would be better placed to enjoy them than the working man. But if the rich did benefit more by the scheme (which need not be so), why turn a blind eye to the other privileges enjoyed by the rich? By definition, the rich form an economic elite. They already live in grander houses, in a better environment. They eat better food, wear better clothes, enjoy personal servants, own expensive jewelery and paintings, and they travel in style to the best places while others of their countrymen remain destitute in an environment made increasingly desolate by the products of enterprises in which the rich have shares. If one is against economic privileges there is far better sport to be found outside my modest scheme. These would-be growthmen do not even have the goodness to admit that the problem of "tourist blight" is primarily a problem of numbers. Given the limited space on earth, it will arise *under any distribution of income* they care to imagine.

* It is a trifle mortifying for an Englishman to record that the "poverty-level" income in the United States today somewhat exceeds average earnings in Britain.

People would recognize that forever putting off the day of reckoning by claiming the need to grow richer is as transparent an instance of self-deception as that of the miser who claims the need to hoard more so as eventually to give more to charity. One need bear in mind the vast current expenditures on "demerit goods"—the "expendables," "regrettables," the "inimicals" and "near-garbage" that absorb so large a proportion of our resources—to recognize the moral implications of society's political choices.

And yet the case for spending more on environmental improvement would hold even if no such "demerit" goods were produced by the modern economy, and if our moral behavior as a community were already impeccable. As I have indicated above, the economic case for such improvements presumes, indeed requires, an excess of social benefit over resource cost. The case for their introduction then depends no more on the rate of economic growth than it does upon the level of aggregate income or its distribution. Whatever the rate of economic growth—positive, zero, or negative—and whatever the aggregate level of income and its distribution, if there is an economic case for reducing pollution levels or enhancing the environment, the case is for doing so now.

Finally, insofar as ecologists and environmentalists reject sustained economic growth as a desirable social goal for the West, they are reminded by economists of the difficulties that arise when the economy does not grow. In each of the short-lived periods of stagnation of the American economy, for instance, there has been an appreciable rise in the number of unemployed, a decline in the share of labor income (except perhaps during the prolonged depression of the thirties), particular hardship among the poorest section of the populace, a frustration of people's expectations, and increased conflict among the working classes. But these recessional features are not pertinent to the issue. For they are peculiar to a growth-bound economy, one in which a period of no growth or decline in growth arises from market failure and inadequate monetary and fiscal policies, and necessarily entails unemployment, stagnation and, consequently, increased frustration. Those concerned primarily with the quality of life have never proposed to create unemployment in the growth economy as a means of slowing economic growth. Rather they seek to persuade the public to abandon the pursuit of economic growth in favor of a stable or steady-state economy within which there is explicit consideration of the factors that enhance the quality of life. The actual means whereby a steady-state economy is to be brought into being—the rationing of raw materials, the controls on technology etc.,—and the level of affluence to be sought are important subjects of discussion. But in the existing state of social awareness, they are perhaps premature. Immediate concern must be with the revolution in thought and feeling that is necessary if men's aspirations toward the good life are ever to be realized. Thus the aim of the ecologist and environmentalist is not a no-growth economy per se.

It is to win *acceptance* by the public at large of a no-growth economy. Once the ethics of a no-growth economy are accepted and the competitive striving for more, ever more, is a thing of the past, it will be that much easier to remove the wretched poverty that still lingers in Western countries, to redirect expenditure away from current extravagance and waste, and to bring about a more equal distribution of income.

Monument to Pangloss

Another and more general objection to environmental concern has it that existing social problems cannot really be too critical, for if they were, people would go to the trouble of solving them.[12] Those which go unremedied do so, therefore, simply because the costs of implementing remedies are expected to exceed the benefits. This Panglossian view of society was, doubtless, held to be true on the eve of the French Revolution. But, though it is hardly more than a tautology, the *cost* aspects deserve closer scrutiny.

True, any alternative organization open to society that was manifestly superior to the existing one would be adopted without hesitation if it were clearly perceived and if the transition were costless and painless. But a feasible design for some social improvement may not in fact occur to anyone for some time and, when it does, initiative, effort, and expenditure will be required to persuade others of its desirability. Greater efforts and expenditures yet may be necessary in order for it to triumph over highly organized commercial interests and other vocal opposition groups. It follows, therefore, that even if feasible and eminently worthwhile proposals are advanced they can founder for lack of funds and sustained endeavor.

Commercial interests are, of course, interested in change too, but in change of a particular kind—technical innovation, product innovation, and new methods for influencing consumers' wants—for which task they are admirably equipped and organized. Indeed this fact makes their opposition formidable whenever a body of reformers seeks public support for measures that are likely to hamper their commercial activities. Estate developers in particular have advantages, incidental rather than deliberate, in that each of their forays into the environment, each of their plans for demolition and rebuilding, for modernizing and extending, is by itself too small to engage the passions of more than a few local inhabitants and their sympathizers. Piece by piece, then, in each of a hundred small towns and villages, building interests prevail. Quaint and historical buildings are reduced to rubble to create sites for plate-glass supermarkets, car parks, and office blocks. Roads are widened and extended, and detours are created to accommodate the traffic generated by mounting automobile sales. Within a few years, some quiet resort or charming village has been transformed at great expense into a stretch of urban blight through which runs a tawdry, jangling, main street soon to be strewn with dust and rubbish, soon to be shattered by engine noises.

This process of events, though uncoordinated, is tantamount to a policy of divide and conquer. Over a decade the face of a country is scarred by cumulative alterations which, had they been presented to the public all at once as the features of a coordinated plan, would have been rejected out of hand as an outrage by any standard of aesthetic propriety. They manage to slip through the meshes one at a time to be discovered later as a *fait accompli*—as but one more instance of that commercially triumphant philistinism that has spread over the land and filled the hearts of men with sorrow and despair.

Now it transpires that the chief factors that appear to make this process of rapid environmental erosion so difficult to check—namely, defective public vision, and the risks and high costs of organizing opposition to simultaneous acts of vandalism scattered throughout the country—all follow from the prevalence today of obsolete laws that continue to ignore the substantial loss of welfare suffered by the public at large in a period during which commercial and industrial developments have become powerfully instrumental in endangering its health, thwarting its senti- ments, and destroying its amenity. A single factory can pollute the once pure waters of a stream, thereby rendering it unfit for drinking, bathing and fishing. A single diesel saw can shatter the stillness of a whole valley. A single transistor radio on the beach pours its sounds into the ears of hundreds of families. A single building firm can so transfigure a small market town as to wound the pride and mar the pleasure of thousands. A single air route can disturb the sleep and infest the nervous system of hundreds of thousands.

Had the law been spillover-repressive rather than spillover-permissive, had all commercial activity that was unable to compensate potential victims for their loss of health and amenity been prohibited, the pattern of industrial development would have been vastly different from what it is today. Yet it would be no less economically justifiable than the existing pattern. Such a law would shift both the burden of proof and the cost of redress from the general public to the industries responsible. Instead of the public having to go to the trouble and expense of pre- venting environmental degradation, of preserving existing amenities, of safeguarding unique and historic buildings, industry and commerce would have to incur sizable expenditures in research in order to devise adequate preventive technology and in continuing attempts to persuade communities either to accept their proposed or modified plans or else to accept com- pensation for the residual losses they bear.

Although industry should be given advance notice to avoid the charge of retroactive legislation, and special plans would have to be made in the interests of generations yet to come, the principle of putting the full burden of accommodating environmental change on those who initiate it rather than, as at present, on those who must suffer it would meet the principle of equity, would maintain social welfare, and would incidentally go far to preserve that which has aesthetic and historic value.

Under such a dispensation the appropriate Panglossian observation would be that the frustrations of businessmen and gadget owners, in finding their schemes continually balked, could not really be that severe, else they would make the efforts and incur the expenditures necessary to remove them.

The Significance of the "Jones Effect"

So much for the opposition to environmental concern and for calls for the prior need for more growth. We now draw attention to a phenomenon that is formally included in the category of spillover effects and plays havoc with the claims of growthmen.

In an affluent society, people's satisfactions, as Thorstein Veblen observed, depend not only on the innate utility of the goods they buy but also on their status value. Another way of putting the matter is to say that the satisfaction a person derives from his current expenditure depends not only on the goods he buys but also on the goods bought by other people; not only on his own income but also on the income of others. Thus to a person in a high consumption society, it is not only his absolute real income that counts but also his *relative* income—his position in the structure of incomes. It may not be irrational then for a person to agree to a 5 percent reduction in his income on condition that the incomes of others are reduced by more than 5 percent. He may even feel aggrieved at receiving a 10 percent rise in his income if he then discovers that the incomes of others have risen by 20 percent.

The more this attitude prevails—and the ethos of our society tends to promote it—the more futile is the objective of economic growth for society as a whole. For it is obvious that over time everybody cannot become *relatively* better off. Thus, once people's satisfactions come to depend almost wholly on relative income or on some other index of status, a sustained rise in the levels of consumption—though it may well be necessary for maintaining the momentum of powerful corporations—yields little additional satisfaction to society, even in the absence of all other spillovers. Indeed, obsessive concern with status and income and, in consequence, a lifetime devoted to nursing one's prospects, go far to drain the joy from one's spirit.

To take account formally of this rather devastating spillover, the economist can, of course, spin his optimal equations. But he has no means of measuring the damage in terms of the resulting sense of futility, and no nostrums to offer within the context of a liberal and wealthy society. Since the extent of these wealth-dissipative effects are virtually unmeasurable, estimates over the years of increments of "real" income or "measured economic welfare" have to be dismissed as unacceptable.[13]

The thing to notice, of course, is that insofar as this Jones effect is operative, society has been collectively gulled into struggling on, accumulating, destroying, innovating, to no intelligent purpose. The goodies proliferate but society feels no better off: it has to fall back on challenges and other heroics. But if we could wean ourselves from the institutionalized habit of continuous invidious comparisons on every level, we should the more clearly perceive just how absurd the policy of sustained economic growth is for a Western nation.

Other Intangible Spillovers

Included in the formal category of spillover effects are, finally, those less tangible consequences of the particular shape that economic growth takes in the West. They defy measurement. But their impact on society's sense of well-being can hardly be exaggerated.

If it is acknowledged that, once subsistence levels are passed, the sources of men's more enduring satisfactions are to be found in mutual trust and affection, in giving love and accepting it, and, in any civilized society, are augmented by the sense of wonder inspired by the unfolding of nature, by the perception of beauty inspired by great art, and by the renewal of faith and hope inspired by the heroic and the good; if this much is acknowledged, it is just not possible to believe that sustained attempts to harness the greater part of man's energies and ingenuity to the task of amassing ever larger amounts of material possessions—fashion goods, gimmickry, motorized implements, novelties, and tasteless inanities—can add much to people's happiness.

On the other hand, it is entirely plausible to believe that the competitive pressures of the technological society, the stifling specialization that makes material progress possible, and the insatiability and discontent that are the precondition of sustained economic expansion will come to grind ever harder against the grain of men's intuitive needs. Beyond a point in technological progress, and we are already beyond it, the innate capacity of ordinary people for open and warm-hearted enjoyment of each other begins to shrink. Sublimation translates into alienation, specialization into disintegration.

Apart from these unsalutary characteristics evolved so as to maintain the pace of economic growth in already wealthy countries, much of the technological innovation associated with economic growth is such as to diminish over time the opportunities for direct and informal communication among people. Human contacts decline with the spread of labor-

and time-saving machines. They decline with the growth of supermarkets, cafeterias, vending machines, private cars and airplanes, with the spread of transistor radios and television sets, with computerization in offices and patient-monitoring machines in hospitals, with closed circuit television instruction and teaching machines. Sanctioned by a restricted interpretation of economic efficiency, the main thrust of consumer innovation since the turn of the century appears to have been directed toward producing for us a push-button world in which our trendy whims are to be instantly gratified while our psychic needs are increasingly thwarted. The vision of such a world—a universe humming with recorded instructions and electronic devices that will herd the multitude along moving belts and through sliding doors, that will feed and tend and lull each one of us without so much as a human twinge—may inspire the technocrat and elate the growthman. But the unavoidable consequence is that the direct flow of sympathy and communication between people becomes ever thinner. And to that extent the quality of their lives becomes ever poorer.

A Concluding Remark

No one need trouble to declare that I have not *proved* that the pursuit of policies and the adoption of institutions that promote the existing economic expansion in the West will issue in a decline of social welfare, in an unhappier life, or in a less civilized one. I do not claim to prove things that can be neither proved nor disproved. What I have done is to attack the traditional presumption in favor of economic growth. In doing so I have sought to bring into the arena of debate some serious questions that cannot be readily resolved by scientific inquiry and, for that very reason, do not disturb the agenda of the Technocratic Enlightenment. In the process I have given utterance to a pessimism about the future that is evolving about us which others are beginning to share—a pessimism in which, however, is embedded a small seed of hope, one that can strike root only as that pessimism sinks deeper and spreads wider.

REFERENCES

1. This man's expressed desire to serve the multitude did not, however, prevent him from using up resources in commercial advertising in the endeavor to persuade people that they ought to want what he happened to be producing.

2. A heavy enough tax on smoking would curb the practice. A heavy enough tax on private motoring would increase the demand for public transport.

3. H. J. Barnett and C. Morse, *Scarcity and Growth* (Baltimore: Johns Hopkins Press, 1963).

4. No historian denies that the German people had the right in 1933 to vote for Hitler. And no historian today argues that they made the right choice.

5. Rudolph Klein, "Growth and Its Enemies," *Commentary*, 53 (June 1972), 37-44.

6. The allocative argument need hardly be qualified by a consideration also of alleged *beneficial* spillovers. But clearly the argument about *a balance* of advantage in economic growth does depend *inter alia* upon the composition of the spillovers it generates and the cost of internalizing them into the economy.

7. On a strict interpretation, an adverse spillover (or external diseconomy) is one that cannot be avoided without incurring expenses. However, the costs of avoiding some of the more ubiquitous spillovers are prohibitive for ordinary people.

8. A spillover-repressive law is simply one that requires full compensation for the victims of pollution.

9. Thus no artificial product would be given a "clean bill" unless tested exhaustively over a long period for all conceivable side effects, and shown by all the relationships tested to have negligible significance levels.

10. W. Beckerman, "Why We Need Economic Growth," *Lloyds Bank Review*, No. 102 (October 1971); A. Crosland, "A Social Democratic Britain," *Fabian Pamphlet*, 404 (1971); and R. Klein, "Growth and Its Enemies."

11. A. Crosland, "A Social Democratic Britain."

12. Edward C. Banfield, *The Unheavenly City* (Little, Brown and Co.: Boston, 1968).

13. Beckerman ("Why We Need Economic Growth") is under the impression that he can recruit the relative income effect to the cause of growthmanship. Conceding that, in its extreme form, economic growth cannot improve the lot of all persons in a country, he nonetheless rationalizes economic growth for the country as a whole on the grounds that unless the nation maintains its international position it will feel worse off.

   Some slippage must have occurred in his reasoning at this point, since his arguments for an individual and for a country are perfectly symmetrical. On this hypothesis, only if a person's income grows relative to the average increase does he feel better off, and only if a country's per capita income grows relative to the increase of that in other countries does it feel better off. *Per contra,* if the person's income increases less than the average increase of income he feels worse off, and if the country's per capita income grows less than that of other countries it feels worse off. And just as all individuals in a country cannot simultaneously feel better off, so also all the countries being compared cannot simultaneously feel better off.

KENNETH E. BOULDING

The Shadow of the Stationary State

THE IDEA OF a stationary state is an integral part of the "economic imagination." It is a particularly significant part of the world view of the classical economists from Adam Smith to John Stuart Mill. Any society must be progressing, stationary, or declining. Both the progressing state and the declining state, however, were thought of as self-limiting, in the sense that in each the rate of progress or of decline would diminish until it was zero and the stationary state was reached. On the whole, the classical economists certainly thought the progressive state was preferable to the others. Mill perhaps had a slightly rosier view of the stationary state than Adam Smith, who thought it would be "dull." They would all have agreed with Adam Smith that the declining state was melancholy, but none of them believed for a moment that the progressive state could go on forever or even for very long, for they thought that all progressive states would come to an end in the stationary state. Indeed, Adam Smith thought there were many historical examples of stationary states—in his own day, for instance, China.

In the neoclassical economics following Alfred Marshall, the equilibrium concept became more a construct and a heuristic device than a description of something which it was expected would be realized. Marshall's long-run equilibrium is not really the same thing as the classical stationary state. It may be a reaction against the static equilibrium theory of the neoclassicals that has led in the last twenty years to an obsession with growth and with growth models in economics in which the ultimate consequences of growth are lost in the discussion of the process itself. The tide has now turned again. Professors Jay Forrester, Donnella and Dennis Meadows, and the Club of Rome have restored the Malthusian gloom of classical economics, invoking the old devils of population expansion and resource exhaustion, along with an additional devil in the shape of expanding pollution. There has been a sharp revival of interest therefore in the problems of the "no-growth economy," which is just another name for the stationary state.

The human race indeed is passing through what I have called a "crisis of closure," with the realization that it is expanding, both in numbers and in artifacts, into a niche which is by no means infinite although it is still quite large. The "shades of the prison house" of earth are closing in upon us, and we realize that the process of expansion, which has been going on now for perhaps a hundred thousand years, will very shortly, as reckoned by historic time, come to an end. It may come to an end in one hundred years, as Forrester thinks, or we may have a little longer than that, but even under the most optimistic conditions conceivable, the present process of expansion cannot go on for very long. In the perceivable future the human race must come to terms with what I and some others have called the "spaceship earth," an economy in which all materials must be recycled and in which ultimately the sun is the only source of energy. The development of fusion power, of course, might postpone this condition for a very long time, but we are by no means sure of this, and even the development of fusion power would not exempt us from the necessity of using energy in ever increasing proportions for the recycling of materials as easily available concentrated resources are used up, and as the progressive accumulation of waste products becomes an increasingly serious problem. It would not exempt us either from the necessity of dealing with waste heat.

The basic theoretical model underlying both classical and neoclassical economics, as well as the Forrester projections, might be called the "bathtub model," illustrated in Figure 1. The stock of anything is like the water in the bathtub, A. Into the bathtub comes inflow from the faucet, P (production in the case of goods, births in the case of populations), and there is an outflow, C (consumption in the case of goods, deaths in the case of populations). If the rate of inflow exceeds the rate of outflow, the water in the bathtub (the stock) will increase. The simplest method of control is that of the *niche*, in which the bathtub has a fixed size and inflow can exceed outflow only as long as it is not full. As soon as the bathtub is full, the excess of inflow over outflow pours over the top (also in the form of consumption or death) and becomes outflow. This is a very common ecological pattern and it is also essentially the classical Malthusian system.

Price theory, from Adam Smith on, has perceived a regulatory mechanism (shown in Figure 1) relating the level in the bathtub to the inflow and outflow. If the level of water in the bathtub rises, this shuts off the inflow valve and opens up the outflow valve. At some level, inflow and outflow are equal and the system is in a state of stable equilibrium. The intervening mechanism of price theory is of course the price of whatever is in the bathtub: as the stock rises, the price falls; this turns off production and expands consumption. There are some interesting and still unresolved problems here about the nature of the mechanism, but some such process is essential to all control systems involving stocks with inflows and outflows. If the control mechanism, whatever it is, does not operate fast enough, there may still be an excess of inflow over outflow when the bathtub is full. Then the "niche" principle takes over and the overflow will raise the total outflow until it equals the inflow.

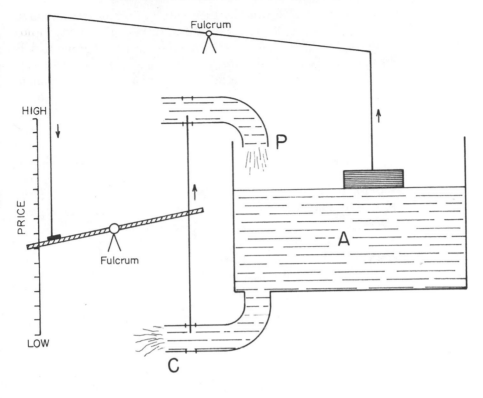

Figure 1

The question of what defines the niche is of great importance. In the biosphere there seem to be two major niche-defining systems: territorial and nonterritorial. Some species, like the robin, limit their population by territoriality. Each individual or pair stakes out a territory and fights off any other members of the species who invade it, so that any member of the species that cannot find a territory does not survive. Food supply is not an important limiting factor if the territory staked out contains, as it usually does, an ample supply. In nonterritorial species, the food supply tends to be a limiting factor, as in the case of deer or herring. Perhaps the most dramatic example of the distinction is that between house cats and alley cats. The population of house cats is defined completely by the number of territories—that is, of cat lovers. The kitten that cannot find a home does not become a house cat. Alley cats, on the other hand, are limited mainly by the food supply and are nonterritorial. It is clear that, from the point of view of the welfare of the individual, territoriality is by far the superior strategy. One rarely sees an unprosperous looking robin or house cat, while alley cats are almost universally starvelings. It should be observed that only individual territoriality is desirable in this way. The practitioners of group territoriality get the worst of all worlds; they have to fight for territory and may still expand within it until they starve. The distinction between territorial and nonterritorial species corresponds roughly to the Malthusian distinction between preventive checks and positive checks on population. It is much better to limit population by a housing or "place" shortage than by a food shortage.

The moral of all this is that the quality of a stationary state depends almost entirely on the nature of the dynamic functions relating the stocks to the flows. At one extreme we have what I have called the "dismal theorem," that if the only check to population is starvation and misery, the population will grow until it is miserable and starves. Its even more ferocious corollary, the "utterly dismal theorem," is that if the only checks to population are starvation and misery, then any improvement, in productivity for instance, is only temporarily beneficial, and will ultimately only create a larger population living in starvation and misery. The dismal theorem, fortunately, has a cheerful lemma: that if other things than starvation and misery can check growth and population, then population does not have to grow until it is miserable and starves, but can reach an equilibrium with equal numbers of births and deaths, low birth and death rates, and a high expectation of life.

All stocks, of course, do not have to be stationary at the same time, and we can postulate a number of quasi-stationary states in which some elements of the system are stationary while others are not. Thus we might have a stationary population with increasing capital stock. We might have a stationary population and a stationary capital stock with increasing income because of technical change—that is, a change in the character of the capital stock might permit a larger throughput and a larger production and consumption with the same overall size of the capital stock. We might have an overall stationary population in which the composition of the population changed, in which for instance one group had an excess of births over deaths while another had an excess of deaths over births, so that the first group would gradually replace the second. We might have a situation in which both the population and the net value of the capital stock were stationary, but in which goods increased and evils, such as pollution, increased in the same amount. We might have a declining population with a constant capital stock so that per capita stock increased.

Clearly there is a very large number of these potential quasi-stationary states, and some of them are more likely to be realized, or at least approximated, than the totally stationary state. No matter what element in the system is stationary, however, the critical question concerns the nature of the controlling mechanism which keeps it so. Indeed the total system consists of a large number of bathtubs, containing the human population, capital stock, natural resources, pollution, human knowledge, and so on, in each of which there is an inflow and an outflow regulated not only by its own stock, but by the stocks, and perhaps the inflows and outflows, of others.

This in essence is the nature of the world dynamics system of Professor Forrester. In principle, this is a realistic model. The difficulty with it is that the behavior of the model depends very much on the nature of the functions and their parameters. These functions are still largely unknown and may also be subject to quite unpredictable parametric shifts, which makes prediction extremely precarious.

Suppose we take the human population: barring major disasters, the mortality parameters seem fairly stable but fertility seems to be subject to quite unpredictable shifts. Thus, in the United States we had a period of high fertility (1947-1961) which was quite unpredicted, now we are in a phase of low fertility which was equally unpredicted, and we cannot really claim that these changes are well understood. Indeed, the dramatic decline in fertility in the whole Temperate Zone has already made Professor Forrester's projections obsolete. It would be a rash prophet, however, who would assert that there could not be an equally unexpected rise in the future, or even a further unexpected drop, to the point where one country after another would exhibit the "fertility shock" which Rumania went into in 1969, when, apparently, it suddenly hit the Rumanian government that Rumanians might simply die out.

Our evaluation of any potential stationary state, therefore, must depend on the regulatory mechanisms involved, and each of these may involve both positive and negative value elements, or valuation coefficients. Thus, we clearly want a stationary human population with a high average length of life and low birth and death rates. Up to now there has been no automatic social mechanism for achieving this. The only sure-fire method of population control has been starvation and misery. As an alternative, I have suggested, a little tongue in cheek, my "green stamp plan" of marketable licenses for having babies,[1] but, as Garrett Hardin has pointed out,[2] this might be unstable in the sense that if philoprogenitiveness is heritable, either genetically or socially, it will tend constantly to increase in a population, causing the price of the birth licenses to increase constantly also, to the point perhaps where the system would break down.

On the other hand, it may be that with the growth of self-consciousness and what might be called systems-consciousness, mechanisms already exist to change fertility motivations when it is widely perceived that further population increase is dangerous. There seems to be some evidence that this is already happening in the developed countries. However, relying on personal morality to take care of this problem involves the danger of dysfunctional selection. Virtuous people who have social self-consciousness and who act in order to preserve the system have a low birth rate and die out, whereas the irresponsible riffraff who follow purely selfish desires breed like mad and eventually take over. Within the system, therefore, the question of the birth and death rates of virtue becomes extremely important. If the virtuous are persuasive enough to persuade all the riffraff to become virtuous then perhaps we do not need to worry. But clearly we had better know something about these functions. Indeed the problem of dysfunctional selection* is beginning to emerge as perhaps *the* major long-run problem of the human race, and its solution, in terms of the social institutions that have to be developed to counteract it, is still largely unknown. This is an area where Forrester's counterintuitive systems—that is, systems which run counter to common sense impressions—may be of great importance, and where what is obviously right may ultimately be disastrous.

A potentially serious by-product of a stationary population with high expectation of life is the nature of the age distribution which this implies. In traditional societies, a great deal of premature death results in a triangular age distribution, with large numbers of young people, smaller numbers of middle-aged people and very few old people. With the elimination of premature mortality—up to, say, the age of seventy—the age distribution becomes something like the Washington Monument, with almost equal numbers in each age group up to the age of about seventy, and a pyramid of rapidly declining numbers after that.

This movement has gone a long way in the United States as Figure 2, contrasting the age distributions of 1870 and 1969, clearly shows. The social consequences of this change are substantial and we are not fully aware of them. For example, hierarchies tend to have a triangular structure, with large numbers of people in lower levels and diminishing numbers in each echelon as one goes toward the top. If the age distribution is likewise triangular, then an individual who does not die first has a good chance of rising in the social hierarchy: that is, if he doesn't go out, he goes up. With the rectangular age distribution, however, a good many individuals will go neither out nor up. Then the question of what to do with older people who do not rise in the status or income hierarchies of society becomes very acute.

There is a great deal to be said for the proposition that the ideal pattern for human life is what might be described as a "late peak," that is, a constantly rising level of status and income as long as bodily and mental vigor are maintained. The "early peak" patterns that we often find in the working class, with the highest income and status around the ages of twenty to thirty, are apt to result in a long declining period of increasing misery. In progressive societies the rise in the general income of the society will tend to produce more late peaks in the individual experience. In a stationary population with a rectangular age distribution, however, early peaking may become such a serious social problem that the grants economy

---

* This is more likely to involve cultural rather than genetic transmission and selection, though the genetic problem cannot be ruled out.

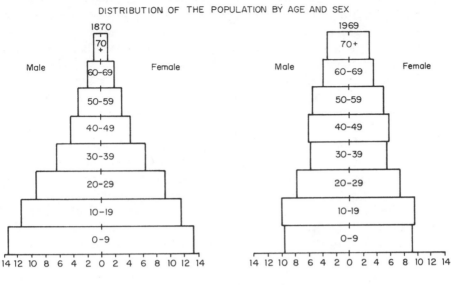

DISTRIBUTION OF THE POPULATION BY AGE AND SEX

Figure 2

may have to be invoked through, for instance, a tax system in which the tax burden of the individual diminishes with age, in order to shift life patterns toward late peaking.

Redistribution between the old and the young is but one aspect of the general problem of redistribution which is likely to become extremely acute in the stationary state. One reason why the progressive state is "cheerful" is that social conflict is diminished by it. In a progressive state, the poor can become richer without the rich becoming poorer. In the stationary state, there is no escape from the rigors of scarcity. If one person or group becomes richer, then the rest of the society must become poorer. Unfortunately this increases the payoffs for successful exploitation—that is, the use of organized threat in order to redistribute income. In progressive societies exploitation pays badly; for almost everybody, increasing their productivity pays better than trying to force redistributions in their direction. One can get ten dollars out of nature for every dollar one can squeeze out of a fellow man. In the stationary state, unfortunately, investment in exploitation may pay better than in progress. Stationary states, therefore, are frequently mafia-type societies in which government is primarily an institution for redistributing income toward the powerful and away from the weak. Therefore, the problem of building political and constitutional defenses against exploitation may emerge as the major political problem of the stationary state. This, of course, is part of the larger problem of building defenses against dysfunctional selection.

Many of the problems which are associated with stationary populations are also associated with a stationary capital stock which can be thought of as a stationary population of artifacts in which the birthrate of goods (units produced) is equal to the death rate (units consumed). There are, however, special problems in economic and social organization involved in the disappearance of net investment. Since net investment is the increase of capital stock, if there is no increase, net investment must be zero. This means that aggregate saving must also be zero—that is, there can be no increase in aggregate net worth. In any one period there may of course be individual saving—one individual may be increasing his net worth—but this must be offset by a diminution in the net worth (dis-saving) of others. The problem of how to achieve these offsets is a difficult one, especially in a free-market society.

Thus, for a market society, there is a real danger that even the approach of a stationary state and the diminution of net investment could result in a very serious crisis of the kind which occurred in the United States between 1929 and 1932. What happened then was that a system of disequilibrating feedback got started. An initial decline in net investment reduced profits, which caused a further decline in net investment, which reduced profits further, and so on, until by 1932 net investment was practically zero and profits were negative. We have no very good defenses against this happening again. The relative stability and high employment of the American economy in the last thirty years are closely related to the fact that gross private domestic investment has been a relatively stable proportion of the gross national product.

In the absence of any net investment, gross private domestic investment (now about 14 percent of GNP) would have to be equal to the capital consumption allowance (now about 8 percent of GNP). If unemployment is not to expand, this 6 percent decline would have to be compensated for by an expansion in some other component of the GNP, like household consumption or government, and this might not be easy to do without substantial government deficits which would put inflationary pressure on the system. Furthermore, if there is no net investment, as we have seen, there is no net saving, and this means there can be no net business saving unless there is household dis-saving. Indeed insofar as business savings are in effect allocated to households, this really means there can be no business saving— that is, businesses as a whole cannot increase their net worth.

This means of course that all profits must be distributed. If one business saves—that is, if it holds back some of its profits in an attempt to increase its net worth—then either some other business must dis-save or there must be a general destruction of profits. If there cannot be any aggregate business savings, the only way to frustrate the attempt on the part of businesses to save a portion of their profits is for aggregate profits to fall. Under these circumstances it is by no means impossible to slide down toward the position

of 1932. Whether a substantial tax on undistributed profits would be sufficient to prevent business saving we do not really know. Our experience
with such a tax in the thirties was not very encouraging, but it needs to be
studied further and the reasons for the failures of the thirties better understood. It would be well for the no-growth enthusiasts to remember that the
depression of the thirties was attributed to "secular stagnation," which is
pretty hard to distinguish from no growth.

Centrally planned economies should, theoretically, have less difficulty
with no growth simply because profits are a less important motivator, although they are always essential in a rational decision-making process.
The Czecho-Slovak experience showed, however, that even centrally planned
economies run into severe difficulties when their rate of economic growth
slows down. We should not conclude hastily therefore either that adaptation
to a no-growth economy is impossible within market-type societies, or that
a centrally planned economy is necessary to solve this problem. We still
have to work on the problem of how to reconcile the real advantages of
market-type societies, in individual freedom and social adaptability, with
the necessity of preventing pathological movements of the total society
toward involuntary unemployment or uncontrolled inflation.

Perhaps the most fundamental and intractible problem of the stationary
state is, as Adam Smith saw so clearly, that of dullness. The second law of
thermodynamics, the principle of increasing entropy, is a special instance
of a much more general principle which might be described as the "second
law of practically everything." This is the principle of the exhaustion of
potential, that once a potential has been realized it is "used up" and cannot
be realized again. In thermodynamics the potential for work arises because
of temperature differences between two bodies. Once the work has been
performed, the temperature difference is eliminated and the work cannot
be done again. Similarly, we have a principle of increasing material entropy.
Man has inherited the earth with a certain endowment of concentrated
deposits of ore and fossil fuels. At present, he is engaged in spending this
endowment by diffusing the concentrated materials and by burning up the
stored energy.

One could postulate a second law of cultural dynamics, that creative
acts are essentially nonrepeatable, that once they have been done they
cannot be done again. Once Beethoven has written the Ninth Symphony,
no one else can write it. Many activities of course are repeatable. We can
perform the Ninth Symphony indefinitely, just as we can grow food and
eat it indefinitely. The progressive state, however, puts a high value on
creativity which is the main reason why it is cheerful and hearty. In the
stationary state creativity may become pathological. Often toward the end
of an old cultural or artistic period, the frenetic search for the new produces
things that are worse than the old. Culture moves toward a stationary state

as the cultural potential that gave rise to a particular pattern is exhausted. In the past we have always escaped this fate by developing new cultural potential: a new style, a new vision of the world, or a new religion.

When our potential for creating new cultural potential is exhausted, then we are in a real stationary state. Under these circumstances, creativity can only go off in corrupt forms, making things worse instead of better. In the stationary state everything new would be bad. There is a parallel to this in genetic equilibrium, in which all genetic mutations are adverse. One of the real puzzles of the world is why true stationary states do not seem to have occurred. Why, for instance, has every temporary equilibrium, either of the ecosystem or of the cultural system, been disturbed by the creation of new evolutionary potential? Since this process seems to have been going on for some four billion years, it is not unreasonable to suppose that it will continue; that every time something that looks like a stationary state is reached, some new "revelation" or creation of evolutionary potential will upset the orderly, stable, dull applecart and permit the cheerful and hearty progressing state to reestablish itself.

In spite of the moderate cheerfulness aroused by the contemplation of the long history of the evolutionary process, it is hard to avoid a little nagging doubt and anxiety. The very rapid progress in knowledge, power, and comfort which the human race, or at least about 25 percent of it, has undoubtedly made in the last two hundred years is a very rare phenomenon, not only in human history but in the history of the planet. We may never have achieved a true stationary state, but the normal rate of evolutionary development seems to be very much slower than what we have experienced in the last two centuries. Do we not, therefore, have a great slowdown ahead of us? Should we not expect the restoration of a pace of change that seems more normal in the light of evolutionary history? The probability of this would seem to be very high. We certainly cannot go on increasing in population as we have done in the last two hundred years. Forrester is undoubtedly right that we cannot go on increasing capital and income the way we have been doing without reaching the limits of the niche of the earth's resources and capabilities.

The adjustment to slow growth may be just as difficult as the adjustment to no growth. All the problems of adjusting to a stationary state which we have mentioned above also apply, perhaps in a slightly lesser degree, to adjusting to slowdown. There are, however, some additional features in the dynamics of general slowdown which would not necessarily be present in a true stationary state. Mainly these problems involve a diminution in the heterogeneity of the world which a general slowdown almost necessarily implies. The extremely rapid development of the last two hundred years has greatly increased the heterogeneity of the world. Thus, at the beginning of the eighteenth century it is probable that the richest country was not much more than five times as rich, in terms of per capita real income, as the poorest country. Today the richest country is at least forty times as rich as the poorest country. The reason for this is not increasing exploitation. Indeed, quite the reverse; there was probably much more exploitation in the sense of imposed redistribution in the seventeenth century than there is today. The increasing heterogeneity is a result of the fact that the developmental process itself has been more successful and prolonged in some parts of the world than in others: the rich countries have been getting richer faster and longer than the poor countries. While there may be some cases of real retrogression, on the whole the poor countries have been staying where they are and the rich countries have been getting richer.

Now suppose we go into a general slowdown. We may expect the rich countries to stop getting much richer: their rates of development will decline as the evolutionary potential which gave rise to their increase in riches is exhausted. The poor countries, we suppose, have not exhausted this potential, and hence we can expect to see the poor countries getting richer and the rich countries staying where they are. This is certainly what we would like to see. We cannot rest easy when the world is as heterogeneous in terms of economic welfare as it is at present.

Nevertheless, another possible but very disagreeable scenario must be faced, in which the present division of the world into rich countries and poor countries is stabilized, and the world separates out into a rich temperate zone capable of maintaining both its power and its riches, and a poor tropical zone which cannot make the transition into development and which remains in a stationary state of poverty and impotence. One could almost wake up in the night in a cold sweat thinking of a world tyranny of the rich and powerful, whether under the name of free markets or of communism, resting unshakably on the foundation of social science and an accurate world information system.

After a good cup of coffee in the morning, however, cheerfulness begins to reassert itself. The rich countries are going to exhaust their own exhaustible resources first, and indeed they are rapidly doing so. This means that the price of exhaustible resources will rise sharply, and, since most of those remaining will be in the poor countries, the poor countries' terms of trade will improve. Such an improvement is no royal road to riches, but at least it gives the poor countries a better chance. The success of Japan, for instance, is not unrelated to the lucky accident that at the end of the nineteenth century the silk disease in Europe substantially increased the price of Japanese silk.

I have characterized the present period as the moment in the history of the planet when exhaustible resources have to be turned into enough knowledge to enable us to do without them. This is as true locally as it is globally, and the critical question is whether increases in the relative price of resources as they move toward exhaustion will stimulate an increase in the right kinds of knowledge in the right kinds of places. What we have, then, is grounds for hope, but not grounds for complacency. It would be all too easy to end up with neither the resources nor the knowledge. We cannot even be sure that increases in the relative price of exhaustible resources will benefit the poor countries. The oil shales and oil sands, the lignite and low quality ores which we will have to turn to may lie just as much in the rich countries as in the poor. At least part of the problem of the tropics is their general lack of resource endowments. How important this really is I do not know. One endowment which may be of increasing significance is climate and amenity. Man is, after all, a tropical animal by origin, even though development is very largely a product of the temperate zone. Chichen Itza, Zimbabwe, and Angkor Wat all testify to the precariousness of development in tropical ecosystems. Improved technology in medicine, however, has already made the tropics much more agreeable as a habitat. Who in his senses, for instance, would live in Chicago or Moscow if he could have the same health, income, energy and stimulation in San Juan or Tahiti? If we conclude that the situation in the tropics is not hopeless, only desperate, we may not be far from the truth.

The probability for solving all these problems depends in a great degree on the potential of the human race for political invention, at both national and international levels. The main function of the political system is to provide public goods and a framework which diminishes the probability of pathological selective mechanisms—mechanisms, that is, which select the bad instead of the good. The cost of conflict, for example, easily becomes pathologically high, simply because it is much easier to escalate the costs of conflict than the benefits. There are those who argue that the inevitable strain of a stationary state, or even of a slowdown, will produce an obscene Hobbesian kind of world in which the only political answer is tyranny, a political system, that is, with a very high component of credible threat and low components of consent and participation. While this is a view that must be taken seriously, it is a challenge that, as Malthus suggests, should lead to activity rather than to despair.

We certainly cannot presume that there is nothing to learn and nothing to invent in the political system. Indeed I have argued that precisely because existing institutions—political, economic, educational and religious—have exhibited survival value in a very rapidly progressing society, their survival value in a slow or stationary society is an open question. The mere fact of their present survival is no proof of their future survival value, although it is no disproof either.

A critical question here is how political form relates to political substance. On the whole, political thought in the West has emphasized form: constitutions and procedures, who is to do things rather than what is to be done. Socialist thought has emphasized substance to the neglect of form, at least in the light of a particular ideology, with the result that socialist societies have found themselves defenseless against tyranny. All societies have been defenseless against incompetence. Both form—who does it—and substance—what is to be done—are important and we must give increasing attention to both if the next hundred years is not to be a disaster.

REFERENCES

1. K. E. Boulding, *The Meaning of the Twentieth Century* (New York: Harper and Row, 1964).

2. G. Hardin, *Exploring New Ethics for Survival: The Voyage of the Spaceship Beagle* (New York: Viking Press, 1972).

RICHARD ZECKHAUSER

The Risks of Growth

ECONOMIC GROWTH, until recently a goal which elicited near universal agreement, now gets a bad press.[1] This decline in reputation was to be expected. Little new has been added to the progrowth argument, while the anti forces have presented much new evidence. Advocates of growth retardation or arrest have surveyed the societal ills that have accompanied our recent years of growth, then extrapolated, perhaps a bit too quickly, from correlation to causality, and attributed them to the processes of growth. Furthermore, these advocates tell us, history reveals but a fraction of the dangers; they have peered into the future, and discerned that matters will become bleak indeed if we continue in the ways of growth.

In this essay I am cast as the defender of the out-of-fashion view that growth is not pernicious but desirable. I shall make arguments in three areas. (1) Ground Rules: Many objections to economic growth would vanish if appropriate terminologies were defined and ground rules established. (2) Predictions: There is no convincing evidence that slowing growth would create a rosier present or future. (3) Distribution of Welfare: An antigrowth policy would help some groups and hurt others, and there is no compelling argument that the groups it would help are more deserving than those it would harm. I conclude with a discussion of the risks of economic growth, and some significant qualifications regarding the restricted scope of my analysis.

Ground Rules

What we are discussing is growth of the total economic product. Appropriately defined, this is the total value to the individuals in a society of all the goods and services they consume, including not only the commodities traded on the market, but also those like congestion, health, leisure, and pollution which are not. Since nothing that people value economically is left out of this total economic product, we might label its growth "economic improvement."[2] Growth in GNP would not merit that label, for that measure has two shortcomings. First, it explicitly leaves out valued goods and services that are not traded on the market. Second, it includes intermediate market-traded goods, like defense and commutation expenditures, that are merely inputs to the production process rather than final contributors to economic welfare.

Recently, William Nordhaus and James Tobin have defined a statistic called the Measure of Economic Welfare (MEW)[3] that avoids these failings. Unfortunately, we have no experience with MEW statistics, and it is evident that, given our present lack of sophistication, many arbitrary decisions will be needed to compute them. The choice between MEW and GNP as guides to policy is a choice between an appropriate but insufficiently understood indicator and a biased but familiar and relatively unambiguous one. If we had equal facility with the two, we would all opt for MEW. What are the potential dangers if we rely instead on the expedient GNP? Unfortunately, GNP and MEW do not rise and fall in perfect harmony.[4] In fact, one argument for slowing growth is that gains in GNP have become so expensive in terms of omitted or double-counted factors that they actually shrink MEW.[5] Thus, employing GNP as our guide could lead us astray.

What is to be done? The ideal solution, in concept at least, is to provide incentives so that MEW is automatically maximized. This could be accomplished if we could clock all valued variables, not just the subset that is counted at present, through the turnstyle of the market.[6] Presently excluded variables would in this way gain admission to economic activity statistics. More important, decision makers, acting in their own self-interest, would be led to take account of the true social costs of such variables.

Some first steps toward providing appropriate incentives are obvious. It is surely right to establish congestion and effluent charges to discourage the present charge-free fouling of common property. A greater stride would be to eliminate misguided public expenditures by assessing taxes on a benefits-received basis. Then taking a giant step, we could develop an arrangement for taxing leisure at the same dollar rate as work time. This, in effect, would impose a system of lump-sum taxation on individuals; no longer would one's work-leisure choices be influenced by the fact that income is subject to a discriminatory government levy. Myriad economists with years at their disposal might be able to implement these ideas. For the time being, we must recognize that it is more difficult to restructure incentives to achieve efficient outcomes than to recognize that such restructuring would be desirable, could it be accomplished.

I suggest that agreement on the following points would establish some ground rules for growth-rate discussions: A measure like MEW, such that its growth represents a true improvement, is the appropriate index of economic welfare. It is difficult, however, to compute an MEW index and well nigh impossible to assure its automatic maximization. Finally, the GNP, although its use is expedient, is a possible source of error.

Predictions

Accurate predictions are the foundation of robust policy judgments. A reasoned evaluation of the antigrowth argument requires that we determine the consequences of a policy of growth retardation. In a decentralized, predominately capitalistic society like our own, the growth rate is hardly a variable subject to control by central decision-makers. Rather, it is determined by a confluence of decisions by millions of citizens. Policy-makers can take a limited range of actions, and they can alter the incentives for action by others. Still, it would take an extraordinary piece of social engineering for them to create a no-growth society. Perhaps those antigrowth advocates who propose that the government take direct action to slow the growth rate have been encouraged by the paradigm of neoclassical economics, which despite its long-standing attachment to little people making little decisions, has produced Big Brother growth models. In these models, a central decision-maker, using the investment rate as a throttle, can ease us onto a Golden Age track. In this world of graphs and equations, if the growth pace is too swift, a few adjustments in aggregate policy variables can put us on a slower course.

In the recent past, however, when growth was a sacred objective, we discovered that the government could actually do very little (at least with present knowledge of economic dynamics) to accelerate it. Boosts that were achieved, say with investment credits, in no way altered the basic structure of economic relations. The major effects they did achieve may simply have been transfusing growth from future booms back to present slumps. This implies that slowing growth by policy measures that were mere reversals of previous boosting efforts would be equally difficult. Effective long-run retardation would require experimentation with unaccustomed devices and procedures. In order to achieve the basic goal of less output, either the input levels would have to be contracted, or the level of output for any given inputs would have to be reduced. The government would probably have little difficulty contracting the inputs by triggering periodic depressions; big boosts in taxes without accompanying government expenditures would do the trick. More in the microeconomic area, it could pass edicts reducing the work week, or discouraging or prohibiting overtime.[7] As an alternative, it might try to reduce the rate of capital accumulation by creating a more consumption-oriented society, perhaps through subsidies for consumption or heavy taxes on savings. Within our present economic structure, except for extreme measures such as government-sanctioned sabotage, there seems to be little we could do to reduce the level of output for any given inputs. If we merely wish to shrink the potential level of future output, however, we might achieve some success by slowing down technological progress. We could, for example, curtail government funding for research and development and squash science and engineering in the universities;

more indirectly, we could give corporate research and development expenditures a new special status so that they would no longer be tax deductible.

These policies may look ridiculous, in part because they are, but also because they are unfamiliar. Their effects are hard to predict.[8] These policies might turn out to be more powerful than we expected, or they just might knock the economy out of kilter, producing an entirely inappropriate mix of goods and services. (When confronted with the antigrowth philosophy, even economists who normally cold shoulder the invisible hand are likely to experience stirrings of fondness for market-guided outcomes.)

What, then, can be the argument of those who favor slowing growth? First, they consider economic growth and MEW to be, in aggregate, negatively correlated. This proposition alone, however, does not lead to the conclusion that growth itself should be retarded, for it would be far preferable merely to discourage those components of economic growth that contribute negatively to MEW. Such people must also subscribe to the proposition that more refined procedures are too weak and that the best way to boost MEW is through a blunt curtailment of GNP growth. To establish these two propositions, however, an impressive body of evidence, or a series of logical arguments will have to be marshalled. Empirical data that have been gathered to date do not support the antigrowthites' view,[9] since decline is not yet upon us, but rather, they predict, just around the corner. These advocates of growth retardation would have us rely on the gloomy predictions of their analytic and computer models.

Let me turn to their darkest prophecy, that regarding exhaustible resources. They observe that exponential growth, always a formidable enemy, has loosed its terrors on resource consumption. The perceived dangers are enormous. If economic growth continues its exponential course, we will soon outstrip our energy capacity and exhaust our resource supplies. The popularity of this prophecy is frightening not because of its predictions of doom, but because of what it says about its supporters' willingness to abandon analytic thinking processes. Consider a simple parable. A land is blessed with substantial reserves of readily accessible (zero extraction and refining cost) underground oil. When its oil runs out, it will have to turn to an expensive nuclear process for its energy needs. How should this society view its oil? It is a one-time only gift, much like a one-time only shower of manna on a community that otherwise must labor to produce its food. Clearly, that society should use up its manna, just as ours should use up its oil.

Continuing with the parable, let us analyze how the market would function. Once the oil is gone, let us say that it will take five man days of productivity (the amount F), to supply an individual with a year's worth of energy. If oil is going to run out this year, no well owner will sell a year's worth of oil for less than F, and no buyer will pay more. But if the well owner can sell oil a year before exhaustion, he can invest his receipts in something else and earn the interest rate r. Thus he need receive only $F/(1 + r)$ for his oil in the penultimate year to be indifferent as to whether he sells then or a year later. Following this induction process backwards, we see that, in a perfectly functioning economy, the equilibrium price of oil or any other exhaustible resource should rise at the rate of interest, which is, of course, the rate of return on investment.

In real life there will be deviations from this projected optimal pattern.[10] Indeed, rough observation indicates that the rate of increase in the price of depletable resources has been below the rate of return on investment. If we really believe in policy intervention to correct the misperformance of markets for natural resources, then this observation would suggest a proposal that seems particularly heretical against the background of contemporary discussion. To depress present prices relative to future ones, we should supply greater amounts of exhaustible resources to current markets, thereby boosting their consumption rates.

What of a resource for which there is no substitute, say a metal whose properties cannot be reproduced? Recycling is a useful palliative measure.[11] The cost of recycling sets the ceiling price; thus it plays a role equivalent to the nuclear generating cost in the energy parable. If recycling is ruled out because it is unproductive or extremely costly, the efficient pattern of use would, at some future point, exhaust the total stock of a good (unless there remains finite demand for the good at almost infinite prices). Then we might have to build thicker bridges or slower planes, but the world would not come to an end.

In their great devotion to natural resources, antigrowthmen have been relatively neglectful of the other factors of production: capital, labor and land. But growth can be achieved by increasing the inputs of these factors as well. How should we feel about using more of them in our productive processes? Our primary interest in capital derives from its interaction with people, an interaction which may be significant: witness the Lordstown linemen, the IBM executives, or the victims of auto accidents. But, for the most part, machines and buildings are machines and buildings, and we don't care how many of them are in existence.

Labor plays an interesting dual role. Population growth brings us increased labor input, but creates more claimants on the production process as well. Do more people each getting less (in terms of space as well as output) represent an improvement? This sounds like a theological question. It can be ducked for now, since our subject is economic growth, and we do not yet understand how economic growth influences population growth. If we did know, and if the relationship turned out to be strong, this might well dominate our thinking about economic growth.[12]

Land is the one factor of production that causes problems for the advocates of growth. Land has special structural properties. Short of filling the oceans, humans cannot manipulate the total stock of land, although they can affect its quality. More important for the present discussion, that stock has a utility independent of its productivity; the members of society, quite simply, care what landowners do with their asset. Given this externality, market forces alone will not provide an adequate guide to its optimal use. Economic growth, it would seem, could prove pernicious here in that it shifts the incentives for land use, probably to the detriment of the bulk of our citizens who enjoy scenic beauty and open space more than parking lots and shopping malls. Could this provide an argument for slowing growth? I don't think so. Measures like zoning, or taxes and subsidies on land use can go a long way toward assuring appropriate land use without creating as many harmful side effects as would slowing the growth process itself.

Economic Growth and the Distribution of Welfare

The analysis thus far has been directed to the aggregate effects of growth. In a society that adheres to traditional liberal values, however, the appropriate way to evaluate growth policies, or any policies, is to examine their effects on the welfare of different individuals. Usually the choice of one policy over another benefits one individual or group more than another. Modern welfare economics, however, has provided us with the clear negative conclusion that we have no satisfactory procedure for weighing the interests of different individuals in order to arrive at an aggregate measure of welfare in our society: Benthamite utility calculations cannot be implemented. We could throw our hands up in despair or retreat to mysticism. But it seems more reasonable to list the consequences of different policies and to seek *ad hoc* procedures for evaluating the resulting lists.

It seems unequivocal that an individual's welfare is not solely determined by the bundle of goods and services he consumes. What matters very much, in addition, is his position vis-à-vis the others in his society with whom he can compare his condition. Considered in this light, for example, the typical American ghetto dweller is worse off than a wealthy African tribesman, despite the fact that he may have more of the vast majority of material goods. In order to compute the effects of economic growth on individual welfare, we certainly want to know how each individual is faring relative to his near and not-so-near neighbors. We would also like a comparison of his present status with the way things used to be. The fact that economic matters are getting better and better may make up for a relatively low position on the income totem pole; on the other hand, it may boost dissatisfaction by increasing expectations. (I would be uncomfortable trying to document my speculation that the first force predominates.)

When growth and distribution are discussed together, the usual concern is the welfare of different generations. From the standpoint of equity as well as the political exigencies of decision making, it seems equally important to identify the welfare of different income classes both at present and in the future. Consider the distributional implications of the stationary state, a limiting case of no growth. Assuming it could be achieved, it would allow very little room for departure from one's present position in the income distribution. And one's sons and daughters probably wouldn't be able to stray very far either. The distributional effects of growth, on the other hand, are more difficult to predict. But we can say with some confidence that the types of societal changes that would come with growth would mix things up a bit. New skills and talents would become desirable; old ones would go out of style. Furthermore, the patronage-nepotism-old-boy system might lose some of its power when the old boys found their share of the market substantially diminished. Growth produces many gainers and, at least if relative position is important, many losers as well. The choice between growth and no growth may depend on whether our concern is greater for the present or for the future poor, with the present poor being the natural advocates of growth. Let us examine, in turn, what retarding economic growth would do for the present poor and for future generations.

The ecology and antigrowth movements have many common objectives. This suggests that their members and major beneficiaries might come from the same classes. If, as is often alleged, the ecology movement has a middle and upper-class orientation, can the same bias be detected in its antigrowth offspring? Is the antigrowth movement founded on values that are particularly appealing to the upper strata of society? Are the areas of improvement it seeks those that our more privileged citizens are likely to value highly? Does it drain government funds from projects that would benefit the poor relatively more?

A look at the goals of the movement provides the answers. Antigrowth promotes stability, insulation from rapid technological change, and acceptance of *status quo* living conditions. The most significant improvements it offers are in the physical environment. It would also protect us from certain societal disasters that would affect all members of society. If the movement were successful, however, it would eliminate the automatic revenue growth that is reaped by the federal government. New social legislation would be harder to secure, for it would have to out-wrestle old programs for funds.

A no-growth society would work most severely against the interests of the poorer members of society. To improve their position, they would have to scrap over the fixed pile of societal resources; any absolute gain they achieved would be somebody else's absolute loss. If zero economic growth were imposed on the current structure of the American economy, Lester Thurow has calculated, "the distribution of family income would gradually grow more unequal, blacks would fall farther behind whites, and the share going to female earnings would fall below what it would otherwise be."[13] Not only would the poor lose the constant moving and shaking created by the natural economic processes of a growth-oriented society, but the political values of the more privileged classes would be likely to take a more conservative, perhaps even an oppressive turn. Traditionally, the increasing affluence of the lower strata of society has worked to the benefit of society as a whole, but in a no-growth society, any promotion of economic opportunities for the poor would work directly against the interests of the affluent.

Just as growth or no growth affects politics, so politics can affect the type of growth we are likely to see. I argued above that we should evaluate the results of growth policies in terms of their effects on individuals. Growth is a people mixer. Though it may increase average welfare, it will also hurt some people. If the potential losers can foresee this, and if they can inhibit growth, then they will do so. Consider the advent of the automobile and the millions of jobs it created. Surely the makers of buggy whips would not have welcomed this development; indeed they may have tried to stop it. At the very least their plight must have been covered in the newspapers. But who could have been photographed to represent the future automobile workers who would surely benefit from this innovation? It might have been confidently predicted that there would be thousands of them, but they were not identifiable at that time. Therefore, they could exert no political influence to counterbalance the pressures of the opponents of change.

But could not some individuals discern that they were among the ranks of potential gainers, that although nothing was certain, on the average they would benefit from the introduction of the automobile? Surely the answer is yes. But no specific individual's expected gain would be likely to equal the expected loss of any of a number of already identifiable individuals. A first dictum of pluralism is that small groups with heavy interests count more than large dispersed groups with small interests, even when the total interests of the latter are greater. Therefore the losers often exert a disproportionate influence in the political struggle.

Where technological change is concerned, we would expect losers to be identified while gainers were not, a situation, I would argue, which tends to inhibit the types of technological change that would, on the whole, promote growth. Taken alone, this implies that we would be likely to have too little growth. Better seers than I would be needed to make confident predictions about the long-run distributional effects of this phenomenon. I would speculate though, that to succeed in preventing change, the identified potential losers would have to have significant power. Thus they would be unlikely to be among the underprivileged groups in the present society.

Future generations are most fortunate, at least from the standpoint of political argument. Their self-proclaimed supporters include both proponents and opponents of growth. The proponents argue that our only legacy to the future is the value of the capital stock we convey to them. Since, as Einstein has demonstrated to the skeptics, goods cannot be passed backwards through time, there is no way that future citizens can pay us. An increase in the capital stock we leave the people of the future must unambiguously increase their welfare.

Some spiritually motivated members of the antigrowth lobby might reject even the principles of this argument. They could argue that bequeathing more capital stock and hence more material goods income to the people of the future might prove downright detrimental because of its tendency to undermine social values. Something that we expected to be good might prove to be bad, because other things are particularly unequal.

Even those antigrowthites who concentrate on economics rather than values need not consider a bountiful captital stock a boon. The difficulty they perceive relates to measurement. An increase in capital stock, as conventionally measured, may be accompanied by increases in environmental degradation and decreases in the levels of unexploited resources—undesirable movements which are not included in the definition of capital stock. The long-run picture the antigrowth forces perceive is particularly dreary. They confront us with a choice of suicides: drown in our refuse or perish when our resources run out. I take a less alarmist view. The resources that are privately owned, as I have discussed above, provide no problem whatsoever. And we are improving our capabilities to place efficient rationing devices on the consumption of such commonly owned resources as ocean fish and environmental purity. Exacting prophecy is required to determine whether at some future time, growth in capital stock will or will not prove detrimental.

However, even in those areas where the problem is not one of prediction, we face extraordinarily difficult questions of a different sort. There can be no disagreement that other things being equal, our future citizens will be better off the cleaner the world into which they are born. Furthermore, we of the present can make sacrifices to preserve or at least to slow down the degradation of the environment. Even assuming that we had a universally accepted welfare meter and that we knew what made it go up and down, what should we sacrifice for our future brethren? In the liberal spirit, we are always interested in making transfers. But if historical trends can be extrapolated, our descendants will exceed us in material wealth. And even those members of the antigrowth lobby who would dispute this contention would not, I think, try to justify environmental preservation as a measure to improve the dynamic income distribution between us and our descendents.

Transfers to the future must be justified on grounds of efficiency; they should be made when, at a very small sacrifice to ourselves—a poorer generation—we can provide a big gain to the wealthier generations of the future.[14] We shouldn't dump garbage in the Grand Canyon, even though the money savings to our generation would more than offset our personal recreational loss. The losses to future citizens, after all, would be enormous.

The decision here is easy, but it gets harder as the ratio of our savings to future loss narrows. Just what tradeoff rate in welfare should we require before we help the future at the expense of ourselves? How should we even address the question?[15] It's hard to know, but on the operational front two things seem clear: one to one is too low a ratio and, given a choice, present society as a whole would be less generous with its welfare than its anti-growth spokesmen would have it be.

One way to get our thinking straight about transfers that we should like to make to the future is to construct an equivalent transfer situation where only present groups are involved. In this spirit, consider two communities etched into the side of a mountain. There is an untraversable ravine that will always separate the peoples of the two communities. The upper community (the present) can exert an influence on the welfare of the lower (the future) by reinforcing against rockslides, maintaining the purity of the mountainside stream, or even floating grain down that stream. But there is no possibility for reciprocal influence.[16] What sacrifice of its own welfare should the upper community make to help the lower?

To answer this question, the upper community could conceivably seek guidance from the social welfare function. Clearly that function would treat the welfare of citizens in the upper and lower communities in identical fashion. If the upper community decided to maximize social welfare, the tradeoff ratio that would guide its actions would be one to one. (This argument extrapolated to the present-future situation would suggest that the discount rate for generations' utilities should be zero.) But it would be highly unusual for an actual community to follow this standard. At present the United States does not see fit to give away even 1 percent of its GNP in foreign aid. Quite obviously we adopt a self-interested point of view with regard to transfers among present groups or, to state the point more gently, we include only a limited population when we exercise our social welfare function. Can we expect, or would we like to see, the present be much more altruistic toward the future?

The Risks of Economic Growth

The predictions of antigrowth forces have been shown to be unduly pessimistic. There is no dialectical force to the argument that economic growth must lead to a diminution in welfare. But the argument that growth, though good on average, raises the probability of various disastrous events, is more convincing. This makes it important to ask: What are the risks and dangers of unhindered economic growth?

In assessing these risks, it is useful to draw a distinction between those, like thalidomide deformation, that fall on individuals, and others, such as the melting of the polar icecaps, that affect society as a whole. Where individual risks are concerned, the economist's concept of *externality* provides the appropriate guide to policy. We do not want individuals imposing risks on others, particularly if those who must bear them will be unable to gain compensation for any losses they suffer either because they live at a far future time, or because causality is difficult to prove, or because transactions costs make claims for suit uneconomic. In discusssing the adverse effects of nuclear radiation, Herman Kahn has argued that "if you can spread the genetic damage over tens of thousands of years, you have done something very useful."[17] But such spreading would impose costs on individuals not represented in the decision process, costs which are not necessarily balanced by gains to them or to others. Where personal gains (whether to a generation or an individual) can be secured by imposing risks on others, there is a natural tendency to take excessive risks. But what if actions risky to one or a few identified individuals hold out promise of great gain to others? In that case, the fact that there is no institutional framework for extracting compensation for conferred benefits is just as threatening. It will tend to prevent enough risks from being taken. In protecting some potential recipients of experimental treatment, for example, the FDA may have slowed the introduction of many beneficial drugs.

Some growth measures create risks for particular individuals; others generate more societal risks. If we are to formulate sensible policies, we must decide whether we prefer to see misfortunes suffered by a few people or by everyone at once. The image of a roulette wheel makes the contrast vivid. Say that each individual in society had to place most of his life's chips on one number, and, if the ball came to rest there, lose them; would we choose to have all individuals play the same number? How do we feel about the choice between "Well, at least some of us will survive," and "We'll all go down together?" If misfortunes were universally shared, we would experience a more equal income distribution and, to the extent that relative income is important, less envy and more welfare. But this shared misfortune concept rules out the possibility of society as a whole having sufficient resources to compensate those who were unlucky. If significant redistribution were feasible, and could be agreed upon before any lotteries were run, then we should like risks to be more individual and less societal.

The societal risks of growth have had the more vocal opponents. We hear that we are going to run out of power, plunder our resources, ransack our genes, or push our society into disintegration. Some such potential crises have been dismissed above. Many others seem compelling and deserve study in much greater detail than is possible here. It seems best to concentrate here on what degree of risk we would like to see society as a whole assume. First, if there are no setbacks, we are not being risky enough. (Bridge experts point out that if all your contracts are succeeding, you are not bidding enough.) In order to reduce risk, we must sacrifice something else we value, perhaps even growth itself. When the price of that sacrifice gets too great (at the margin), we should live with the remaining risks. By way of analogy, economists point out that the ideal traffic safety program involves some traffic and some safety. We could, of course, have perfect safety merely by outlawing the automobile, but that would make travel more difficult.

If the strategy I propose were followed, economic growth would not proceed at a smooth exponential pace, but rather at variable speeds.[18] Once in a great while it might even go in reverse. Since times of sluggish contraction are more painful than equivalent periods of rapid expansion are pleasurable, we should sacrifice some speed of average growth to smooth out fluctuations. But the final result would still be an upward journey.

But what of the far future? We have no conception of the cumulative effects of our actions. There are too many things that could go wrong. When addressing this frequently heard concern, I suggest that one employ an expedient rule of thumb and simply ignore calculated dooms that are more than one hundred years away.[19] They have to take their place in line behind the many potential cataclysms that may intervene between now and then, the most apparent involving some form of warfare. If everything goes smoothly in the interim, the accelerating pace of scientific and technological progress will make our world and its problems almost unrecognizable a hundred years from now. It is hard to conceive of a growth-induced disaster that could not be averted or deflected by some significant scientific innovation. Indeed, nothing more than the successful exploitation of fusion energy would splash rosy paint on many black predictions of recent years. If growth and its risks are our concern, the foreseeable future should be our focus.

Beyond the Economic Perspective

If prescription for social policy is our goal, we should look for areas in which we can improve the present state of affairs. Now the neoclassical model of economics correctly tells us that if markets were everywhere perfect, we would not have to worry about growth or any of the other targets of social policy. The uncoordinated outcome would be efficient. But markets are hardly perfect. Flaws are particularly noticeable in markets for risky assets and capital, key ingredients to the whole growth process. This observation should forewarn us that something may go wrong.

The neoclassical model requires not only that we trade on perfect markets, but that we be utility isolationists and care not one bit about the welfare of others, nor about their decisions. However, where growth, its attractions and liabilities are concerned, no stipulation could be further from reality. In the short run, we may worry that a new factory pollutes the clean air, a situation that an economist might label a static externality. And over the course of time, such matters can be even more consequential.

Henry Ford and other automotive pioneers gave an all-time boost to GNP by initiating mass production technology for automobiles. Our situation will never be the same. More jobs and higher incomes may be the least of the long-term effects. We have noxious oxides; we have a mobile society; we have trysts in motels and back seats. What would our society be like without automobiles? The question is mind boggling because virtually any answer must project a world so different from our own. Assume that we could have stopped the automobile and had this different world. Would we like it? A lot depends on the viewpoint we take. There are always advocates for the good old days, but most of us have been molded into patterns by our present society and its accouterments. It would not be easy to forego our new developments. Economic growth goes hand in hand with new products and new technologies, and these in turn produce changes in society and in its yardsticks for evaluating its own welfare. Here, too, we will need something more dynamic than the neoclassical paradigm which deals with a single society where tastes don't change.

From a policy standpoint, this discussion has focused primarily on economic welfare. In that limited domain, it is evident that slowing growth will not produce the optimal situation. But MEW and income distribution may not be all we care about. Religion, justice, independence, racial equality and brotherhood, the strength of the nuclear family, and sexual liberation are perhaps more important to our welfare.[20] If we could demonstrate an adverse causal relationship between economic growth and these social variables, we might wish to slow growth despite the economic consequences.

One of the nice things about economic growth is that it is observable and measurable. Not only that, but each individual picks up his own share. He can see clearly how he is doing. Social decline, on the other hand, is a fuzzy concept, difficult to observe, and not personal to the individual. This contrast introduces a danger into the growth debate. Where we are surely making progress, economically, progress can be documented. Where we may be backsliding, socially, we can hardly tell where we have been. Our politicians can fool us, and we can fool ourselves. Some people might argue that we were better off in the good old days with fewer material goods but better values and a more cohesive society. Nevertheless, if we had to vote, I doubt whether many people would go back. And that is probably the way our future brethren will feel about our time.

If, in fact, growth is not in the best interest of society, economists should not be the ones to tell us, for economists are the gurus of growth, with the assignment to further it and guide it in profitable directions.

Growth in return is supportive of the central concern of the economics profession, the material well-being of society. The limited jurisdiction of economists, therefore, cannot support a very stimulating discussion on the merits of growth. It's time other tradesmen joined the debate.

REFERENCES

1. My Kennedy School colleagues have provided me with helpful comments.

2. This terminology may seem to prejudge the issue. That is exactly what Thomas Schelling, who proposed it to me, intended.

3. W. Nordhaus and J. Tobin, "Is Growth Obsolete?" *Economic Growth* (New York: National Bureau of Economic Research, 1972). This piece provides an excellent scholarly survey of the growth-welfare relationship.

4. Even if they did, there could be some more complex computational problems if we had to worry about sacrificing present for future GNP. We would have to convert to MEW, our true objective, define our tradeoffs, and then reconvert to GNP.

5. A man inclined to chubbiness might point out that his recent gain in weight merely reflected the replacement of low-density fat with muscle of high specific gravity. He might draw an analogy between poundage and GNP. Both are convenient for certain purposes, but neither is what we really want to measure.

6. A logical extension of this approach would suggest that our physicians, like their fabled Chinese counterparts, should receive payment only when their patients are healthy.

7. Those who are interested in preserving the pristine nature of our natural environment might not be so happy about this. People would have more time to litter our beaches and crowd our parks.

8. In my elementary school, twenty-odd years ago, there was a student of excessive height who might have taken growth inhibitors. His parents chose against this course for the procedures were experimental and therefore somewhat dangerous.

9. Nordhaus and Tobin ("Is Growth Obsolete?") indicate that economic growth has been accompanied by an increase in MEW. There is, of course, no logical reason why this pattern couldn't be broken in the future.

10. This parable does not capture the richness of our present energy situation. The production of nuclear energy entails substantial capital costs in terms of research, construction, and learning from inefficient initial installations, costs which could be reduced by delaying the year of introduction. The concentrated and regulated nature of the nuclear power industry further complicates the optimization problem. Despite these factors, I would bet that nuclear power will phase into use in a pattern that roughly approximates what dynamic programmers prescribe.

11. M. Weinstein and R. Zeckhauser, "The Optimal Consumption of Depletable Resources," *Quarterly Journal of Economics* (forthcoming); "The Optimal Consumption of Recycleable Resources," Kennedy School Discussion Paper No. 13B

(October 1972). Recycling is not the solution for oil, because the alternate technology of nuclear power generation is cheaper.

12. Our ignorance is reflected in the traditional economic assumption that population growth is an exogenous variable. In a very rough sort of a way, it seems that as we pass up the industrial development income ladder, children become more of a consumption and less of a production good. This in no way implies that more wealth would mean less population; we know very little about the long-run relation between income and demand for children.

13. Lester Thurow, "The Impact of Zero Economic Growth on Personal Incomes," mimeo, M.I.T., August 1972.

14. An adherent of the fixed-all-time-consumption-of-resources view of economic development would point out that at some point in the future, assuming humans continue to exist, per capita welfare will have to diminish. His decisions in providing for the future might depend on how much he thinks he will be benefiting our more affluent immediate descendants as opposed to the impoverished residents of the far future.

15. Some analysts might argue that the utility from altruistic behavior should be our guide, that if we get sufficient utility from providing for the future, then we should. This is the philosophy underlying some arguments that the social rate of discount should diverge from the interest rate we observe on the market. Starting from a very different philosophical basis, one could argue that the government is the custodian of the future and should take full account of any externalities that will befall it, even though compensation can never be charged. Acceptance of this point of view would lead to a high rate of transfer to the future. A third approach, similar in consequence to the second, would make intergeneration transfer decisions on the basis of a hypothetical contract that would have been agreed to by all future citizens standing behind a Rawlsian "veil of ignorance." The transfers would be equitable, because at the time the agreement was drawn, the parties would not know who would live when.

16. The mountain analogy gets slightly modified if we recognize that generations overlap. Everyone has a fixed spot on the mountain. He can trade with his immediate uphill neighbor; once those transactions are completed, he can trade with the man just below. In this way, each generation can employ its early life wages to purchase the total extant capital stock during its midyears, only to resell it and consume the proceeds before its death. Given natural relationships between generations, particularly within families, much of this capital transfer occurs without recompense. Each generation gives to the next, especially in areas like support in the early years, with little expectation that they will ever be paid back. Indeed, it seems that much of the motivation for each generation proceeds from its desire to continue the process of transfer forward. A sometimes cited externality is the satisfaction older generations (say, grandparents) receive when younger generations pass income forward (say, parents to children). Perhaps this has something to do with desires for immortality; at any rate, it is interesting to note that our society has rules against perpetual bequests.

17. Herman Kahn, *On Thermonuclear War*, 2nd ed. (Princeton, N.J.: Princeton University Press, 1961).

18. There is quite another source of variation. Technological advance is hardly the smooth exponential process posited in most economists' models. An invention like

the transistor, which can provide a measurable boost for the total economy, may come along only once in a great while.

19. Economists' models, relying on unchanging assumptions, frequently show a decline, say, in income beyond some point t'. If this information is to be used for policy, it is important to know whether the real-time equivalent for t' is five, one hundred, or one million years.

20. A survey on this matter might not tell us much beyond identifying areas where consciousness is high. Perhaps people pay the most attention to the objective which they see as potentially most threatened. For example, when asked to name their most valuable consumption item, few individuals would select oxygen or water. Fortunately, for the present, neither seems likely to be taken away.

MARC J. ROBERTS

On Reforming Economic Growth

So viele Fragen. B. Brecht

RECENT ATTACKS on economic growth represent a sharp reversal of traditional concerns. Ten years ago Americans feared that Russian industrial production was expanding faster than their own. More recently, the "threat" of rapid Japanese growth was much discussed. Now, suddenly, growth is the villain. The advocates of no growth, proclaiming a new faith among the heathen, have often been more fervent than scientific. But economic growth has brought too many benefits and too many problems to be either dismissed or accepted without discussion. Antigrowth advocates argue that growth is bad. But is that a fruitful way to pose the problem? Can and should growth be reformed instead of discontinued?

The question is empty if growth is defined as an increase in man's capacity to do whatever he desires. Instead I want to focus on economic growth, broadly defined—on the production of goods and services, whether or not they pass through the market or are recorded in the National Income Accounts. These, unfortunately, do not take account of such outputs as the health effects of air pollution. Thus defined, economic growth might or might not accompany economic expansion as it is conveniently measured by Gross National Product (GNP).[1]

The prospects for "reform" depend in part upon what one sees as "wrong" with growth as we have known it. Some are worried about the availability of *inputs* and others about the effects of *outputs*. Some, like economists, care about the effects on man; some, like ecologists, about the natural world as a whole; and some, like oil company executives bemoaning the energy crisis, about the effects of growth on potential for further growth. Some discussions focus on health, others on aesthetic, others on recreation opportunities, and still others on social, psychological or political ramifications.

Selecting from this welter of issues, I propose to consider four aspects of the growth controversy.

119

1. Are there limited stocks of important nonreproducable natural resources and, if so, what does that fact imply?

2. Is the capacity of the ecosystem to absorb waste limited, and if so, what can we do about it?

3. What is the effect of the limited land area of the earth on the possibility and desirability of future growth options?

4. What are the social and political consequences of growth, and how should we respond to them?

What follows reflects my own ethical views which imply that even for a family living at the exalted level of 1971 U.S. median family income, $10,289, old-fashioned, narrowly defined economic growth still has much to recommend it.[2]

Does the Barrel Have a Bottom and, If So, Does It Matter?

The view that growth is limited by the earth's finite resources is historically familiar and has concerned advocates as well as critics of growth. The problem is not straightforward. Consider the extreme case of a particular steadily diminishing resource without which some types of economic activity could not continue. Perhaps surprisingly, even in such a situation, we would not know offhand whether current rates of economic activity and growth were appropriate. The only way to prevent eventual exhaustion of such a resource would be to stop totally all economic activity that used it. Limited, zero, or even negative growth would only postpone the day of reckoning. Yet ending all use of the resource forever would surely be pointless, for then it might as well be all gone now.

In fact, restricting aggregate economic output is not an obviously effective technique for controlling the use of resources. First, it might not work. Changes in the composition of output could increase the use of any given resource even if GNP were constant. In addition, to limit the production of goods which use little or none of a scarce input seems like a tactic with few benefits but possibly large costs.

In reality, furthermore, the availability of a resource is not fixed, but depends upon how much people are willing to pay for it. Higher prices lead to more output by making higher cost production profitable. By spending more we can, for example, recover iron from lower and lower grades of ore. Even this relationship between cost/price and supply (the supply curve) is not fixed. Improvements in the technologies of exploration, extraction, processing, and transportation can expand the supply available at any given price. Thus far in the United States, technology has kept ahead of increased use, and the relative costs of resource inputs have declined.[3]

Not only does the supply of a resource depend on price and technology, but so does demand. If one fuel becomes scarce and expensive, consumers can and do switch to others. If fuel in general becomes scarce, we can insulate our homes more, drive smaller cars, wear warmer clothing indoors, move south, and so on almost *ad infinitum*. In addition, the availability of alternatives has an important effect on resource use. What is relevant is not the potential supply of a particular resource but rather the set of supply functions for all those materials with similar properties—for example, metals that can carry electricity: copper, aluminum, and silver.

The economy is not a mindless glutton that will devour the last morsel before it notices that the plate is empty. Instead a variety of processes operate within it to allocate resources among alternative uses. These processes respond, albeit imperfectly, to changing balances of abundance and scarcity. At least to some extent, they take into account the value of various inputs in producing various outputs. It would be foolish to argue that the extant allocational system is perfect, or even adequate; government policies and private actions too often prevent the existing mechanisms from efficiently matching resources with uses. As a result, in the relatively short run, disequilibrium shortages of particular resources do develop. Such shortages, however, are evidence of a need not for global limits to growth, but rather for better procedures and institutions to adjust supply and demand in particular sectors.

Limiting economic growth *in toto*, whether broadly or narrowly defined, is a painful and inefficient means of dealing with resource problems. The indisputable finiteness of the earth is, in fact, quite irrelevant to the questions of whether we must limit economic growth to prevent resource exhaustion.

Policies for Altering Resource Use

Given that we should use some of our natural resources, what is the "correct" rate? How much should be recycled? How much should society spend now to develop technologies that could help to overcome resource constraints in the future? These are difficult questions. Unfortunately, most of the relevant literature in economics deals with very simple hypothetical cases. The available results are at best suggestive for making real choices.

In a market economy, the rate of resource development depends upon a comparison between current prices and expectations about the future. When a resource owner expects his goods to be sufficiently more valuable in the future, he will hold onto them before selling. Thus if resource development is proceeding at the "wrong" rate, one could argue that the owners of resources are mistaken in their expectations about future prices. Alternatively, one could argue that, even when they have correct information, the interests and incentives that move resource owners systematically lead them to make choices that are not in the interests of society. To judge such arguments we must devise some way of selecting the "right" growth rate in terms of the interests of society. For example, suppose our basic value is simply to achieve "the greatest good of the greatest number," and someone claims that current investors shortchange the future because they fear their own mortality. Then, in order to determine the best choice of institutions and the "right" growth rate, we need some way to assess and compare the happiness of all members of each generation under the various alternative circumstances.

Holding onto resources for future development is an act of speculation. Speculators and speculative markets are not always perfect, even though participants have strong incentives to predict accurately. The evidence over the last fifty years just does not support the view that resource owners have tended to sell too soon, that they have been too optimistic about future discoveries and technical progress and hence too pessimistic in forecasting future prices. The steady decline in the United States of a whole spectrum of real resource prices over a relatively long period[4] makes it difficult to argue that this is a transitional phenomenon caused by overly rapid development in the short run. Indeed, in most cases, resource owners would have lost money by holding back on sales. It was far better from a narrow financial viewpoint to do what most of them did, develop their holdings and reinvest their profits. As long as a 7 percent return is available elsewhere, unless resource prices double every ten years, an owner loses money by not selling immediately.

The future is always uncertain. The more accurate predictions are, the more they cost, and even the best are sometimes in error. The effort and resources that individuals and organizations devote to making choices are strictly limited—as indeed they should be if decision-making is to be "globally rational."[5] At some point the gains to be expected from making a better decision are not worth the increased cost. This makes it very difficult to determine whether the decision-making process is working satisfactorily. We have to ask not whether a specific choice was correct, but whether the decision-making system produces the best outcomes on the average and in the long run. We must weigh the cost and risks of various kinds of errors against the costs and benefits of avoiding them.

Can one, despite these complexities, argue that development takes place too fast or too slowly? If future shortages were obviously inevitable, why are more owners not holding back on development to wait for the bonanza that future scarcity will bring? Perhaps these entrepreneurs fear instead that continued technical change will lower the value of their holdings. Before the Civil War, the U.S. used mainly wood for fuel, and some writers even then wrote worried essays about the possibility of running out.

Unless growth does become decline, the future will be richer than the present and it will have a more productive technology. It is not obvious that the citizens of the future, who will be more affluent than we, ought to receive still greater transfers than they now seem likely to from the relatively poor present. Admittedly, mortal individuals cannot expect personally to enjoy the returns on an investment which will accrue in 200 years. But as long as old men can sell their ventures to younger ones, it is not clear that the future is shortchanged as a result.

The problems of conservation and recycling are equally complex. Invoking the "spaceship economy" and calling for lower resource use does not answer the hard questions. Recycling does not give us "free" inputs; instead it requires the use of labor, capital, and other resources. Conservation requires us to give up otherwise desirable activities or goods. Either can be too expensive to be worthwhile. Unfortunately, at the moment the costs of using or of not reusing various materials—the costs, for example, of garbage collection and sewage treatment—are seldom charged to those who use or dispose of them. Similarly, the adverse environmental consequences of using up virgin materials—the air pollution from refineries, the soil erosion resulting from clear-cutting forests—are not borne by those who employ them. Current U.S. policy also furthers resource development by means of such devices as mineral depletion allowances which raise profits, lower prices and encourage resource use.[6]

For these reasons, current markets are probably not giving very good signals to producers about the social costs of using various materials or of choosing between recycled and virgin materials. Correcting this does not require a limit on growth, but an effort to reshape procedures. Ending depletion allowances and imposing taxes on packaging which winds up as garbage are two of many steps which might be taken to make prices more accurately reflect all costs, including environmental ones. Limiting overall output is like burning down the house to cook the pig trapped inside.

In addition, some government support for research aimed at relaxing resource constraints seems justified. Modern corporate managers often appear to be too conservative when faced with large risky research projects, for success may bring only moderate gains, while failure can have very high personal costs. Furthermore, despite the patent system, the benefits of research efforts are not always fully captured in a company's increased product sales.[7] Developing the technology to help sustain growth is not, of course, inevitably worth whatever it costs. We must balance the gains against the costs of giving up whatever might have been achieved by using the resources involved in other ways.

Can We Have Production Without Pollution?

The evils of pollution have been cited to justify controls on growth, both because pollution harms the ecology and because it has an adverse impact on man with regard to aesthetics, health and recreation. Ecologists argue that the purpose of the world is not simply to improve man's lot. They see the good society as one which fits into a larger set of balanced, interdependent, stable, and varied ecological communities. In contrast, the classical liberal-utilitarian viewpoint shared by most economists is utterly homeocentric.[8] From this perspective, correct measures to ameliorate the growth/pollution situation are simply those which would bring about a situation in which some people were better off than they had been, at least in terms of their own perceptions.

In practice, some utilitarians are not easily distinguished from ecologists. For example, one could argue that individual choices are often imperfect since most people have only limited time and expertise. Thus, a person's choices might well change as his tastes are developed by additional experience. Alternatively, suppose that there are grave risks of ecological disaster. Even a believer in consumer sovereignty might not want the interests of the future considered in the policy process solely according to the tastes and preferences of current society members.

Moral assumptions aside, pollution is not one but many different and complicated problems. Previously, we explored the possibility of maintaining growth while minimizing the use of certain resource *inputs*. Now the issue is, can we have growth while lowering the *output* of various objectionable materials? Often there is a significant choice about the amount of waste material produced per unit of primary output. Smokestack precipitators lower dust emissions from powerplants by 99 percent. Good sewage treatment processes routinely eliminate 65 percent of the organic material they take in. Some components of automobile exhaust emissions are already being reduced to 25 percent of their former levels. Often redesign of the entire production process produces the best results. For example, one study of beet sugar mills clearly indicated that it was possible to eliminate waste water output almost completely.[9] Cleanup usually does cost money. But the cost often turns out to be less than was initially estimated. Until recently no one has had much incentive to curtail waste emissions. Once controls are imposed, new technology has often been developed which accomplishes cleanup, or even production itself, at less cost than was previously thought possible.

What matters in pollution control is not waste output per se but its impact on the chemical and biological character of the receiving ecosystems. That impact and its significance for man is often not very well understood. However, we can predict that as economic growth continues, if waste output per unit of production remains unchanged, many ecosystems will steadily deteriorate due to rising waste loads. We will, in other words, have to provide better and better pollution control just to stay in the same place.

Most "polluting" substances are found to some degree in nature. Some of these waste products and materials will ultimately be assimilated by the environment. Such biodegradable materials, like human sewage, represent a flow problem. This year's difficulties depend on this year's waste. When additional discharges stop, the waste already in the system is soon assimilated and the problem "goes away." Often, about substances like these, we can usefully ask, "How much can the ecosystem handle without serious harm?"[10]

In contrast, other substances, like DDT and mercury, break down slowly or not at all. The stock of these materials accumulated in the biosphere does the damage, and any discharge may mean additional damage. Yet many of these substances, like pesticides, are used because they appear to provide benefits in health or production. If they turn out to be harmful, the harm may not become apparent until it is too late. Even if the use of DDT were now completely stopped worldwide, DDT would continue to accumulate in higher animals for years as previous applications moved up the food chain.[11]

Nonetheless, it does not follow that economic growth should be limited because it leads to the development and use of such substances. New substances are just one kind of change in technology. Furthermore, while technological change and economic growth have been associated in the past, they are simply not the same thing. Growth could proceed with a constant technology if inputs were expanded. Alternatively, even with no growth, technological change could occur, making it possible to produce a constant output with an ever smaller flow of inputs. Our current market system does not give the developers of new technologies, like that of the SST, much incentive to worry about long-range ecological consequences. Certainly, given the dangers, both caution and new controls appear to be in order. Controlling growth, however, is a very roundabout and ineffectual approach. It would neither end DDT use, not guarantee that its replacement won't be even more dangerous.

Not every suggestion that has been made about the limited capacity of the environment to assimilate human by-products is equally sensible. Consider the view that the energy use of modern society implies an inevitable and disastrous increase in the "entropy" of the earth system as a whole. In fact, the earth is not a closed system. It receives enormous energy from the sun—energy that can be used to *decrease* entropy. And why should small changes in the earth's total entropy matter anyway?

There are serious pollution problems, ones that pose major threats to human health and well-being. But in our enthusiasm to solve them, we must not engage in "ecological overkill." Limiting worldwide economic growth is just not the correct response. The way to control pollution is to control pollution, not growth.

Controlling Pollution

Our economy is apparently unable to organize voluntary transactions to take care of pollution control, a clear case of market failure.[12] Why is it that we don't have spontaneous arrangements whereby people can buy pollution control the way they buy bread and airplane trips? Two reasons seem crucial. First, voluntary transactions are expensive and difficult to organize since many individuals are affected simultaneously by waste discharges and the impact on each person is small. Furthermore, the incentives facing individuals are perverse. Calculating people may well refuse to contribute to such efforts, since they know that they will benefit from any cleanup that occurs whether they participate or not. Since the legal system generally gives a would-be waste source the right to use the air or water as he chooses, in the absence of voluntary transactions, we end up with the pollution problems characteristic of the United States today. Use of the environment for dumping waste remains free, and no one has any incentive to economize on it.

There is an obvious role for government here. Although government is hardly a perfect social choice mechanism, it does at least, since it is not financed by voluntary contributions, minimize the force of perverse incentives.[13] In addition, government is an efficient mechanism for arranging social bargains. One set of representatives can deal with many issues thereby lowering the transaction costs of reaching any particular agreement.

Picking the correct response to pollution is not easy. The properties of the natural systems we are trying to protect vary over time due to changes in climate, rainfall, and so forth. Thus a pollution control policy is really a lottery ticket. A sewage treatment plant that is more than adequate in a wet year could be quite insufficient in a very dry one. In addition, the ecosystem has to have the capacity to withstand small variations or else the normal changes noted above would continually disrupt it. Thus there may be threshold effects: in technical language, the damage functions are often nonlinear. A little waste has no impact, neither does a little more, or a little more—and then a bit more and the whole system goes haywire.[14] Furthermore, the social value of one policy often cannot be judged independently. The effect, for example, of eliminating sulphur oxide emissions from power plants depends heavily on how much dust (particulate matter) is also discharged.

There are many many alternative strategies for pursuing pollution control: regulations, fines, tax incentives, subsidies, and so on. We could also rely on direct public cleanup, as is often done for garbage disposal. Or we could simply appeal to people's moral sensibilities as in antilitter campaigns. Others have suggested rationing the use of the environment, or creating artificial markets for the trading of carefully restricted waste disposal rights. And many have proposed indirect approaches—for example, giving subsidies to expand the supply of trained sewage treatment plant operators. To choose among alternatives, we have to ask how the policies will work in practice, what they will cost to adminster, who will pay for them, and how clean the environment is likely to be as a result.

Short of direct cleanup, the government can choose between two major options: regulations or fiscal devices. Proponents of regulation, the method most often followed, argue that it will get the job done. Economists, however, contend that simple regulations will lead to needless waste. They argue that regulations will be costly to enforce and that some very expensive measures will be undertaken while cheaper alternatives are not utilized. They feel that the levying of fees based on waste discharges will be both cheaper and more effective. It would also allow people not to clean up where cleanup is too costly, but to pay the fees instead.[15] The differences between the approaches can be understood by asking what happens in each case to a waste source as he varies his waste discharges. Effluent fees present him with smoothly varying costs for disposal while regulations present him with no external penalties if he complies with them, and perhaps high fines or jail if he violates them. The choice between the two strategies depends in part upon how sure we are about what each waste source should do. If we know we want no DDT at all discharged, why bother trying to figure out a price for its use which will bring about that result? On the other hand, if small variations in outcome are less serious than the possible waste of resources that the use of oversimple regulations might cause, then charges seem a more appropriate tactic.

The administrative cost of various approaches is also relevant. Regulations require government to monitor waste discharges and prosecute violators. Yet economists who advocate effluent fees don't always recognize that these would require a similar checking and enforcing apparatus.[16] In either instance, self-reporting requirements combined with selective review (as for income taxes) could shift some of the data-gathering burden to the private sector. Such a shift, however, is quite different from avoiding the burden entirely.

In a number of cases, we should consider direct public provision of waste control. The costs of having one organization do all the cleanup can be much less than those of proceeding in a decentralized way. For example, there appear to be substantial advantages to public action in water pollution control, if only we could create agencies that were responsible for all the waste discharges into a river. These advantages depend not only on the potential economies of scale, but also on the ability of an agency to use processes that operate directly on the river, which no one source of waste has any incentive to undertake. In addition, such an agency could respond more flexibly to variations in actual ecological conditions than would a system of effluent fees or rules.

In other situations, such as automobile air pollution control, some decentralized method is probably required. We now have rules about the allowable air pollution from cars, enforced by careful testing of a few vehicles from each manufacturer. Perhaps we would do better, despite the administrative costs, by putting a tax on the actual emissions of each automobile as determined in annual inspections.[17]

Whatever we do, it is important to make sure that industrial and commercial polluters pay both for cleaning up and for the damages caused by any emissions that are not abated. Otherwise, the price of commodities whose production causes pollution will be too low, a situation which will encourage purchasers to buy more of such goods, thereby increasing pollution.

By allowing the environment to be used free of charge, we also fail to give firms sufficient incentive to use or develop production processes that produce less waste to begin with, or to recover and reuse waste material, or to consider disposal costs in deciding between virgin and reused materials. For these reasons, where we do have public provision for sewage treatment or solid waste disposal, it is essential that industrial and commercial customers pay service charges based on the costs of handling their output.

The system is complex and our knowledge of it imperfect. Real firms and households may not respond to fees or rules in ways that minimize their costs, although economists invariably assume that they will. Mistakes, limited time, the costs of obtaining information and making decisions, and the special interests of some participants may all prevent very "fine-tuned" adjustments from taking place. We very much need a better understanding of what we can and cannot expect from consumers and producers. For example, suppose electricity prices rise to reflect environmental costs. Will consumers take these price changes into account and consider the differential operating costs of various air conditioners when purchasing such devices? If not, perhaps we need to rely more on standards (like minimum efficiency levels) than on the price system for limiting inefficient use of the environment.

Decisions may be irrevocable once buildings and machinery have been constructed to implement them. This makes it hard to search out the correct policy by successive approximations. Furthermore, waste loads will shift over time, so that correct choices today require due allowance for what will happen tomorrow. All of this makes it very hard to discover either the "right" level of ambient environmental quality, or the actions needed to bring it about.

The possible impact of such policies on the income distribution is also a cause for some concern. Charges for pollution control act like a sales tax and have a regressive impact. The burden on lower income families constitutes a higher percentage of their income. That is one reason why we should not try to accomplish household sewage control through effluent fees. Another is that people can do very little to alter the amount of sewage they generate so that the incentive question does not arise, except perhaps in the case of garbage grinders and disposals. And, in any case, individual household monitoring would be far too costly. Distributional considerations also suggest that the maximum possible use be made of more progressive federal taxes, as opposed to state and local taxes, to finance these activities.

Surely we need better social choice mechanisms. We need to find ways to relate the often unformed and uninformed feelings of the mass of citizens about their environment to the highly technical choices that must be made about the biological and chemical condition of various ecosystems. This must be done even though most individuals are amateurs at the enterprise of government and their elected representatives are amateurs about these esoteric problems. Unfortunately, recent environmental politics have been characterized by a search for "good guys" and "bad guys" and a trust in very simple rules of the form "Thou shalt not. . . ."[18] We will have to do better if we are not to waste resources, become disillusioned, and possibly abandon our efforts. And if the success even of subtle techniques is problematical, consider the pointlessness of trying to accomplish our aim by simply limiting economic growth!

Running out of Room

Even if we can limit our use of other resources, can we do the same for land? Land has three major roles: it is a direct input into production, especially in agriculture; it is a location for other activities; and it is a source of aesthetic pleasures. Obviously we can to some extent economize and use substitutes like multi-story buildings and houseboats. There have been proposals recently for putting nuclear power plants on barges offshore. And the supply of land can quite literally be expanded by building dikes or filling in low-lying areas. In the longer run, however, does the indisputable finiteness of the earth's surface imply either that there are limits to the earth's potential for economic growth or that there are reasons to limit that growth?

Although land is central to agricultural production, it is not the only input. Yields can be increased by employing more labor, machinery, fertilizer, or other factors. And technology is continually being improved. Our capacity for food output is sure to grow over the course of time. Whether our needs nonetheless outrun that capacity in the next century or so depends on many things: on the development, diffusion and ecological impact of new grain varieties; on the level of ocean harvests; on consumer acceptance of new, even artificial, food products; and on population.

No one can confidently predict that food production can or will expand to provide world-wide abundance in the face of any conceivable future pattern of population growth. But the solution to potential difficulties lies in expanding agriculture output and in controlling population, not in limiting economic growth. Even if one believes that we will eventually encounter limits to agricultural output, why deliberately seek to contract them and why attempt to limit nonagricultural production? Until recently, the United States has indeed tried to limit agricultural land use in order to increase farm sector income. But as world-wide food markets are more fully developed, this situation appears to be changing quite rapidly.

The use of land as an input to other activities does depend to an extent on economic growth. In advanced societies, economic growth generally increases household incomes. If the choices of current higher income households are any guide, when the incomes of lower income families increase, we can expect them to seek more land for residential purposes. Even in the absence of population growth, then, economic growth could lead to some additional conversion of land to housing uses.

But it hardly seems morally defensible to oppose economic growth because it will enable more people to enjoy amenities. Suburbanites share many values with ecofreaks in rural communes (space, clean air, a chance to grow things). And in the absence of population growth, the net effects of economic growth on residential land use seem likely to be small enough to tolerate. Similar arguments apply to the increase in land use for other production purposes which economic growth could also bring about, even with a constant population.

It is possible that our technology and housing choices are both too land intensive because existing allocational processes do not take enough account of the externalities (effects on third parties) of all land development decisions. In controlling land use, our patchwork system of zoning laws, licensing processes, and liability rules may not adequately correct such market imperfections, particularly in such complex problem areas as power plant siting and coastal zone management.[19] But if new measures are called for, why not deploy our capacity to economize and adjust to changing supply and demand balances? Again, limiting economic growth would be a blunt and very costly instrument. If residential development patterns are inappropriate, or if not enough land is being preserved as green space, let us attack those problems directly.

If we want to locate more economic activity close to a downtown area we can build taller buildings or improve transportation and communication so that land further away is a better substitute for land closer in. We can also substitute other inputs for land in agriculture. But for aesthetic, recreational and ecological purposes, there is less substitutability. There is only one Yosemite Valley.

Altering or developing undisturbed natural areas is not exactly the same as using up the stock of an ordinary resource. True, from an aesthetic and ecological viewpoint, once developed, an area is just as used up as a mined body of ore. If left undisturbed, however, such places provide a continuing flow of services, unlike a vein of unmined coal. Thus irreversible development may be very costly indeed in terms of lost opportunities. In addition, we can expect the social value of undisturbed ecosystems to be even greater in the future than it is today. The supply of unspoiled nature can only decline and, as population and incomes increase, the demand will certainly rise.

Unfortunately, existing market arrangements may not correctly reflect the value of land used for purposes other than development. By developing his property, an entrepreneur can expect to capture more of its value than by not developing it. Unlike building lots, the satisfaction distant citizens derive from knowing that, say, Mineral King Valley is preserved, cannot be sold off. That is one reason we have national parks. Because economic growth will accelerate such pressures in favor of development, further interventions and reform are called for.

The irreversible alteration of unique ecosystems poses still other problems. When we mine a mineral deposit, we impose on the future the need to use higher cost alternatives. If we turn the Belle Isle marsh in Boston Harbor into an oil refinery, we prevent future citizens as well as ourselves from enjoying that system in its natural state. Is the ethical significance of the two choices fully the same? A strict utilitarian would see no difference: both actions simply lower future consumer satisfaction. Yet, as James Tobin has noted,[20] the society does appear to be more concerned about the distribution of certain specific goods—education, health and the like—than about the general level of income. Whether such "specific egalitarianism" does or should extend to the environment and to the intergenerational transfers of undisturbed ecosystems is a relevant question, although one of ethics not science.

Furthermore, the choice is not simply between development and preservation. We must decide what land uses are to be allowed or encouraged. The preferences of the camper owners and the backpackers must be balanced against each other and against the limited capacity of the ecosystem. National park campgrounds and even high country hiking trails are becoming overcrowded. Growth has given more and more people the resources and leisure to take up outdoor pursuits. Yet surely that is not a bad result.

Education and income level seem to be closely related to a preference for preservation and minimum development. This implies that choices about what uses to allow will have an impact on the distribution of well-being in the society. The minimum-use/wilderness strategy benefits upper socio-economic levels most.[21] These effects will be made worse if we use prices or markets to solve these allocational problems. Do we really want to control overcrowding at campsites in Yellowstone by charging

$35 a night?

Many of these land use problems are affected less by economic growth than they are by population growth. Indeed experience in Western Europe and the United States demonstrates that economic growth can help in the control of population growth. Higher wages mean that more income is lost when parents spend time on child rearing. Similarly, the relative price of purchased child care and educational services has increased like that of other activities in the economy that enjoy little or no technical progress.[22] Of course, the decline in fertility which has occurred in France might not occur in India, where children are less a consumption item and more an investment in future productive capacity.

While additional population can advance economic growth—when, for example, it means more labor doing useful work—it is hardly a necessary prerequisite. And if the additional workers cannot be as productive on the average as those already employed, if, for example, there is not enough farm land to go around, then average income will decline because output will increase less than population. Thus in a society where there is already surplus labor, expanding the work force will have little or no impact on output. Indeed, population growth can retard economic growth if the additional people use up resources that might have been invested to expand production. Clearly then, one can oppose zero economic growth (ZEG) and still support zero population growth (ZPG). I can hope to improve the lot of all living individuals but still wish to limit the number I need to worry about.

Whatever approach we take to controls on the preservation and use of land, limiting overall economic growth is not an attractive or effective option. There is not even reason to believe that such limits would resolve these problems. The demand for nature, campsites, and ski resorts could continue to expand even in the face of constant output if this were accompanied by technical change, increased productivity and leisure, and a shift in tastes toward nonmaterial values.

Meanwhile, the fragmentation of the current system of land use controls, divided among market, legal, and administrative procedures, creates serious difficulties. Externalities and interdependencies are pervasive and poorly accounted for. Allocative mechanisms operate with an almost complete lack of coordination. We seek to resolve complex optimization problems through inappropriate case-by-case litigation. Yet choices are made, often irrevocably, to drain or fill this marsh, or to create a new resort community in some unspoiled valley. Clearly, action is required on various fronts. We need to find better choice mechanisms than any we now possess. Ending population growth would help some. Controlling economic growth in toto, however, would help little, if at all. The problems of land use control are just too complex to be resolved by so simple a tactic.

The Nonmaterial Ramifications of Material Growth

Some oppose economic growth for social reasons, because of its impact on people and on the social and political order. They claim that these results arise from the individual's participation in a growing economy both as producer and consumer, and from the structural characteristics of such an economy.

Economic growth, however, does not uniformly make labor more unpleasant or hazardous. New machines can be less taxing and less dangerous than those they replace. And this dimension of technology too can be altered independently of economic growth. We do have a history of efforts to improve industrial health and safety which, if imperfect, have not been totally ineffectual. Indeed any new technology that increased workers' misery more than their output would not even contribute to economic growth, broadly defined.

A more profound issue is the influence of various reward, authority and task structures on an individual's view of himself and the world. An economy produces people as surely as it produces goods and services. Inevitably, it inculcates certain habits, attitudes, and values. What message does a worker get if his value in the production process is measured by ability to perform mechanical tasks exactly as anyone else would perform them? Is it just self-selection that salesmen so often turn out to be the salesman type? One need not be a Marxist to recognize that a market economy does help to create people who "know the price of everything and the value of nothing." Does an economic system enjoying high rates of growth inherently foster materialism, competitiveness, and dissatisfaction? And does this lead to alienation and feelings of inadequacy and anger among the losers?

Many of these effects, it seems to me, are due more to the social and physical structure of production itself, than to growth. I see no reason to believe that ten years of slow growth in GNP or even a major recession would lessen alienation or materialism. Quite the reverse seems more likely. Ironically, protests against materialism are most fervent within those nations and social groups with the most material security. Indeed, no doubt most Americans live better than most eighteenth century aristocrats did.[23] High rates of productivity make it possible for many more people to take the time for education, reflection, and self-fulfillment. But crime, drug abuse and restlessness all indicate that growth has not produced the best of all possible worlds. Clearly the issue is one of consciousness, not just of condition.

Mass production and high productivity do depend on standardization and hence on limiting the discretion of those involved in production. Growth has also meant, however, that an ever smaller fraction of the work force must do production line work. And even the situation of the production line is not immutable. Some recent experiments giving production workers more autonomy and responsibility, both individually and in small groups, have yielded substantial benefits in both psychic and productivity terms.[24] Similarly, many large organizations have found that decentralization accompanied by performance-based rewards works better as a form of management than a system in which superiors consistently tell inferiors in detail what to do.

Growth, or at least affluence, also has an impact on individuals as consumers. When incomes are higher, time becomes more valuable. As Steffan Linder has brilliantly discussed,[25] the change to higher incomes is, in a sense, coercive: it becomes too expensive to take the time for time-intensive leisure activities. If one insists on taking the time anyway, one's income declines more than it would in a lower wage economy. And the psychological impact of that lower income may be very different from what it would have been when everyone lived at a lower level. Furthermore, growth might produce changes in relative prices which in turn would alter the significance of relative income levels. If richer societies require more pollution control expenditures which are ultimately paid for by price increases which fall disproportionately on necessities, then the poor will be relatively worse off. On the other hand, if growth increases average incomes and hence the demand for and the price of luxuries, the previously wealthy may find themselves less well off.

The social system too is affected by high and rising levels of output. Efficiency may require very large facilities with still larger organizations to administer the work, secure the needed inputs, and arrange for disposing of the outputs. If political power is to control such large economic organizations, it too must often be concentrated. The states continue to take over functions from the cities, and the federal government to supersede both. Functions shift further and further from people both in geography and in responsiveness. This has been occurring steadily for many years, from the creation of the Interstate Commerce Commission in the nineteenth century, which superseded state efforts at railroad regulation, to recent legislation which has sharply limited local choices about sewage treatment. And, as organizational scales increase, both the feeling and the reality of individual powerlessness and insignificance increase also.

In the past growth has often been accompanied by social change. New technology altered the demand for various skills and the locational advantages of various regions. Mobility was often the result. Those who valued stability, order, and the old ways and situations were distressed. Those who moved encountered a lack of community and suffered a sense of discontinuity. Why not, then, seek material satisfactions and possessions which at least in the short run you could "take with you"?

Yet it is not clear how many of these ills could be corrected by slowing, stopping or reversing economic growth. Even if the growth process in the past did foster materialistic values, it is not clear that the relationship is effectively reversible. Some of these ills, like the effects of large-scale economic units, are a function less of the growth of economic activity than of the level it has already reached. Even stopping growth would in no way guarantee an end to, or even a decrease in, production line work. If we are concerned about social mobility and change we could try to alter or limit them within the context of a growing economy. But in considering possible policies we must ask who will benefit and who will be harmed. Perhaps we should limit our attention to tactics that expand opportunities (like rural development) as opposed to approaches which restrict them (like length of residency requirements for welfare support).

And what of the costs of lower growth in nations that are not yet affluent? Their societies may be more solidaristic, but also less egalitarian. Their citizens may have the opportunity to appreciate nature, whether they do or not, but they are also frequently hungry and many die young. Surely they live close to nature, if by that we mean they lack plumbing, electricity, transportation, education and modern medicine. Is growth really undesirable in such contexts?

In the United States, growth could probably be reformed to respond to these social concerns. We could redesign jobs to make work more meaningful, or at least less destructive. We could institute social insurance programs to help lessen material insecurity and hence the need people feel to accumulate large assets. For those who find the society too materialistic, we could seek to discourage the pursuit of wealth by making wealth less easy to come by, perhaps by establishing higher tax rates for capital gains, imposing limits on charitable deductions, and raising inheritance taxes.

Whether we should go further and try to alter tastes and attitudes directly is a very difficult question. Our knowledge of why people believe what they do is very limited. How do we choose who is to decide how people are to be educated? Last year for example, Orthodox rabbis protested a TV show, "Bridget Loves Bernie," because it presented interfaith marriage in a desirable light. This raises some very deep questions. To date the society has limited the ability of any one group consciously to control the socialization process partly by refusing to admit that it occurs. But do we like the particular pattern of socialization that has come about as a result?

This discussion has focused on what is possible, not what is likely. We could do better by reforming economic growth than by stopping it, but there is no guarantee that we will. Unless we do act, continued growth as we have known it could cause serious problems. If we wait until the last minute, and then demand very rapid readjustments from the economic system, we may be very disappointed with the results. New technology takes time to develop; so do new capital facilities even when constructed with proven technology.

Growth has important benefits. Ending it will not guarantee the achievement of the goals desired by most critics of growth. Nevertheless, it should also be clear that some, often drastic, reform is required. A growing waste load and a deteriorating environment will, and a growing population might well accompany a growing economy—unless we insure that they do not.

REFERENCES

1. An interesting attempt at creating a broader definition of Net Economic Welfare is J. Tobin and W. Nordhaus, "Is Economic Growth Obsolete," *Fiftieth Anniversary Colloquium V*, National Bureau of Economic Research (New York: Columbia University Press, 1972).

2. U. S. Department of Commerce, *Survey of Current Business*, 53, No 4 (Washington, D.C.: U. S. Government Printing Office, 1973), Table 1, p. 17.

3. H. Barnett and C. Morse, *Scarcity and Growth* (Baltimore: Johns Hopkins Press, 1963).

4. *Ibid.*, esp. pp. 202-216.

5. H. Simon, "A Behavioral Model of Rational Choice," *Quarterly Journal of Economics*, 69, No. 2 (February 1955), 99-118.

6. M. Gaffney, ed., *Extractive Resources and Taxation* (Madison: University of Wisconsin Press, 1967).

7. R. Nelson, M. Peck, and E. Kalachek, *Technology, Economic Growth and Public Policy* (Washington, D.C.: The Brookings Institution, 1967).

8. A classic paper on this subject is A. Bergson, "A Reformation of Certain Aspects of Welfare Economics," *Quarterly Journal of Economics*, 52 (February 1938), 310-334.

9. A. Kneese and B. Bower, *Managing Water Quality: Economics, Technology, Institutions* (Baltimore: Johns Hopkins Press, 1968), pp. 44-49.

10. *Ibid.*, pp. 18-27.

11. O. Loucks, "The Trial of DDT in Wisconsin," *Patient Earth*, eds. J. Harte and R. Socolow (New York: Holt, Rinehart and Winston, 1971).

12. R. Coase, "The Problem of Social Cost," *Journal of Law and Economics*, 3 (October 1960), 1-44.

13. The fact the real governments do routinely circumvent the "free rider" problem has not always been clearly understood by economists. See J. Buchanan, *The Demand and Supply of Public Goods* (New York: Rand McNally, 1968), Ch. 5.

14. For example, some fish are unaffected by changes in the dissolved oxygen level in a stream until it falls below some critical level. See J. Jones, *Fish and River Pollution* (London: Butterworth, 1964).

15. R. Solow, "The Economist's Approach to Pollution and Its Control," *Science*, 173 (August 1971), 998-1003.

16. For the contrary view, which I find unconvincing, see M. Freeman, R. Haveman,

and A. Kneese, *The Economics of Environmental Policy* (New York: John Wiley and Sons, 1973), pp. 104-106.

17. A comprehensive review of automobile pollution problems is provided by H. Jacoby and J. Steinbrunner, "Salvaging the Federal Attempt to Control Auto Pollution," *Public Policy*, 21, No. 1 (Winter 1973), 1-48.

18. The recent water pollution control legislation, which requires "best available" treatment regardless of individual circumstances has this character. See M. Freeman and R. Haveman, "Clean Rhetoric and Dirty Water," *Public Interest*, No. 2 (Summer 1972); C. Barfield, "Environment Report," *National Journal*, Jan. 15, 1972, pp. 84-96, and Jan. 22, 1972, pp. 136-147.

19. Bar Association of the City of New York, Special Committee on Electric Power and the Environment, *Electricity and the Environment*, (St. Paul: West, 1973).

20. J. Tobin, "On Limiting the Domain of Inequality," *Journal of Law and Economics*, 13, No. 2 (October 1970).

21. E. Mueller and G. Gurin, *Participation in Outdoor Recreation*, Study Report No. 20 for the Outdoor Recreation Review Commission (Washington, D.C.: U. S. Government Printing Office, 1962).

22. The underlying economic process that brings about such price changes were highlighted by W. Baumol and W. Bowen, *The Economic Dilemma of the Performing Arts* (New York: Twentieth Century Fund Publications, 1966).

23. Just consider the differential availability of food, shelter, transportation and medicine.

24. *Work in America*, Report of A Special Task Force to the Secretary of Health, Education and Welfare (Cambridge, Mass.: M.I.T. Press, 1973).

25. S. Linder, *The Harried Leisure Class* (New York: Columbia University Press, 1970).

HARVEY BROOKS

The Technology of Zero Growth

THIS ESSAY WILL be concerned not with the desirability or ecological necessity of zero growth, whether of population or of GNP, but rather with its feasibility and possible secondary consequences. Many advocates of zero growth have a strong antitechnology bias, assuming that zero growth can be achieved merely by the arrest of scientific and technological progress. Indeed, zero growth probably could be achieved in this way, but only at a high price in human suffering and social coercion. My proposition is, in fact, the opposite, namely that zero growth at acceptable human and social cost, if it is attainable at all, can be achieved only by the use of very sophisticated technology and scientific understanding, including, of course, social as well as physical and biological technology.

I must begin with a word about what I mean by technology. Technology is essentially a specifiable and reproducible way of doing things. It is not hardware but knowledge, including the knowledge not only of how to fabricate hardware to predetermined specifications and functions, but also of how to design administrative processes and organizations to carry out specified functions, and to influence human behavior toward specified ends. The key element in all technology is the capacity to specify how to do something in a publicly communicable and reproducible way. The term "technology" does not span the whole domain of human action, but only that part which can be communicated and specified in a replicable way. Thus it excludes many human skills and arts which, at least at the present time, cannot be codified, but must be learned from experience and by doing.

The technical feasibility of zero growth and the technology it will require are strongly dependent on the time scale on which it is to be achieved. There are few who would deny that the human population must eventually reach, in relation to its environment, a steady state, defined not as a static condition, but rather as a dynamic one in which growth in some activities is always compensated by decline in others, and in which the only input is solar energy or geothermal heat, and all other materials are recycled. The controversy then is whether such a steady

139

state is so far in the future that it is not useful to talk about it now because of unforeseen evolutionary changes in technology and society which will take place in the meantime, or whether it is imminent and must be consciously designed within the next half century or so unless uncontrollable disaster is to overtake humanity.

Many models of zero growth, especially zero economic growth, are nostalgic, harkening back to an earlier and simpler technological situation. America in the early- or mid-nineteenth century is frequently looked upon as the model of a nearly ideal society, with a wide distribution of the minimum necessities, a high degree of personal freedom, and a minimum impingement on the rights of some by those of others. This may be questionable, however, if one takes into account the high incidence of disease and death, particularly among infants and women. But, even if we accept uncritically the idyllic picture of the past, we cannot retrace human cultural evolution any more than we can retrace biological evolution. The development of the great civilizations of the ancient world, as well as of modern Europe and America, was based on the exploitation of indigenous, abundant, and highly concentrated resources, which are now depleted. The flowering of the Age of Pericles was based in part on the famous silver mines of Laurion. During its industrial dominance in the nineteenth century, Britain was the foremost world producer of lead, copper, tin, iron, and coal. From 1820 to 1840 it produced 45 percent of the world's copper, and from 1850 to 1890 50 percent of the world's iron and steel.[1] Now most of these stocks of high quality minerals are exhausted and Britain is overpopulated relative to its own resources; nevertheless, it is still relatively prosperous because it can trade services and value added in manufactures for resources from elsewhere.

In the U.S. our industrial and technological development has rested on using up the richest and most available resources, on skimming the cream from a rich and underpopulated continent. Today we are running out of this cream and are on the threshold of rapidly increasing our imports of raw materials and energy fuels. We spent $8 billion for energy fuels and raw materials in 1970, but we will spend more than $38 billion by 1985, and could easily spend double that by the end of the century, even at today's price levels.[2] By 1985 we will depend on imports for more than half of our supply of nine major minerals, and by 2000 of twelve minerals if present trends continue. These are essentially irreversible changes.

Only the U.S.S.R., China, Canada, Australia, and the African and South American continents have any potential for "cream skimming" today, but they are not as rich relatively speaking, as were the present most industrialized countries at the beginning of their industrialization. Rural America of the early nineteenth century could virtually dig iron in its back yard and smelt it with charcoal made from local forests; simple labor-intensive technologies were sufficient to make the metal hand tools and simple iron machinery needed by a rural society. To recreate the American society of the 1830's, however, would require a wholly new kind of science and technology, dependent on transportation and on the processing of low concentration ores or the import of raw materials. In addition the viability of nineteenth-century American society depended on a rapidly expanding population resulting from the large families needed to work the farms, on an open and expanding frontier to provide land for the next generation when it grew to adulthood—a nonsteady state situation—and on extensive imports of manufactured goods, capital, and technology from a more industrialized Britain.

Could the decentralized rural and small town society of early nineteenth-century America be recreated without a drastic reduction in population? It is difficult to say with confidence, but clearly it could only be done by means of much innovation in our production and distribution system. One can imagine the country spotted with modest-sized towns joined by an immensely sophisticated information network so that people could communicate face to face without traveling, and production processes in many small local plants could be controlled and integrated remotely. Some bulk materials would still have to be supplied through a transportation system, but their transformation would be affected locally by nonpolluting, remotely controlled processes. We would have learned how to design production processes so that economies of scale would not be especially important. Many kinds of goods would be made almost exclusively from materials that could be manufactured locally; plastics, for example, would be manufactured from cellulose rather than petroleum, and the cellulose would be produced by artificially catalyzed photosynthesis. Energy, mostly solar or geothermal, would be generated, transformed and stored locally. Most food would be grown by intensive culture in a controlled environment, and much of the surrounding land would be restored to a natural state. One can imagine such possibilities, though they seem very distant. Certainly, any return to past patterns of living with present population sizes would require an extremely sophisticated technology.

Interaction Between Population and Economic Growth

P. Ehrlich has emphasized that it requires more than a proportional economic growth to maintain the quality of life with a growing population.[3] He estimates that it requires a 4 percent growth in national income to accommodate a 1 percent growth in population, especially in the most advanced industrial societies. While little credence can be placed in the quantitative estimate, qualitatively the argument is almost certainly valid. There is a variety of reasons for this. In the first place, as resources are depleted it takes more and more energy and effort to obtain them, a situation which, other factors remaining equal, is exacerbated by an accelerated demand. In the past other factors have not remained equal, since the requirement for increased energy and effort has been offset by advances in labor-saving technology and by the declining cost of energy. Thus, historically, raw material prices have, if anything, declined in comparison with the prices of industrial products. However, there is reason to believe that this situation cannot continue. As less and less concentrated ores are mined, the amount of material that has to be processed increases, as does the cost of minimizing damage to the environment, even if increased environmental standards are not imposed, although the fact that ore mining can be less selective helps to keep costs down. In addition, the declining cost of processing raw material has resulted mainly from the substitution of energy at rapidly declining unit cost for human effort. It seems unlikely that this trend will continue, again due to the rising environmental costs of energy production, the world-wide price increases in fossil fuels due to the improved bargaining position of supplying countries, and to the apparent unlikelihood of further improving thermal efficiency in the conversion of fuel to available energy.

It is true, of course, that the saturation of thermal efficiency improvements may be only temporary. Technology still offers many opportunities for improved efficiency in transportation and in earth-moving equipment, for example. Large improvements are also possible in the amount of energy needed to win metals from their ores. Thus, although nothing can be said with certainty, it seems less likely than in the past that raw material prices will continue their relative decline.

Similarly the costs of environmental protection tend to increase at least geometrically, and often much faster, with the amount of improvement over ambient air or water quality which is required. Thus as the rate of emission of pollutants increases, the cost of maintaining a given level of environmental quality may increase more rapidly than proportionally.

In a world with a relatively fixed amount of total arable agricultural land, the use of synthetic fertilizers and pesticides must be increased more rapidly than the additional yield per acre they produced. For example, the amount of chemical fertilizer required increases approximately as the 2.5 power of the yield per acre. Even with a ceiling world population of about 7.5 billions, synthetic fertilizer would certainly be required to feed the world population. The trend to substitute biological methods of pest control for broad spectrum chemical pesticides is another factor which will cause the cost of food production to increase more rapidly than in proportion to yield per acre.

In hundreds of ways—in the management of traffic and the administration of municipal services in larger and larger urban conglomerations, in the increased requirements for transportation and communications and information storage, in the protection of an increasingly delicately articulated society from disruption by nuts and cranks—increases in population require more than concomitant increases in GNP if the quality of life is not to deteriorate. No doubt some of this can be balanced by changes in lifestyle over time, although there is presently little understanding of such a possibility in quantitative terms.

The other side of the coin is that zero population growth is not something that can be achieved overnight. Even if the world fertility rate were to drop to the replacement rate of a little over two children per couple, it would be nearly a century before the population would reach a steady state. Meanwhile, the U.S. population would grow by more than 30 percent, not including the effects of immigration, and world population would grow by 50 percent or more. If one makes the more plausible assumption that fertility will gradually decline to a replacement rate over the next fifteen years, the ultimate population in a typical underdeveloped country such as Mexico would level off at 2.5 times its present magnitude, as would about two thirds of the world's population.[4]

In an essay in this issue, Norman Ryder presents some of the bizarre demographic consequences of trying to achieve zero population growth immediately. As he explains, accordionlike fluctuations in the size of successive age cohorts would have to occur for literally hundreds of years in order to maintain a steady population starting immediately. Such fluctuations in age distribution would result in enormous strain on economic institutions, and in very wasteful use of capital and labor, particularly that associated with education and other special services to the young. Many investments would have to be abandoned or to remain idle for a generation, only to be replaced at forced draft in the succeeding generation. Furthermore, the immediate achievement of the birth rate necessary for zero growth could scarcely occur spontaneously, but would require an unprecedented degree of social coercion.

Controlling population on a global scale imposes more severe problems than controlling that of the U.S. alone. Because of the greater youth of populations in less developed countries, the accordion phenomenon in successive generations would be more severe. The large youthful population in poor countries is already causing massive unemployment among youth and an impossible load on educational systems. Even with quite high rates of economic growth, the poor countries are unable to absorb a youthful labor force which is growing at several times the population growth rate, at a rate which is without precedent in the history of any society. It has been estimated that an annual economic growth rate of 9 to 11 percent would be necessary to absorb just the annual increase in the labor force in most such countries and that a considerably greater growth rate would be necessary to absorb the accumulated backlog of unemployment.[5] There is some evidence that the Chinese have partially solved this problem through intensive development of the agricultural sector, and through parallel development of rural and urban industrialization, but without any apparent high addition to their growth rate.[6]

In summary, the dynamics of demography are such that even under the most optimistic assumptions population growth must continue for the greater part of a century. Hence, some continuation of economic growth is inevitable in most parts of the world to avoid either totally unacceptable suffering and loss of life, or a politically and economically impractical transfer of resources from the rich countries to the poor countries.

Interaction Between Economic Growth and Income Distribution

Democratic societies have been able to sustain considerable internal inequality in income largely because economic growth has provided sufficient opportunity for upward mobility. I suspect that economic growth generates hope not so much by raising the minimum level of the poorest as by providing opportunities for selected poor individuals to rise into more affluent groups. In the U.S., for example, since the end of World War II, the number of individuals in professional and technical occupations has increased at over three times the growth rate of the labor force as a whole. Between 1950 and 1970, for example, the percentage of the work force in professional and technical jobs increased from 8.6 to 14.5 percent (as compared with about 4.5 percent in 1900). Such jobs have increased at about the same rate as has the total number of college graduates. Thus economic growth provides opportunities for talented or ambitious people to rise in social status and income without depriving others of status. The greater the rate of growth, the less economic and status competition is a "zero sum game." The income distribution within industrialized societies is surprisingly constant from country to country, irrespective of large differences in industrial structure and systems of taxation, although too little is actually known about this to make assertions with great confidence. An apparent exception, Japan has a more equal distribution than Western societies. Little is known about the situation in modern China, but most observers believe that income distribution there is also more egalitarian than that in Western countries.[7]

Most people who argue for zero economic growth assume, quite correctly I believe, that it could only be achieved within the framework of a democratic political system if income were distributed more equally than it is at present. Furthermore, the redistribution required is probably such that a large number of people would be affected adversely, not just a tiny political minority of the most affluent. In 1965 the top 5 percent of family units in the United States received 15 percent of the total pretax income of all families, while the highest 20 percent received 41 percent. If all income in excess of the average for all families were taken from the top

5 percent and redistributed equally to all families, the lowest 20 percent, which now receives 5 percent of the total, would receive an increased share of 7 percent. However, if all income in excess of the present average for the second highest 20 percent of consumer units were taken from those who made more than that amount and redistributed equally among all families, then the income share of the lowest 20 percent would be doubled. Clearly such a redistribution would affect adversely something in excess of 30 percent of all consuming units.

Only in wartime has it proved possible to persuade such large political blocs to sacrifice their own living standards for a common societal goal. The large redistribution that has apparently taken place in China required sustained social discipline facilitated by virtually complete isolation from the outside world and constant propagandizing about an external threat. Interestingly enough, income distributions in developed countries have remained fairly stable during times of peace; they have flattened out during wartime, and tended to remain flatter after the war. But political conditions in wartime are highly artificial; people are willing to accept a degree of political and economic regimentation which is considered impossible in peacetime. Furthermore, it is doubtful whether such regimentation is sustainable over long periods. The ingenuity of individuals simply begins to design around it, through black markets, corruption of political officials, and other modes of political degeneration. Perhaps a profound change of values toward a more collective and less individualistic orientation could result in the acceptance of such extensive redistributions without violence and political coercion. Some observers profess to see evidence of such a profound value change among youth in the industrialized societies, but I have doubts as to the degree of survival of these values as present cohorts of young people get older, and I also suspect that these egalitarian values are confined to a relatively small upper layer of youth from already affluent families. Even in a country like China, except for the confiscation of the wealth of a tiny minority, income redistribution has been achieved primarily by a process of leveling up. In Western societies, a process of leveling up over a period of a generation or more of continuing economic growth might make a slowdown of economic growth politically more feasible at some point in the comparatively distant future.

Large changes in income distribution in a country like the U.S. could not be achieved without big changes in industrial structure and in patterns of living in cities. The composition of demand for industrial products and services is quite dependent on income levels, and any rapid change in income distribution would cause some industries to decline and subject others to inflationary demands. Very large shifts in capital and in technology would be required to accommodate to new distributions. For example, mass transportation would have to be substituted for the automobile on a considerable scale, and the resulting redistribution of population would make many dwelling structures obsolete or useless and create demands for new structures in new locations. The U.S. barely accommodated such a shift during World War II because railroads and mass transit systems had not yet decayed to the point where they could not be temporarily revived, while the explosion of the suburbs had only just begun. Very little is known, in fact, about the relationships between industrial structure and income distribution, but it seems clear that redistribution, if it is to occur, will require very sophisticated social engineering, as well as new kinds of "hard" technology. For example, a large part of the housing stock would probably have to be converted to higher density occupancy. Many consumer durables, such as automobiles and home appliances, would have to be more standardized to achieve a more universal distribution, thereby leveling up rather than down with respect to mechanical services which have become almost necessary to decent living. Cheap and universally accessible communications would have to be substituted for personal transportation to a large extent. Technologies would have to use energy and materials more efficiently in order to offset the increased demands on them resulting from the fact that a more equitable income distribution would make certain physical goods and uses of energy available to more people. Again, such changes would be technically much more feasible if they were extended over a sufficient time period. In the U.S. it is estimated that about 8 percent of total capital stock is replaced each year, but this replacement rate varies widely for different kinds of capital. Residential buildings, for example, last much longer than this.

What I have been talking about so far is income distribution within a single country. The citizens of a single nation are equal before the law, and this creates the major pressure for economic equality as well. Increasingly, however, the same pressures that operate within a nation are operating across national boundaries. Already there have been many confrontations between developed and underdeveloped countries, and they are bound to increase as the economies of developed countries become more dependent on natural resources within the political control of the underdeveloped countries. When maintenance of the American standard of living requires us to import a major and increasing share of our raw material and energy fuel requirements from countries with lower living standards, we will no longer be able to turn aside pressures from the rest of the world for a larger share of trade, wealth, and political influence, pressures of the same kinds that now operate between the poor and the rich within our own nation. Furthermore, improving communications and transportation will cause the inequities to tug more and more at the consciences of the rich nations, particularly of their youth, who, having grown up in relative affluence without struggle, perceive the injustice of the present distribution with greater feelings of guilt than their parents did. There may be greater conflicts over distribution between nations differing only moderately in income level than between the very rich and the very poor. Such a pattern appears in our country, where pressure for "soaking the rich" comes mostly from moderate to upper income professionals, while conflict with the very poor is experienced mostly by the skilled labor group, more recently removed from the lowest class themselves.

It is no simple matter to transfer resources from rich countries to poor countries. In today's world, wealth lies in productive capacity. It is not a fixed quantity, but rather an asset whose capacity to produce a stream of income is strongly affected by its distribution. Wealth is only transferable to the extent that the productive capacity it represents is not impaired in the transfer process. Some goods can be exported, but many others, such as housing and other construction, and most services, cannot be without exporting people and skills as well. Attempts to transfer technology from rich to poor countries have not been very successful, except possibly in the case of private investment by private corporations. But in practice this form of transfer generates political difficulties that often end in expropriation. Only in a few relatively small countries such as Taiwan, South Korea, and Malaysia has private foreign investment succeeded over an extended period, and the scale there is small relative to what would be required for large-scale redistribution. Private investment followed by expropriation might be an effective form of transfer temporarily, but it would soon dry up if the practice of expropriation became widespread. In fact there appears to be no modern historical case of a really large scale transfer of wealth or technology from one nation to another. It was attempted from Germany to the Soviet Union in the form of reparations after World War II, but it largely failed, since the wealth lost most of its value in the process of transfer.

With the depletion of natural resources under the political control of industrialized wealthy countries, the relative bargaining position of those poorer countries which control key resources will improve rapidly; they will be able to increase the income stream to their peoples, especially if the industrialized nations compete with each other in bidding for limited supplies. We see this process going on already with respect to Middle East petroleum. The income thus achieved is used for internal development or for investment in the productive capacity of the rest of the world. In either case it will constitute a form of redistribution.

Moreover, as rich countries become more concerned about the impact of industry on their environments, they will tend to build polluting industries in countries which are environmentally less vulnerable and less concerned, a process we can already see beginning with regard to United States oil refineries. This is in itself a form of transfer of wealth. Its real value to the recipient country, however, depends ultimately on how much learned skills are transferred along with wealth and technology.

One problem not usually mentioned in connection with the redistribution of wealth is that of population growth. Much is made of the fact that the relatively small and slow-growing populations of the Western countries now preempt a large share of the world's natural resources, but one must also ask the question, both within and among nations, whether those who breed the fastest should have a superior claim on the world's future resources. Perhaps this conflict is not a real one in the long run because greater affluence among the poor will lead to lower fertility, but in the short run it does raise an ethical question not usually considered.

Need for Models of Alternative Economies

One of the difficulties in discussing zero growth is that most growthless utopias have been invented by literary people who are not quantitatively minded. There is a great need to study quantitatively and in detail the economics and technology of such utopias, looking at the flow of materials, communications, and people in a self-consistent manner. This is a challenge to economic modeling and systems analysis. Most such analysis today deals with relatively minor variations of existing economic and social structures. This is partly because public policy is largely concerned with incremental changes in what exists, and partly because, to inspire confidence, a model must be testable against an observable system on which statistical data are available. Unfortunately, the theoretical structure of economics and sociology is not deep enough to warrant confidence in models of systems which differ radically from existing arrangements. Yet, crude as it may be, the attempt should be made. Models of utopia may not help much in pointing the way to what is feasible, but they should help to reveal assumptions which are not internally consistent, and to eliminate proposals which are not technically or economically feasible.

For example, one theme that keeps recurring in many utopias is that of a more decentralized society. In Western industrialized societies, considerations of economic efficiency and economies of scale have largely determined patterns of investment and industrial location. The resulting structure reflects the fact that energy utilization and transportation technologies developed before communication and information technologies. Given the building blocks of modern communications and information processing, as well as higher speed transportation, is it possible to envision new patterns of settlement in which there are no agglomerations larger than, say, half a million people? Would it be feasible to set a limit to the further growth of our modern conurbations, insisting that any additional population growth occur in new settlements?

Is it possible to model an optimum world population which maximizes freedom and material well-being for the individual, and is capable of indefinite self-perpetuation on the basis of foreseeable resources and energy supplies and environmental absorptive capacity? If so, is there any credible process by which we could get there from here without intolerable political and social strains? These are the kinds of questions which responsible scholarship has almost never addressed. There are few credible utopias.

The Problem of Employment

As long as labor productivity continues to increase at the present historical rate, the U.S. economy must expand at a rate of 4 to 5 percent a year in order to maintain a tolerable level of employment. Indeed it is a remarkable phenomenon of recent years that, although our economy has absorbed more new entrants to the labor force than at any time in our history, the rate of unemployment has been increasing. This is largely the result of the postwar baby boom, which has been flooding the employment market in the last few years. With zero population growth, or even a gradual approach to a steady-state population over the next century, the rate of economic expansion required for full employment would gradually decline. Once the population stabilized, the growth rate would only have to match the rate of increase in labor productivity; in other words, it would only have to keep the number of man hours worked per year constant. Furthermore, as the economy shifts its emphasis from goods to services, the rate of increase of labor productivity may decline so that, with zero population growth, we might not have to absorb a yearly increase in GNP of more than about 1.5 percent. This assumes that improvements in our ability to measure growth in service productivity do not reveal that the accepted hypothesis of low productivity growth in services is mistaken. But even if optimistic projections regarding population are correct, this situation would not come about for some time. Certainly the pressure for full employment is one of the most persistent and fundamental political pressures operating in every country, and no policy on population or economic growth which results in unemployment, even temporary structural unemployment, is likely to be politically acceptable.

The most obvious and most frequently suggested alternative is to reduce the number of man hours worked per year through shorter work weeks, or through much longer annual paid vacations, or possibly through systems of socially subsidized sabbaticals for all workers. If the average time worked per year were reduced enough, productivity on a per worker year basis would cease to grow. Historically, however, the average number of hours worked per week has declined much less rapidly than the nominal work week for people use a large part of their released time to increase their earnings either by "moonlighting" or by working overtime. In addition, longer vacations and more leisure have created a boom in recreational products and travel and have overloaded public parks and wilderness areas. The snowmobile, the outboard motor boat, the trail bike,

and the mobile camper are enjoying an unprecedented boom and probably place greater stress on the environment than other consumer goods
and services. Any further move to reduce man hours worked per year
in order to spread employment without increasing GNP would—at least
without other measures—exacerbate many of the very problems that we
now associate with continuing economic growth.

A system of sabbaticals has, perhaps, more to recommend it, especially
if the time were used for continuing education or retraining, and therefore to increase the potential mobility and adaptability of the work force.
Any measure that increases labor mobility and adaptability tends to reduce
structural unemployment, and thus to reduce the political pressure against
regulatory measures which generate temporary unemployment by dis-
placing economic activities. Thus sabbaticals for retraining might fit in
well with stringent environmental regulations and income redistribution
policies which would drastically alter patterns of demand and, in the
absence of greatly improved adjustment mechanisms, produce structural
unemployment.

Of course, since much of the secular growth in labor productivity
is attributable to technological change, it might be argued that restraining
such change would reduce the need for the economy to generate new employment opportunities. Most innovative technological activity occurs in
the capital goods sector of industry, and it is mostly this sector which
contributes to productivity growth. If this innovative activity were diverted
to other areas, especially toward improving social services, the link between innovation, employment, and growth might be broken or at least
attenuated. In a society which placed greater emphasis on services as
compared with material goods, economic growth might still occur, but it
would be less demanding of resources and environmental absorptive capacity. The most important technological inputs to services—those associated
with the generation, processing, storage, and transmission of information—
tend to be much less environmentally demanding than the more traditional
technologies which are concerned primarily with the utilization of energy.
Indeed, by making environmental standards and resource conservation
criteria more stringent we could raise the price of materials and energy,
while at the same time permitting information technologies to become
cheaper. There may, in fact, be an automatic shift of the economy and
especially of innovative effort in this direction.

Since modern industrial nations are less and less self-sufficient, however, especially with respect to their material inputs, they are increasingly
forced to earn foreign exchange to survive, and hence to increase labor
productivity in order to compete with other countries. At the same time
their individual economies must grow to maintain full domestic employment. It seems to follow inexorably that any policy which involves less
efficient use of manpower in order to limit GNP growth will have to be

enforced by some sort of international regime—something that seems rather distant at the present time. Deliberate economic inefficiency is a bad term in international economics, and yet it seems a necessary condition for any scheme that would result in limitation of overall GNP growth without adverse effects on employment. It must be acknowledged that in the field of agriculture the developed countries have tolerated an extraordinary degree of economic inefficiency in order to preserve their individual rural economies. However, this type of negotiated inefficiency is not regarded tolerantly outside the agricultural sector.

Again, what is difficult for sophisticated industrial societies looks virtually impossible to less developed countries. Even with high rates of growth, often higher than those of developed countries, these nations face an unemployment problem of catastrophic proportions. To tell them to limit growth is very difficult, unless the pattern of recent Chinese economic development is transferable to other developing nations. Even to tell them to grow in an environmentally responsible manner, not repeating the mistakes of the developed countries, is useless if doing so will have the slightest negative impact on employment.

Conclusion

One of the main purposes of zero growth is to achieve a better balance among population, resources, and environmental stress. However, it seems fairly clear that the best way to attack problems of resources and environment is directly through the allocation of investments and the manipulation of consumption patterns rather than through any overall controls on growth. Environmental standards already legislated in the U.S. will require appreciable but not enormous channeling of investment toward environmental protection, particularly in the field of energy generation and consumption. This will slow the growth of GNP, but probably not by more than 0.1 or 0.2 percent out of a projected growth rate of about 4 percent.[8] According to most studies this channeling of investment will actually improve the environmental quality of air and water. If due attention is paid to environmental standards and resource conservation as desirable social goals in themselves, zero growth will probably be reached over a very long period simply in the natural course of events, without any attention to growth per se. Environmental protection should be looked upon as a product one buys like any other. Because it is not counted in measuring GNP, it appears to be bought at the expense of economic growth, but this is really illusory.

Probably the greatest single obstacle to more rapid introduction of environmental standards arises from competition in international trade without agreement as to common standards. Such an agreement would not mean that the standards of developed countries would have to be applied to the poor countries, or even that standards would have to be the same everywhere, but it would mean that countries would have to give up a considerable measure of national sovereignty. Trade policy, macroeconomic policy, and environmental policy are intimately related; each has repercussions for the other, and policies therefore cannot be made in isolation by nations acting unilaterally.

The question of the technical feasibility of zero growth cannot be answered in any simple way because it is so dependent on the time scale involved. We understand so little about potential national or world economies that differ more than marginally from existing ones that it is very difficult to foresee the outcome of changes in policy which are more than incremental. One thing that seems clear is that we cannot simply retrace our past industrial and technological progress back to some simpler society. Past progress has involved many irreversible changes, and the future will therefore be quite different from the past. It will probably involve the decline of many existing technologies, such as that of the automobile, which are now regarded as sacrosanct, but it will also involve rapid advances in other technologies, such as communications, which are less resource intensive. In looking at modern societies we sometimes forget that to arrive where we are has involved the decline or disappearance of many technologies which at one time were expected to go on growing forever.

REFERENCES

1. T. S. Lovering, "Mineral Resources from the Land," *Resources and Man,* Committee on Resources and Man, National Research Council (San Francisco: W. H. Freeman, 1969).

2. Karl Kaiser, "Europe and America, the Future of European-American Relations," paper presented at the Aspen Institute for Humanistic Studies, December 7-10, 1972.

3. P. Ehrlich and J. Holdren, "Impact of Population Growth," *Science,* 171 (March 1971), 1212-1217.

4. R. Revelle, ed., *Rapid Population Growth* (Baltimore: Johns Hopkins University Press, 1971).

5. James P. Grant, "Marginal Men, the Global Unemployment Problem," *Foreign Affairs,* 50, No. 1 (October 1971), 115.

6. Jon Sigurds, "Rural Economic Planning," *China's Developmental Experience,* ed. M. Oksenberg, 31, No. 1 (American Academy of Political Science: March 1973), 68-79.

7. Tang Tsou, "The Values of the Chinese Revolution," *China's Developmental Experience,* p. 35.

8. R. C. d'Arge and K. C. Kogiku, "Economic Growth and the Environment," *The Review of Economic Studies,* No. 1 (January 1973), 61-77.

LESTER BROWN

Rich Countries and Poor in a Finite, Interdependent World

OVER THE PAST two decades the global scale of economic activity has nearly tripled. In 1950, the goods and services produced throughout the world were valued at just over a trillion dollars. By the early seventies, they were worth nearly three trillion. While it has been more fashionable to focus on the population explosion of the postwar period and the resultant growth in claims on resources, clearly there has also been an enormous growth in individual consumption of goods and services in much of the world. The combined effect of these two trends has been an overall growth in consumption that causes the global economy to double every sixteen to eighteen years.

The continuing expansion of economic activity depends on a number of the earth's critical resources. It depends on the earth's capacity to provide fresh water; to produce food, forest products, and marine protein; to supply minerals and energy fuels; and to absorb waste. In many parts of the world, the scale of economic activity is beginning to put pressure on at least some of these resources. When the earth's capacities are exceeded either locally or globally, certain undesirable and sometimes irreversible changes occur.

The costs of exceeding the earth's various capacities take many forms. Among these are the eutrophication of fresh water lakes and streams, a rising incidence of environmentally induced illnesses, the progressive deforestation of the earth, soil erosion and abandonment, the extinction or threatened extinction of various species of plant and animal life, inadvertent or deliberate climatic alterations, either locally or globally, and growing scarcity of some raw materials. Among those resource constraints which are most immediately limiting the continuing expansion of economic activity are the supplies of fresh water and marine protein, and the available waste absorptive capacity.

Fresh Water

In many countries, the expansion of agricultural and industrial activity is impeded by a scarcity of fresh water. The principal constraint on the spread of high-yielding wheats—the Green Revolution—in a number of

153

countries ranging from Mexico to Afghanistan has been the limited supply of fresh water. The lack of water is also a serious constraint on Soviet efforts to expand crop and livestock production.

Competition for waters of various rivers and river systems which cross national boundaries has become intense in recent decades. India and Pakistan required several years to negotiate mutual rights in the allocation of the Indus River waters. Competition between Israel and the Arab countries for the water of the Jordan River is intense. Protracted negotiations were required to allocate the Nile waters between the Sudan and the United Arab Republic. Use of the Colorado River waters continues to be a thorn in the side of relations between the United States and Mexico.

Soviet efforts to expand domestic food supplies have been seriously handicapped by a scarcity of fresh water. When the virgin lands project of the late fifties failed to live up to expectations, the Soviets attempted to expand their food supply by intensifying production on existing cultivated areas. The consequent need for more water led them to devise plans for diverting southward the flow of four major rivers which now flow north into the Arctic Ocean. Once these plans became public, however, the international meteorological community was quick to respond. Meteorologists urged the Soviets to abandon these plans, arguing that to interrupt this flow of warm water into the Arctic would alter the climate in the Arctic, and in turn trigger compensatory adjustments throughout the global climatic system. One study estimated that rainfall in central North America would be measurably reduced if the Soviets were to proceed with these plans. For the time being, at least, these plans are being held in abeyance and the Soviets are importing grain.

Within the United States, the state of Florida recently contracted with a rain-making firm to increase rainfall in Florida in order to break an extended drought that was damaging agricultural crops and threatening wildlife in the Everglades. The interesting question is: What if Texas were to sign such a rain-making contract? How would this affect relations between the United States and Mexico? What if Ceylon, in an effort to become self-sufficient in its production of rice, were to hire a rain-making firm to increase its share of the monsoon rainfall at the expense of India?

The Food and Agriculture Organization projects that global demand for fresh water will increase 240 percent by the end of the century. Needless to say, this could generate great pressures on countries to use whatever technologies are available or can be developed to expand their fresh water supplies. National efforts to expand fresh water supplies by using advanced technologies often have transnational if not global consequences. In our ecologically interdependent world, we must now seriously consider regulating national interventions in the climatic system to expand fresh water supplies, particularly when this may be done at the expense of another country.

Marine Protein

Another resource for which competition among countries is becoming increasingly intense is the world's marine protein supply. As population increases and incomes rise, the demand for animal protein is increasing at close to 3 percent per year. The world fish catch expanded from 1950 to 1968 at an average rate of nearly 5 percent per year—more than double the rate of growth in the population. Since 1968, growth in the world fish catch has slowed significantly, which suggests that growth in marine protein supplies might fall behind the growth in population, not to mention the growth in global demand generated by rising incomes.

Many marine biologists now feel that the world catch of table grade fish is very close to the maximum sustainable limit. A UN sponsored conference convened in 1948 to survey the condition of world fisheries concluded that only a few table grade species, and these rather exotic ones, were being overfished. A contemporary examination suggests that a large number, perhaps a majority, of the thirty-odd leading species of table grade fish may now be overfished. Reports of the recent annual conventions of the fifteen-member International Commission for the Northwest Atlantic Fisheries (ICNAF) provide some insights into the deteriorating condition of fisheries in the northwest Atlantic, traditionally one of the world's richest fishing grounds. Overfishing is the principal cause of this deterioration.

Even more disturbing is the growing number of situations in which countries cannot agree on a limitation of the catch and on the allocation of this catch among the countries involved. Competition among countries for the ocean's fish supplies is evident in daily newspaper headlines. Within the ICNAF membership, Britain and Iceland are in continuous conflict over the fishing rights off the coast of Iceland. Conflicts between U.S. and Soviet ships off the Atlantic coast of North America are frequent. Expanding Soviet and Japanese fishing fleets compete for limited supplies in the North Pacific. American fishermen deeply resent the intrusion of Soviet, Korean, and Japanese trawlers off the West Coast of the United States. Scores of U.S. fishing trawlers have been confiscated off the west coast of Latin America by the governments of Ecuador and Peru. Brazil has insisted on a treaty regulating the terms on which U.S. fishermen are permitted within its 200 mile offshore territorial limits.

Complex social and political issues are raised by the prospect that the world catch of table grade fish may be at or close to the sustainable level. One sticky international political issue is how countries share the catch of those species where the catch must now be limited. The principal division among countries is likely to be along economic lines. The rich countries are likely to insist on allocating the catch according to a historical base. Such is the case within the ICNAF in instances where agreement has been reached. Most quotas set by the Commission are distributed among member nations

according to a formula which allocates 40 percent of the total catch in proportion to average catches over the previous ten years, 40 percent in
proportion to average catches over the previous three years, 10 percent
to coastal states and 10 percent according to special needs. This formula
has not always been acceptable to all countries involved. Failure to agree
on the allocation among countries has generally resulted in a continuing
decline in the stocks and catch of the species in question within the
ICNAF region.

The poor countries, many of which are just entering the world fisheries
on a large commercial scale, can be counted on to resist formulas based
largely on historical shares. They are likely to counter with proposals to
allocate the catch on some other basis, perhaps according to coastal
proximity or population. Historically based allocations would mean that
the rich countries would maintain the lion's share of the world fish catch;
population based allocations would mean that the poor countries would
get the major share since they have an overwhelming majority of the world's
people. Political leaders in some poor countries are certain to request first
claim on this common global resource because their people are suffering
from protein malnutrition.

One of the great difficulties in assessing the future of world fisheries is
the lack of reliable data on which to base projections. If the rate of growth
in the world fish catch falls significantly below the level of the past two
decades, as it now seems certain to do, how will this affect prices of marine
protein? How will it affect efforts to eliminate protein malnutrition in poor
countries, and relationships between rich countries and poor as rich countries use their superior purchasing power to bid protein resources away
from the poor ones?

Waste Absorption

Another of the resources on which the expansion of economic activity
depends is the earth's waste absorptive capacity. Utilization of this resource
may have a greater impact on the relationships between rich and poor
countries than almost any other, with the possible exception of liquid
fossil fuels. Those countries which are highly industrialized have now
reached a situation in which local waste absorptive capacities are often
being exceeded. The result is eutrophication of fresh water lakes and
streams; a rising incidence of environmentally induced illnesses, particularly
respiratory illnesses in urban areas; and the threatened extinction of a
number of plant and animal species.

The unwillingness of local populations to bear the environmental consequences of excessive waste discharge has resulted in the passage of a
vast amount of legislation in recent years limiting the waste discharge of
industrial and other activities. Within the United States, this includes

national legislation such as the Clean Air Act, the Clean Water Act, legislation in almost every state, and ordinances at the local level. The net effect of compliance with these new laws is to raise the cost of production, particularly in some of the more pollution-intensive industries.

One of the industries affected most in the United States is petroleum refining. Between 1972 and 1975, seven new oil refineries will be needed to meet the projected demand for refined petroleum products in the northeastern United States. It is highly unlikely that any of these refineries will be built there. In some communities in the region the construction of oil refineries is prohibited regardless of the pollution abatement technologies used. In others, the cost of complying with regulations would raise the cost of production so much that oil company executives are locating their new refineries elsewhere—in the Caribbean, the Middle East, or, in the case of one firm at least, in Indonesia.

Other industries are carefully assessing the impact of environmental legislation on their production costs. Increasingly, we can expect that multinational corporations will respond to pollution differentials in much the same way they have responded to income differentials over the past fifteen years. They will locate the pollution-intensive phases of their operations in poor countries in much the same way they have located the labor-intensive aspects of their operations in the same countries to take advantage of lower wages.

Japanese industrialists, operating in a country faced with perhaps the world's most serious national pollution problem, are beginning to think of systematically locating pollution-intensive activities elsewhere. Plans devised a few years ago to construct feedlots in Japan have been altered, and investment by Japanese firms is now scheduled for countries where coping with feedlot waste will be easier.

Some developing countries are beginning to perceive of their underutilized waste absorptive capacities as a resource to be exploited in international economic competition, in their efforts to expand exports and to attract new investment by multinational corporations. Brazil, for example, has publicly invited multinational corporations to locate their plants in Brazil where there is as yet relatively little pollution and where there are few pollution regulations. Rich countries, feeling the impact of this relocation on their own rates of economic growth, levels of employment and balance of international payments, will undoubtedly try to insist that all countries, rich and poor, adopt the same environmental regulations in order to nullify this potential economic advantage of poor countries. Many poor countries will argue that their unutilized waste absorptive capacity is a resource to be exploited in international economic competition, like mineral reserves, fertile soil, or tourist attractions.

We have examined briefly three of the resources on which global economic activity depends: fresh water, oceanic protein, and waste absorptive capacity. As long as the hydrological cycle produced more fresh water than man could ever hope to use, there was no competition among countries for fresh water supplies. As long as there were more fish in the ocean than man could ever hope to catch, the entry of another country into a given fishery or the addition of a few more fishing ships to the world fleet was of little concern. But today, with overfishing becoming widespread, such additions may represent a serious threat to world fisheries.

Similarly, as long as the ecosystem could absorb far more waste than existing scales of economic activity could produce, there were no problems. We have now reached the point, however, where the expansion of economic activity is beginning to press against the limits of the earth's resources, locally and globally. As it does, the interaction and interdependence among countries rise. The question of how those resources which are in limited supply, or which can be expanded only at considerable cost, are divided among countries becomes a critical international political issue.

Raw Materials

Those countries which industrialized earliest are beginning to deplete and, in some cases, exhaust their indigenous supplies of raw materials. Among these are several European countries and the United States. Japan, of course, has been heavily dependent on other countries for raw materials ever since it began to industrialize. Europe today is heavily dependent on imports for its supplies of petroleum and for most of the principal minerals. Even with the North Sea oil fields in full production by 1980, Great Britain will still depend on imports for half of its petroleum supplies, and for continental Europe the percentage is much higher.

Within the United States, dependence on imported energy fuels and raw materials has been rather limited until recently. In 1970, for example, the United States was only marginally dependent on petroleum imports. In some years during the past generation it was actually a net petroleum exporter. Projections show, however, that by 1985 the United States will be dependent on imports for more than half of its supplies of petroleum and natural gas. This is closely paralleled by the situation in minerals supply. It is projected that by 1985 the United States will be dependent on imports for more than half its supplies of nine of the thirteen basic industrial raw materials. Among these are iron ore, aluminum or bauxite, and tin. In 1970, imports of energy fuels and minerals cost the United States $8 billion. By 1985, this sum is projected to increase to $31 billion, assuming constant prices, an assumption which, needless to say, is no longer considered realistic.

Some exportable reserves of energy fuels and raw materials are located in industrial countries such as Canada, Australia, and the Soviet Union, but the great bulk of them are located in nonindustrial countries. Exportable petroleum reserves are controlled almost entirely by the eleven members of the Organization of Petroleum Exporting Countries (OPEC), all nonindustrial countries. Four poor countries—Chile, Peru, Zambia, and Zaire (Congo)—supply most of the world's exportable surplus of copper. Three others—Malaysia, Bolivia, and Thailand—account for 70 percent of all tin entering international trade channels. Cuba and New Caledonia have well over half of the world's known reserves of nickel. The main known reserves of cobalt are in Zaire, Cuba, New Caledonia, and parts of Asia. And Mexico and Peru, along with Australia, account for 60 percent of the exportable supply of lead.

The prospect of collective bargaining by raw-material-exporting countries is a very real one in those instances where a few countries control most of the world's exportable supplies. The success of the eleven-member Organization of Petroleum Exporting Countries (OPEC) in bargaining for improved terms for supplying petroleum to the international community is a model which other raw material exporters can be expected to attempt to emulate. Copper exporting countries are attempting to organize. There is talk within the aluminum industry to the effect that the politics of oil may become the politics of aluminum. Coffee producers are beginning to consider negotiating collectively, independently of the importing countries, to set world coffee prices. How many of these efforts will be successful remains to be seen, but the existence of a highly successful model is encouraging other groups to try.

As industrial societies deplete, or in some cases exhaust, their indigenous reserves of important raw materials, they are becoming heavily dependent on nonindustrial countries for raw materials. This in turn is transforming the relationship between rich and poor countries from one in which the poor have been heavily dependent on the rich for capital and technology, to a more genuinely interdependent one, in which the rich are becoming dependent on the poor for raw materials and for cooperation in environmental and other matters.

Social Justice at the International Level

The rapid expansion of global economic activity against the backdrop of increasing environmental pressure is thus compelling mankind to address the issue of social justice on a world scale and in a new context. Hitherto, the rich could urge the poor at home and abroad to wait, arguing that the benefits of growth would eventually trickle down, that the supply of a given resource could always be expanded. And it is quite conceivable that yet-to-be-discovered technologies will make this possible. Indeed, the difficult adjustments which must be made in economic systems—both domestic and international—are immensely easier in a growing economy than in a static one. But when opportunities for further expansion of a given resource are limited, the issue becomes not how to expand the resource, but how to divide it. Given what we presently know and can foresee about the availability of resources and the state of the environment, it may be possible to narrow the global poverty gap only by slowing the growth in consumption of material goods among the rich while accelerating it among the poor countries.

Traditionally, rates of economic growth in nonindustrial countries were closely tied to those in the industrial countries. A slowdown in industrial countries was usually followed by a slowdown in nonindustrial ones. In part this was because rates of economic growth in nonindustrial countries often correlate closely with growth in their export earnings. The close correlation in growth rates between the two groups of countries may be diminishing. At least some of the nonindustrial countries are benefiting from the rapid growth in exports of energy fuels and minerals to the industrial countries, from their improving export terms for some key raw materials (such as petroleum), from a gradually expanding share of processing in exported items; and from their growing trade with each other.

Control over the major share of the world's exportable supplies of many important raw materials ranging from petroleum to tin is giving the nonindustrial countries leverage in the international economic system which they have not heretofore enjoyed. The terms on which they make resources available are influenced strongly by their desire to attain a more equitable share of the global economic pie. Numerous efforts are under way to increase their share of processing raw materials. Poor countries seem most anxious to abandon as rapidly as possible their traditional "hewers of wood, drawers of water" role in the world economy. For example, Turkey and Japan have made an agreement whereby Japan is building a 50,000 ton per year ferrochrome alloy plant in exchange for a million tons of chrome ore to be delivered over a ten-year period.

Increasingly the poor countries are invoking the need for greater social justice at the international level in their economic relationships with the rich countries. Algeria took over control of the French oil and gas interests in the Algerian Sahara with the express desire of providing an acceptable level of living for every family in Algeria. They knew that if these resources remained in French hands, this objective would not be fulfilled.

In Chile, President Allende linked his terms of compensation to the copper firms, whose holdings his government had expropriated, to the needs of the Chilean people. He claimed that there are 700,000 children in his country who will never develop their full physical and mental potential because they were deprived of sufficient protein in the early years of life. The copper companies, he argued, have invested a paltry sum in Chile, but they have taken out $400 million in profits. This sum, President Allende pointed out, would be sufficient to fill the protein deficit in Chile for as far as one could see into the future.

In Peru, Foreign Minister Edguardo Marrin justified the extension of his country's offshore limits to 200 miles in terms of Peru's needs. The fish from the rich fishing grounds off the coast of Peru provide much of the protein consumed by the Peruvian people and earn most of the country's foreign exchange. He argued that industrial countries such as the Soviet Union, Japan and the United States are able to invest in sophisticated technologies such as sonar, floating fish-processing factories, and auxiliary fishing fleets to roam the world's oceans taking fish wherever they can find them. Peru, on the other hand, lacks the capital and technology to compete in these ways. It can protect its share of the world's oceanic protein supplies, he maintains, only by extending its offshore limits. Political leaders in other maritime developing countries are taking similar positions.

The relationship between rich countries and poor is not at present a particularly happy one. Although nearly all poor countries have achieved political independence, many do not feel that they have yet attained full economic independence. Many feel that political imperialism has simply been replaced by economic imperialism. They cite the trade negotiations of the postwar period as an example. The Kennedy Round of trade negotiations was very much of, by, and for the rich countries. Broad reductions in tariffs on industrial products were made, but little liberalization was achieved on the agricultural commodities which the poor countries export. At present, the duties levied on imports into the industrial countries from the poor countries are roughly double those levied by the rich countries on imports from each other. Economic assistance from the United States and the Soviet Union, two leading industrial societies, has fallen sharply in recent years. The share of the GNP which these two industrial giants make available in economic assistance to poor countries is less than one half of one percent.

In the monetary area, when it came time to allocate the new international reserve currency, the Special Drawing Rights, among member countries of the International Monetary Fund, the lion's share went to the rich countries, thus reinforcing the existing global maldistribution of wealth. As the United Nations Conference on Trade and Development in Santiago in May 1972 and the U.N. Conference on the Human Environment in Stockholm in June 1972 indicated, the poor countries are increasingly dissatisfied with their position in the world. They can be counted on to try to improve their position by exercising every bit of leverage they can get in the form of control over raw materials or refusal to cooperate in various international efforts.

Population Growth Versus Rising Affluence

The issue of what share of the pressures on global resources is attributable to population growth and what share is attributable to rising affluence is becoming an issue between rich and poor countries. Political leaders in the rich countries with low rates of population growth focus attention on the rapid population growth in the poor countries as a source of stress on resources. Their counterparts in the poor countries point to the pursuit of superaffluence in the rich countries as the principal source of growth in claims on global resources.

In fact both are important. At the global level, the growth in annual consumption of goods and services—about 4 percent per year—is allocated rather equally between population growth and rising individual affluence. If the 4 percent rate of economic growth of the past two decades were to continue to the end of the century, the gross world product, now just over $3 trillion, would expand to $9 trillion. Even the increase of global economic activity from $2 trillion to $3 trillion greatly increased both pressure on resources and competition among countries for those increasingly scarce resources on which the expansion of economic activity depends.

As we look to the future, we must ask ourselves how we can accommodate ourselves to the earth's ecosystem, the natural life support systems on which our existence depends, and the finiteness of many resources. Clearly one way is to slow the growth in individual consumption among the more affluent, something which might be done without in any way impairing their well-being. Another way, of course, is to move toward a stabilization of world population as rapidly and systematically as possible.

A part of the conventional wisdom within the international development community has long been that the two billion people living in the poor countries could not aspire to the lifestyle enjoyed by the average North American because there is not enough iron ore, petroleum and protein in the world to provide it. Even while accepting this, however, those of us in the United States have continued the pursuit of superaffluence, increasing our consumption of resources as though there were no limit to the amount that could be consumed.

Political leaders in the poor countries are beginning to ask with disturbing frequency what right Americans, who constitute only 6 percent of the world's people, have to consume a third of the earth's resources. This question is being raised in the various international forums where access to and allocation of resources among countries is discussed.

Within the United States we must examine carefully the presumed link between our levels of well-being and of material goods consumption. There is growing evidence that this relationship is at best a tenuous one. At low levels of income and consumption, increases in material goods, such as food or household appliances, do very much affect one's level of well-being, but after a point improvements in well-being are scarcely perceptible. For a man with only a crust of bread, the acquisition of a second crust greatly improves his well-being. For a man with a loaf of bread, an additional crust has little impact on his actual well-being.

The technologies underlying our economic system evolved in a situation of relative resource abundance. We have reached the point now where we need to reexamine these technologies in the light of growing resource scarcity. Could we retain our current level of individual mobility with a much smaller volume of resource use merely by limiting the size of automobiles? Could we greatly reduce energy consumption with a properly designed public transport system? Should we be building skyscrapers, with their enormous energy requirements, or should we abandon the competition to see who can build the tallest building in each major city? We must reexamine the use of our public budgetary resources and the maintenance of a global military establishment. The issue may no longer be whether the U.S. taxpayer can foot the bill, but rather, whether mankind can afford such a frivolous use of resources.

In a global economy which is increasingly integrated and interdependent, countries compete for common global resources of energy, minerals, marine protein, forest products, and agricultural commodities. Under these circumstances, the more of us there are the less each of us has. As recognition of this spreads, efforts to slow population growth and achieve population stability may acquire a new urgency. We must ask ourselves how we can stabilize world population sooner rather than later.

Given recent trends, it is relatively easy to envisage a strategy which would lead to population stabilization in some of the wealthier societies. In Europe, population has recently stabilized in East Germany, West Germany, and Luxembourg. Other countries, such as the Netherlands, the United Kingdom, the United States, and the Soviet Union, may well stabilize their populations within a decade or two if the recent decline in birth rates continues. Japan's population growth is slow enough so that it too could stabilize within the foreseeable future—given the appropriate policy decisions. In summary, we can envisage a situation in which, a decade or so hence, population growth in the wealthier countries might come to a halt.

What is far more difficult, however, is to envisage a rapid slowing of population growth in the poor countries in the foreseeable future. Birth rates do not usually voluntarily decline in the absence of a certain minimum level of living—an assured food supply, literacy (if not an elementary school education), at least rudimentary health services, and reduced infant mortality. What we may witness is the emergence of a situation in which it will be in the interest of the rich countries to launch a concerted attack on global poverty in order to reduce the threat to our future well-being posed by continuous population growth.

The costs of doing so are not as formidable as one might think. The evolution of the global economy has reached the point where this may have become a realistic undertaking. For example, according to UNESCO estimates, it costs approximately $8 to enable a person to become literate in a developing country. For a billion illiterates, this would require an expenditure of $8 billion. If this were spread over a five-year period to minimize annual outlays, it would come to $1.6 billion per year. Shared by several wealthy countries, it would amount to a few hundred million dollars each per year at most. This might be a very cheap price to pay to achieve one of the preconditions for a major slowdown in global population growth.

The Chinese experience in providing health services, including family planning, to the countryside has been instructive in this connection. By using limited available resources to train paramedical personnel, they have apparently succeeded in providing at least rudimentary health services to the great majority of their vast population, although income per person averages only $140 annually.

Following World War II, the United States took a major global initiative and decided that it would use its food-producing resources to intervene anywhere in the world where famine threatened. It has followed this policy over the past twenty-five years, even when, as in India in 1966 and 1967, a fifth of the U.S. wheat crop was required to forestall famine. Perhaps the next step should be not merely to avoid famine, but to work systematically toward providing a minimum nutritional intake for everyone in the world. Again the Chinese experience is instructive for it seems to have permitted the achievement of adequate nutrition at an exceedingly low level of income.

In summary, we may now have reached the point in the evolution of global society, in the expansion of economic activity, and in the deteriorating relationship between man and the environment where we must give serious thought to the need to at least attempt to satisfy the basic social needs of all mankind. At first glance this seems terribly ambitious. It may, however, be much less costly than we would at first think if we utilize some of the new technologies and new approaches now available. It may be one of the cheapest ways of insuring our own future well-being.

WILLARD R. JOHNSON

Should the Poor Buy No Growth?

NO-GROWTH SOCIETIES—those that experience very little increase in population or per capita income or production—have, historically, been bottom heavy with poor people. The so-called "traditional societies" are the only examples we know. They have emphasized ecological balance and man's accommodation to the forces of nature. Many people consider rapid expansion of production and reproduction to require some special (cultural if not racial) blessings such as the Protestant Ethic, the Spirit of Capitalism, and the Industrial Revolution. Are we now to have a no-growth society composed of rich people or of some mixture of economic classes that includes a substantial number of rich people? The noted British socialist, Anthony Crosland, has stated that the current champions of the no-growth society

are often kindly and dedicated people. But they are affluent; and fundamentally, though of course not consciously, they want to kick the ladder down behind them. They are militant mainly about threats to rural peace and wildlife and well loved beauty spots; but little concerned with the far more desperate problem of the urban environment in which 80 per cent of our citizens live.[1]

Is the superindustrial society going to be like the "traditional society"? Is such a society now, for the first time in history, to be the social condition of the wealthy instead of the poor? What is the proper response of the poor to the call for a return to a no-growth society? Should the poor buy no growth?

In truth, practically nobody, rich or poor, argues for absolutely zero population or economic growth on a universal basis. Interests are not coherent in these matters any more than in most others. Changes in population and income are not always clearly related, certainly not in a consistently positive or negative way, and not in the same way for the aspiring as for the already affluent. Rich people desire no population growth for the poor, but continued money growth for themselves and perhaps even for the poor if it does not dampen their own. The poor want to expand the ranks of the rich by at least their own number, but they do not want further income growth for the already rich. Some poor people think increases in their own

165

numbers enhance their chances of becoming richer through political advantage in developed countries, through increased productive labor resources in developing countries. They may regard efforts to reduce their rates of population growth as motivated by genocidal or antidemocratic intentions. Of course, many of the poor do wish to have fewer children; they recognize the grain of truth in the adage, "The rich get richer and the poor get children." They may therefore prefer selective growth policies which favor growth in the numbers but not necessarily in the per capita wealth of the rich, and growth in the per capita wealth of the poor but not in their numbers.

In any case, the question of which policies the poor should prefer is irrelevant. The poor can't "buy" what the rich won't "sell," and the rich hoard all the really effective roles in determining the outcome of such policy debates. It will take power to alter the direction of fundamental economic trends and patterns of resource utilization in the United States and in the world. The numbers of poor do not amount to a sufficient resource to offset the power of wealth. Not yet. Perhaps the rich fear that someday they may and thus, in these debates, they stress population control as a starting point.

No Growth Defined in Terms of Population

Population increase is not the real issue, however, at least not in America.[2] Our projected population profile suggests that the American population will double in about sixty years. While this will obviously put some strain on our resources, it will not overburden them. With only 6 percent of the world's population using perhaps 50 percent of its material resources, there is plenty of room for population growth in the United States. A more important reason to control population growth would be to reduce the level of our resources utilization in order to permit the rest of the world to achieve a standard of living nearer to what current standards call decent. Nonetheless, many Americans are concerned that if we limit population increase to near the zero point, the present basically young U.S. population will grow older without replenishing the youth, and the society will come to resemble a Florida retirement colony.

There is evidence that American women no longer want to have more children than would permit the population to approach nearly zero growth.[3] It seems safe to say that the technology of preventing unwanted births will improve and that soon it will be safe and fairly painless, even morally, to reduce the rate of childbirth to the level desired by the women concerned. It may be that poorer women desire more children than richer ones,[4] or that, in any case, they desire more than the rich wish to see them have. Even so, population growth among the poor will not soon overburden our national resource base; it will, however, strain the resource base that those who control social policy allow to the poor. Thus the real population issues to the poor are the incompatibility of their values and desires with those of the rich, and their lack of power to protect and satisfy their own values. With regard to the population of the domestic United States, though perhaps not to that of the world, it is a ruse to couch the issue in the language of population explosion or overburdened resources.

No Growth Defined in Terms of Production or Income

Mancur Olson has suggested in the introduction to this issue that we define "no growth" as zero increase in per capita net national product (NNP). Such a definition, however, is basically irrelevant to the real issues involved in the no-growth debate. As he himself has pointed out, there are a number of items that would augment per capita NNP that would also enhance the quality of life, even to the no-growth advocates. Indeed many of the controls that would be required to eliminate threats to ecological balance, controls which most no-growth advocates desire, involve money transactions, and thus contribute to an increased per capita NNP. Furthermore, as we assign money values to householding services, or increase our expenditures on education, keeping other things constant, we increase per capita NNP without putting any additional strain on ecological balance.

The real issue is to avoid the type of growth that threatens the future life of the human species and that hampers optimum satisfaction of human wants and needs. No-growth advocates do not arouse the concern of the poor as effectively as they might by calling for stable per capita net national product or even for zero population growth, when so many people still lack so much of what they want and need and of what their countrymen already have. It would be more relevant for them to emphasize the threatened depletion of resources fundamental to everybody's survival and health and to the survival of civilization itself—threats to life support systems and to ecological balance for the species.

Do the poor people in the United States or in the poor countries of the world have any special stake in defending against these threats that the richer populations do not have? Will they suffer sooner or to any greater extent? Are their survival resources any better or worse than those of the richer groups? These are questions well worth returning to. First, however, I will join the debate by discussing the issue that is generally argued, that of the impact of general per capita growth in national product or income on the elimination of poverty.

The Propaganda War in Favor of Growth

The industrial enterprises that are most directly threatened by the depletion of nonrenewable mineral and fuel resources are seldom found among the ranks of the no-growth advocates. In fact, they are in the forefront of a propaganda campaign to convince the poor that their best hope for eliminating poverty is continued economic growth. This seems curious. The most blatant example is provided by the Mobil Oil Company which has invested an impressive sum to sponsor advertisements designed to convince the poor that economic growth is a requisite to the elimination of poverty in the United States. One such ad, quoted by Peter Passell and Leonard Ross in "Don't Knock the $2-Trillion Economy,"[5] runs as follows:

GROWTH IS THE ONLY WAY AMERICA WILL EVER REDUCE POVERTY. . . . While the relative share of income that poor people get seems to be frozen, their incomes do keep pace with the economy. It's more lucrative to wash cars or wait on tables today than 20 years ago. Even allowing for inflation, the average income of the bottom 10th of the population has increased about 55 percent since 1950. Twenty more years of growth could do for the poor what the Congress won't do.

The problem with the logic of this argument is that it fails to give due consideration either to alternative ways of eliminating poverty (such as transfer payments) or to the changes that occur in consumption needs. Things such as telephones and television sets that were not considered necessities twenty years ago are seen as such today. Another Mobil Oil advertisement in the series says:

We can have full employment and true equality of opportunity only in an economy that creates new jobs and new opportunities. We can have decent homes and a decent environment only with proper land use, continuing technological innovation and an adequate and dependable supply of energy.

Still another asserts in a headline, "Growth is not a four-letter word." It quotes British socialist Anthony Crosland:

Even if we stopped all further growth tomorrow, we should still need to spend huge additional sums on coping with pollution. We have no chance of finding these huge sums from near-static GNP, any more than we could find the extra sums we want for health or education or any of our other goals. Only rapid growth will give us any possibility.

The fact that it is Mobil Oil, which admits that "The United States will consume more than twice as much oil in the next 30 years as it has consumed in the entire history of the country's oil industry," that spent the thousands of dollars for these advertisements to convince the poor that their hope lies in economic growth makes the argument suspect in itself.

Economic Growth and Elimination of Officially Defined Poverty

Can we really count on continued increases in per capita GNP or NNP to substantially reduce if not eliminate poverty in the United States? However indignant we might be over the fact that the owners and managers of Mobil Oil or General Motors will benefit more from growth than the poor, we might comfort ourselves if poverty were being eliminated, even if inequality were not. But there is no clear evidence that poverty is or can be eliminated as a consequence of the processes of general economic growth.

It is quite clear that the ranks of the poor have thinned recently during years of significant economic growth. In 1959 there were nearly 40 million people who would be classified as poor by today's Census Bureau standards. This number had fallen to 25.6 million in 1971, a decrease of 14.4 million in twelve years, or nearly 1.2 million a year. It is tempting to conclude that, if similar trends could be maintained, all the poor could be moved out of official poverty in twenty-one years. Alan Batchelder has, in fact, noted that "the drop in the incidence of poverty was so great between 1961 and 1968 that if the 1961 to 1968 trend were to continue through 1981 America would have no poverty."[6] It is not, however, that simple a matter. There have been some important fluctuations in the rate of poverty elimination, as Batchelder's comments indicate. The seven-year rate was higher than the eleven-year rate. The trend may reverse itself. The number of poor rose from 1959 to 1961, and again from 1969 to 1970, and it did not change from 1970 to 1971.[7] Perhaps, despite economic growth, we are now entering a period of increasing numbers of poor. (Some economists, however, feel that statistical techniques account for the rising number of people considered poor.[8])

Structural features of the American economy cause the relationship between growth and the rate at which poverty is eliminated to produce different results at different times. Features of general growth that had a significant impact on poverty twenty years ago have much less today. Batchelder and several others[9] have noted that structured-in poverty will be increasingly difficult to eliminate. The decline in poverty between 1961 and 1968 resulted from an expansion of aggregate demand and increased labor productivity. By 1968, however, the able-bodied poor who were capable of doing so had already worked their way out of poverty. But work, in itself, is not sufficient to remove a family from poverty. In 1970 the heads of nearly three million poor families were employed, but this did not protect them from poverty.[10]

Poverty is a feature built into the current American economy and social structure. It results from social, political and economic discrimination which thwarts needed investment in poor people.[11] It is not due to an abundance of bums who do not want to work but rather to an abundance of businessmen who won't or can't give jobs to those who need them, and of labor unions that won't allow people to acquire the credentials and skills they need to get jobs. Those most likely to be left out of the picture of general growth are blacks (except for young urban black families in the North in which both father and mother work), families headed by females, farm families, and the elderly. The poverty of these groups is relatively impervious to the benefits of general economic progress.[12] Economists are unable to agree as to the extent and reasons why these groups are isolated.

However, the fact is that we prevent old people from working and, in 1970, 4.7 million elderly persons, comprising 4.6 percent of all household units, accounted for 18.2 percent of the poor individuals in the country.[13] We keep blacks from getting jobs: in 1971 nearly one million blacks, or almost 10 percent of the national nonwhite work force, were officially classified as unemployed,[14] and unofficially the figures are probably much higher. In Massachusetts in mid-1972 the unemployment rate for inner city blacks was over 22 percent and among the black youth it was over 35 percent. The black poor are more likely than the white poor to be employed, but both their employment and their education work less well for them. In 1971, nearly 10 percent of the black male heads-of-families with some college education were impoverished, as compared to only 3 percent of whites.[15]

Improving the industrial structure, providing tight labor markets, and holding down inflation would be important public policy objectives in order to improve black incomes. However, economic growth has not and will not improve the situation very much, though recession may aggravate it considerably as it did between 1969 and 1970. Poverty seems to be built into our current social and economic structure. As Theodore Schultz has noted, our most important declines in poverty have been due to increases in income from labor, which are in turn due to increases in the demand for high skills and to the responsiveness of the labor force to this market situation. But blacks, agricultural workers, women, older people and workers in the South have generally been kicked out or held out of these labor markets.[16]

Growth, defined as rising per capita NNP, can have some positive effect on the incidence of poverty for some blacks, less so for whites. Lester Thurow, a leading analyst of measures of poverty, has determined that "General growth results in higher incomes for both blacks and whites," but the key element for blacks in this is the availability of jobs, especially of full-time jobs in the government service and industrial sectors.[17] These are the types of jobs that blacks have been able to get and to benefit from most fully. In the future, however, there is likely to be more flexibility in the service than in the industrial sector, especially if ecological balance becomes a more potent influence on our economic policies.

There are special implications here for the zero economic growth advocates. The industries in which blacks have a foothold and a potential for economic improvement are precisely those where we find the greatest ecological hazards. Blacks are particularly entrenched in the auto industry and many of the industries and services peripheral to it. Blacks constitute 23 percent of nonfarm, nonconstruction laborers.[18] Black workers form substantial contingents in industries which deal with chemicals, fabricated metals, primary metals, and nonelectrical machinery and transportation equipment. Industries like these are closely identified with the problems of poisoned lakes and streams, and with overuse of material resources, especially of nonrenewable resources such as petroleum, natural gas, and other fuels that will become increasingly important as energy sources in the future. Traffic problems, overcrowding, noise, and other invasions of psychic domains are also rooted in these industrial activities. Those whose predominant objectives are ecological may threaten economic progress for blacks as well as for great numbers of nonblack and nonminority poor.

An equally important if not more serious threat to these industries is the fact that the raw materials that feed them are close to exhaustion. This is particularly threatening to patterns of industry in the United States because we account for such high percentages of total world usage. Paul and Anne Ehrlich note, for example:

Estimates of the total American utilization of raw materials currently run as high as 50 percent of the world's consumption, with a projection of current trends to about 80 percent around 1980. Probably 30 percent and 50 percent would be more realistic figures, but in any event our consumption is far beyond our "share" on a basis of population. We number less than 6 percent of the world's people![19]

The Club of Rome's *The Limits of Growth* presents an even more dire picture. Taking into account rates of utilization that are growing exponentially, and even assuming that, somehow, five times the known reserves of needed raw materials will be found, they predict that we will exhaust those materials most crucial to present patterns of industrial civilization within 173 years.[20]

The other way to relate per capita NNP and officially defined poverty is to ask: Would a slackening of growth or a lack of growth especially hurt the poor? Would it wipe out the gains that have already been made? Certainly the periods of stagnation and decline in 1958, 1961-1962, and 1969-1970 have tended to do so. Especially among the black population there were income reversals in each of these periods. The economic progress that poor people, especially blacks, made in the 1960's essentially ended with the Nixon Administration. The percentage of white and black families and individuals in poverty has remained virtually constant since 1968.[21] A lack of continued growth, without substantial change in national policies to facilitate the transfer of wealth and income through transfer payments, tax reform and job development, or vigorous antidiscrimination efforts would probably have disastrous consequences for blacks, and perhaps for the poor more generally.

Economic Growth and Elimination of Unofficial Poverty

The statistical improvements we have been examining are, to an alarming degree, merely a matter of definition. The minimal income level established in 1969 by the Federal Interagency Committee reflects the interest of federal agencies that are supposed to reduce the incidence of poverty. They are more concerned about statistical results than about human needs. In 1971 they considered $4,137 to be the annual income figure beyond which the typical American family (an urban family of four composed of a thirty-eight-year-old husband, a nonworking mother, a boy of fifteen and a girl of eight) was no longer in the "low income" or poor group. Other federal bureaus, with different clientele and interests, define the problem according to other sets of criteria. The Department of Labor has announced that this "typical" American family needed $7,214 a year to maintain the lowest "reasonable and decent" standard of living as of the autumn of 1971.[22] This minimum is far below the $10,971 that they estimated would be needed for an intermediate standard of living, or the $16,000 for a high standard. But it is about twice the average family welfare allowance awarded in mid-1972 in Boston.

No doubt the poor aspire to comfort. We need not argue here whether the "American way" gives one a right to a comfortable level of income. It is apparent, however, that many needs for healthy and sane living in peaceful social settings must go unmet at the levels of income officially used to define poverty. Oscar Ornati has indicated criteria for defining various levels and types of poverty.[23] L. Fishman summarizes his position as follows:

Ornati defines poverty generally as the lack of command over goods and services sufficient to meet minimum needs. These needs are different as seen from different perspectives. The most often used poverty calculations approximate those which Ornati bases on eligibility guidelines for public assistance programs. This level he calls the "minimum subsistence" poverty budget. The federal government makes use of another set of budgets to determine "living wages" requirements. Ornati calls this poverty level "minimum adequacy." Yet a third poverty line can be established on the basis of guidelines that have been used to settle various wage disputes. This level he calls "minimum comfort." All three levels are of "poverty."

The minimum adequacy and minimum comfort budgets reflect the demands and pressures of the population to which they are applied, the organized and working poor, more than does the subsistence budget which is administratively determined for welfare and other public assistance recipients. These budgets have grown over the years in response to rising prices and needs more than the subsistence budget. Thus the number of people with incomes falling below the subsistence budget poverty line has tended to decline without any real lessening of misery or greater satisfaction of need.

Another influence on measurements of the incidence of poverty is the use of constant dollar and value standards to define poverty. Projecting 1960 standards of poverty in 1960 dollar values backwards thirty years would define more people as poor than were considered so at the time. Similarly, if we used the standards of thirty years ago and projected them forward to today, we would find that some of the poverty had dwindled for statistical reasons alone. Ornati concludes that it is more fair and accurate to compare amounts of poverty in terms of contemporary standards.[24]

It seems that the best we can hope for from recent economic trends is to reduce the number of people who live under conditions of abject pov-

erty, below the level of income by which the Census Bureau officially
defines poverty. But how long would we have to wait for those trends to
eliminate poverty even at this unrealistically low level? Lowell Galloway,
writing in 1965, attempted to strengthen the case for using growth as a
tool to eliminate poverty.[25] He criticized the projections of poverty reduction made by the Council of Economic Advisers on the basis that they
assume that a linear relationship exists between rates of economic growth
and poverty elimination, and that all families are either completely unre-
sponsive or equally responsive to economic change. He assumed instead a
nonlinear relationship which enabled him to claim a higher poverty elimination rate although one that declines with additional economic progress,
leaving a residual group who are increasingly impervious to the benefits of
economic progress, including blacks, female-headed families, farm families,
and the like. He makes his own projections, which can be compared to the
CEA ones, based on the differing rates of economic growth and levels of
unemployment in the periods 1947-1956 and 1956-1963. In addition, he
varied his assumptions about the level of unemployment.

Figure 1

Actual and Projected Percent of
Families Below Poverty Line

	Galloway			Council
Unemployed	4% (1947–1956)	5% (1970)	6% (1957–1963, 1971)	
1956 actual	22.2%			22.2%
1963 projected	16.6			18.5
1963 actual			18.5	
1970 projected	12.6		14.2	
1970 actual		10.0		10.0
1971 actual			9.9	9.9
1980 projected	6.4		8.7	10.0

Galloway concluded that growth could not eliminate poverty much below
the 6 percent level but would get us to that level sooner than the Council
had estimated. The actual level of unemployment in 1970 was 5 percent
and since early 1971 has been around 6 percent, and the actual percentage
of all families represented by the poor was 10 percent in 1970 and 9.9
percent in 1971, so perhaps the figures of the Council of Economic Advisers
are closer to the correct ones. It is clear that the rate of poverty elimination
is now virtually zero. Perhaps we have already reached Galloway's impervious hard core, but at 10 percent rather than 6.4 percent of all families.
Poverty is going to continue to be a problem, even as officially defined, for
more than another decade, despite projections of growth. John Hardesty

and others predict that in 1990 there will still be 2.5 million families and 5 million unrelated individuals living in poverty compared to the 5.3 million families and 5 million individuals who were poor in 1971.[26]

Relative Standards of Income and Wealth

We have discussed several concepts of poverty, all of them absolute, based, that is, on definite fixed budgets defined almost exclusively in terms of what it costs to meet certain selected needs. There are also relativistic concepts which define poverty in terms of the incomes of other groups. The absolutistic approach is akin to the legal concept of due process, a minimum standard to which everyone has a right, while the relativistic approach accords with the legal doctrine of equal protection or equity, which seeks to avoid extreme differences in the way the system deals with people. The absolutistic is the less controversial of the two. Since we can predetermine consumption patterns and supply and calculate the cost of living, being poor or rich has, according to this standard, a precise and stable meaning. Ironically, however, a competitive free enterprise system that spurs individualism and egotism makes it harder, not easier, to ignore relative standing. People in our society, especially the poor, value keeping up with the Joneses. Thus it is perhaps more realistic to define poverty in relative terms that take into account the changes in income and expenditures patterns of the general society.

The most common relative standard of poverty is arbitrarily pegged at 50 percent of the median income. Perhaps we accept this standard only out of aesthetic appreciation for its symmetry—half of half. But, defined this way, poverty is less tractable than it is when defined by any but the most generous absolutistic standards. Here we are really talking about reducing income inequality. In the postwar period income inequalities have increased in the American society, a fact which may take on increasing importance because of the exalted place equality has occupied in American myth.

Let us look first at the nation's performance with respect to reducing income inequality. Herbert Gans has observed that in the United States between 1960 and 1970, when the median family income rose from $5,260 to $9,820, the proportion of families earning half the median dropped only 1 percent—from 20 to 19 percent.[27] This is a far less striking improvement than can be claimed when poverty is defined according to the absolutistic measures used by the Census Bureau. The disparity of results produced by techniques of accounting is revealed with great clarity in this example: in 1960 the poverty line did fall at 50 percent of median individual income, but the poverty line was not permitted to rise as median income rose so that by 1970 the poverty line came to only 40 percent of the median. As Gans notes, "During the decade the poverty line rose far more slowly than the median income, and the inequality gap between the poor and the median earners actually widened by a full twenty percent."[28] This permitted officials to claim that the number of poor had declined when almost the same proportion of households had incomes below 50 percent of the median income.

Thurow and Lucas have measured the retrogression of the poor when their income is measured against that of others, especially of the decidedly rich: they note that the gulf between the richest 20 percent of families and the poorest 20 percent (as measured in constant 1969 dollars) widened from $10,565 in 1947 to $19,071 in 1969.[29]

The picture is worse for blacks, a point of particular importance. Blacks have a special interest in the matter of eliminating poverty, not because they are the only poor people—they are a minority even among the poor—but because about a third of all blacks are poor, even in terms of the arbitrarily low official poverty line. Poverty is no less frequent, and no more welcome in black households now than before the antipoverty programs. Since 1948, nonwhite income has made what appear to be spectacular gains, going from $7.9 billion to approximately $46 billion in 1971. But any comparison of black income to white income, whether in terms of aggregate income, or of median level, or of percent of total income compared to percent of total population, shows that blacks have not made much headway; Negroes held 5.1 percent of the total white income in 1948, a mere 6.4 percent in 1963, and only about 6.6 percent in 1971.[30] There is, however, a widening span between the aggregate income by race calculated in dollar amounts: in 1948 white income was $146.2 billion, nonwhite $7.9 billion—a difference of $138.3 billion; by 1963 white income had climbed to $347.5 billion while the Negro's rose to $23.6 billion—a difference which had also

Figure 2

Median Income of Nonwhite Families as a Percent of White Median Family Income, 1950–1071.[31]

Year	Nonwhite	Year	Nonwhite
1950	54%	1961	53%
1951	53	1962	53
1952	57	1963	53
1953	56	1964	56
1954	56	1965	55
1955	55	1966	60
1956	53	1967	62
1957	54	1968	63
1958	51	1969	63
1959	52	1970	64
1960	55	1971	63

expanded to $232.9 billion; by 1971 white income was $649 billion and black income was $46 billion, a difference of $603 billion.[32]

The same picture of lack of progress emerges from a comparison of black and white median family income. Patterns of distribution within each racial group have augmented the disparity between blacks and whites on the lower end of the income scale. Sources since 1950 differ in specifics, but they indicate that in general black median family income has fluctuated in the area of 50 to 60 percent of white median family income. Figure 2 gives the available figures. In addition, the gap in absolute dollar figures between white and nonwhite median family income is actually widening: in 1947 it was $2,174; by 1966, it was $3,036; and by 1971, it was $4,270, more than double the 1947 figure.[33]

Wealth inequalities may be a more significant factor in the no-growth debate than income inequalities: not only are they greater, but they also have long-range effects on income, and are likely to increase with growth. Furthermore, because of the power of wealth, they are less subject to change as a result of politics. Given the lack of strong redirecting forces in the economy, some growth probably gets absorbed into wealth: even the super-rich can only spend so much on current consumption. This absorbed capital acts as a corrective, however, because, by limiting consumption, it dampens growth.

The disparities between white and black family wealth, or net family worth, are very stark. They have been calculated in a tentative fashion by Andrew Brimmer, who indicates an average gap of $16,214.[34] The disparities within the general society, ignoring racial differences, are even greater. Whites have as much cause as blacks to be concerned about them because wealth is highly concentrated in the United States, and is becoming ever more so. Brimmer reports that, in the late 1960's, over half of all private assets were owned by about 9 percent of American families.[35] Gans reports that the country has always had an unequal distribution of wealth: "In 1774, among the minority of Philadelphians affluent enough to pay taxes, 10 percent owned fully 89 percent of the taxable property."[36] While we have made some headway in reducing inequality since 1774, things have not changed very much in this century.

The landmark Lampman study found that in 1953 more than 30 percent of the assets and equities of the personal sector of the economy (about 20 percent of all wealth was government owned) were held by only 1.6 percent of the adult population.[37] They held all ownership of state and local (tax exempt) bonds, more than 82 percent of all stock, 38 percent of all federal bonds, 29 percent of all cash, 16 percent of the real estate holdings, 13 percent of life insurance reserves, and 6 percent of pension and retirement funds. R. J. Lampman's data generate the chart of wealth in Figure 3. Notice how much of the total held by the top 1 percent is actually held by the top 0.5 percent.

Figure 3

Concentration of Wealth in the United States[38]

Year	1/2 of 1% of Adults (Percent of All Wealth)	1% of Adults
1922	29.8	31.6
1929	32.4	36.3
1933	25.2	28.3
1939	28.0	30.6
1945	20.9	23.3
1949	19.3	20.8
1953	22.7	24.2–28.7[39]
1954	22.5	n.a.
1956	25.0	26.0
1958	n.a.	30.0[40]
1962	n.a.	31.0[41]
1969	n.a.	28.0–34.0[39]

In the recent years of renewed economic growth, the number of very wealthy has increased: in 1966 there were over 90,000 millionaires, for example, whereas in 1953 Lampman recorded only 27,000. Part of this is due to inflation which boosts the money value of holdings more than consumption power.[42] But the concentration of wealth has also been increasing, as Figure 3 shows. Gans asserts that the top 1 percent of wealth holders currently own more than a third of all wealth.

In terms of the position of the poor in the no-growth debate, the type of wealth that is concentrated is more important than the degree of concentration. The superrich hold even larger portions of investment wealth than of general wealth, and it is investment wealth which directs the activities of productive corporations; which determines levels of expansion, job creation, prices, reinvestment, etc.; and which has such a profound effect on politics. It has been asserted that the top 200,000 wealth holders own 32 percent of all investment assets,[43] and that 2 percent of individual stock holders own about two-thirds of all stock held by individuals.[44]

The impact of that control is amplified by the extent to which a few corporations dominate the business sector. One-tenth of 1 percent of the almost two million corporations in this country control 55 percent of the total corporate assets; 1.1 percent control 82 percent of those assets.[45] William Buckley has pointed out that the 200 largest firms in America command 58.7 percent of the market place. This is up from the 48 percent in 1948.[46] What does this domination mean? Perhaps it is what leads the federal government to subsidize businesses to the level of $63 billion, a fact determined recently by William Proxmire's Joint Economic Committee; or perhaps it supports the tax loopholes which cost the government $77 billion, according to economists Benjamin A. Okner and Joseph A.

Pechman; or perhaps it is responsible for what populist Fred Harris points to: an estimated $60 billion in overcharges made by shared monopolies which can set prices without much regard to laws of supply and demand.[47]

With this kind of concentrated economic power, perhaps it really doesn't matter whether the poor want to buy no growth or not. The basic decisions are made by the superrich, and can only be moderated by political forces. To the relatively poor, the debate as it is currently argued ignores the real issues. Neither side can offer much relief, certainly not sufficient relief, without resorting to policies calling for a substantial redistribution of income, and perhaps of wealth as well.

Redistribution

As we have seen, no trends allow us to predict in a clear-cut manner just when recent patterns of economic activity will eliminate poverty in the United States. Moreover, those debating growth or no-growth policies disagree about their implications for the poor. Mobil Oil echoes Passell and Ross in asserting that "Growth is the only way America will ever reduce poverty," while noted economist Lester Thurow asserts that "poverty cannot be eliminated without direct income transfers."[48]

A decade of impressive economic growth but meager improvement in the poverty situation makes it an act of wisdom to side with Thurow. The real issue then is to determine the relationship between achieving effective income transfers and economic growth. Is it easier or harder to get redistribution with no growth as the goal of public policy or as the condition of the economy?

It is useful to distinguish the import of the no-growth debate as a debate or clash of values and preferences from the implications of impending real limits to growth. Often the debate is argued as if both sides could assume the possibility of continued growth and thus dispute only the costs of such growth. The "no growthers" point to the problems of continued growth: fouling of the atmosphere, dangers to health, offense to the senses, rising prices for scarce nonrenewable resources and the products that use them, crowding, ugliness, and loss of recreational resources and beauty spots. The "growthers" point to the dangers of no growth: the lack of improvement in economic well-being and the resultant increases in social turmoil among the poor as their convictions that they play in a zero sum game are confirmed; the increased rigidity and more forceful political control on the part of the superrich who neither wish nor feel the need to accept a more slender slice of the economic pie.

Stuart Chase has called this debate over growth an antagonism between partisans of the gross national product on the one hand and partisans of the quality of life on the other, between green-money men and green-earth men. Put this way, I again question whether either side has solace to offer the poor. The money men are holdovers from the days of what Charles Reich calls Consciousness II: a society which contains the seeds of its own destruction and will be replaced by Consciousness III. Consciousness III types are now busy organizing earth days and holding ecology marches; they would rather be honey-seekers than money-seekers, but then they can be both. The revolution they pursue is not likely to involve the partisans of the black revolution who find it hard to drop the concerns of Consciousness II, lest they leap-frog history altogether. The black and white youth of the counterculture quickly fell out with each other.

To be relevant to the needs of the poor, those who advocate growth will have to talk more specifically and effectively than they have to date about specific types and rates of growth that would alleviate the misery of the underclass. Merely saying that growth is good and has not done all it can do to eliminate poverty is not enough. On the other hand, they could take some of the heat off themselves by pointing out the failure of no-growth advocates to deal directly with the problems of the poor.

British economist E. J. Mishan, a no-growth advocate, is guilty of debating the issues in terms of values that, for all their humaneness, ignore the concerns of the poor. He challenges economic growth policies because he questions values deeply rooted in Western society. The trouble with growth, according to him, lies with the materialistic nature of a social order that piles up more and more material goods. He sees this as destructive to humane values and antithetical to human happiness. Growth, to him, is a potentially unbalanced, misdirected, and destructive force in itself. No doubt his concerns feed on a genuine consideration for the quality of life, but they seem to me mistaken about the contribution material goods can make to it.

John Kenneth Galbraith, sometimes counted in Mishan's camp on the growth question, is more concerned about the failure of the post-Keynesian synthesis on which we once relied, at least in terms of expectation, to harness growth to the interest of the general good, including the reduction of poverty. That synthesis coupled Keynes' policies for promoting high levels of employment and high rates of growth with Alfred Marshall's polices for allocating resources and distributing incomes in order to respond to social needs within a private, essentially market-oriented economy. The synthesis was effected by Paul Samuelson, who was not unconcerned about poverty and other socially disturbing imperfections in the economy, but who did not believe that a police state was required to protect advantage, or that fundamental redistribution of income and wealth was necessary to eliminate severe disadvantage. Fusfeld has characterized Samuelson's system:[49]

Much of the system rested on the assumption that competition would prevail and concentrated economic power could not control markets for its own benefit. To ensure competition and prevent monopolies from building up, the post Keynesian synthesis required strong anti-trust legislation, and where natural monopolies existed . . . vigorous regulation by government . . . to ensure full employment and growth by the proper mix of spending, taxation, and monetary policy. . . . Even poverty might be ended by a growing economy.

Galbraith's analysis has revealed the failure of these assumptions to accord with reality. Monopolies did develop in the mature industrial societies, and are continuing to develop at an ever more rapid rate. Big business aided and abetted big government, and vice versa. Inflation became an overwhelming problem, even carrying over into periods of rising unemployment. Galbraith, like Mishan, now attacks economic growth itself; it doesn't work either as a goal or as a safety valve. An economy dominated by private decisions about consumption and production, he argues, tends to starve its public sectors.[50] The society's needs for long-term development, social betterment and general welfare get slighted in favor of luxuries and entertainment. It seems apparent today that big business can pretty much mold consumer tastes and spending patterns to its own needs.

Galbraith and Mishan call for a new synthesis, a reconstruction of economics, to move us toward more humane goals, and to permit us to analyze more realistically the obstacles to that movement. Perhaps they reject less the values growth produces than the values that produce growth.

At this point I should specify what I mean by redistribution, for there are several redistribution schemes, most of which promise great improvement, and it is quite possible to misunderstand their character and their promise. Initially we might, as a nation, choose simply to eliminate what is officially defined as poverty; in 1971 this would have meant eliminating incomes lower than $4,137 for the modal family of four. Later, more humane floors for income might be established. We might also choose to transfer money directly only from the very richest of the population to the very poorest, rather than to spread the burden evenly among the nonpoor. To have done this in 1971 would have required that about $12.1 billion be added to the aggregate incomes of those officially designated by the Census Bureau as low-income families and individuals. To have taken this entire amount from the richest 5 percent of the population would have reduced their pretax money incomes from all nonpublic transfer sources[51] only by 8.2 percent. Their share of the nation's total income would have dropped from 21.6 percent to 19.8 percent. Surely such a restriction of income would be economically and morally, if not politically, feasible.

More far-ranging proposals might reach substantially up into the ranks of those who find it virtually impossible to support their families adequately. These are not broken families, save perhaps in spirit. Heading these families, typically, is a working male, but, although they contain the clear majority of the country's population, they receive considerably less than a majority of the aggregate annual income.

Dr. Harold W. Watts of the University of Wisconsin proposed to the Democratic Party Platform hearings in St. Louis on June 17, 1972, one of the simplest plans yet advanced to aid not only the poor, but also the middle class that is under such financial stress. He proposed to replace the present public assistance and individual income tax programs, as well as all other means-tested programs with a "credit income tax" scheme. Each taxpayer would pay the same basic tax, at the rate of one third of all income received before the benefits derived from the redistribution scheme itself. There would be an additional 6⅔ percent surtax on any annual income in surplus of $50,000, and still another 10 percent surtax on income in surplus of $100,000. Money would then be redistributed back to *everybody* on an equal footing, regardless of income. Each aged and disabled person would receive a payment of $1,560 a year, able-bodied adults eighteen to sixty-four would receive $1,320 a year, children ten to seventeen would receive $660, and younger ones $420. The modal family of four could not have an income less than $3,720. Such a family would break even, that is, receive back as much as it paid in taxes, at an annual income of $11,160. Work incentives would operate all along the road: any person earning $3.00 would keep $2.00 as long as his total income were less than $50,000 a year, and no person, however rich, would lose more than 50 percent of any dollar.

The impact such a scheme would have on the current distribution of income seems startling. Seventy percent of the entire population would benefit, ending up with more money than they did in 1970. The poorest 20 percent of the population would have 10 percent of the total final income, compared to between 7.7 and 7.9 percent in 1970. The next 50 percent of the population would enjoy an increase of 5 to 7 percent over their 1970 income. Perhaps equally important, in terms of the political feasibility of the scheme, the total revenue available to the government would *increase* by about $3 billion over that generated by the present system.[52]

With 70 percent of the populace, as well as the government, coming out ahead under such a scheme, why does it not command the support of the country? Of course the scheme was mauled in the infighting of the Democratic primary candidates and McGovern's other liabilities were involved, but there was more to the opposition than that. As Passell and Ross state, "On the face of it, there should be an easy solution to poverty in the United States. A redistribution of only 5 percent of the national income could bring every family up to a minimum $5,000 income." But they point to the fate of the President's Family Assistance Program as evidence that the idea of "explicit redistribution of income is still political anathema."[53]

Part of the handicap of such proposals, as McGovern discovered, is public confusion about their "costs." Such proposals involve taking money away from some people, perhaps from all income receivers at one stage or another of the operation. That which is taken away is popularly regarded as a cost. The confusion lies in the notion that it is a cost to "the country." Actually the money is taken from some people and given to others. It does not cost the country anything, except the quite limited expenses of the administrative system that supervises the transfers. The important question is whom does it cost? Watts' scheme costs only the 30 percent who receive the highest incomes, and them not very much. But there is an apparent inclination for most people to believe the extremely wealthy, who are in fact threatened, when they scream that the program would cost "the country" the nearly $44 billion in net losses that they themselves would suffer. Such "costs" should properly be measured against the costs of social control, the losses incurred through crime and social turmoil to the extent that it is rooted in poverty and needless deprivation, or even against the $40 to $45 billion that the present system transfers among our people with far less positive results.

Perhaps we have not touched on the deepest pitfall of all for redistribution programs, the attitudes held as much if not more fervently by the poor than by the rich: that to receive some direct benefit from a transfer system is to "get something for nothing" and to get something for nothing makes one "dependent" and therefore less than a man, certainly less than an American.

Here, both the motive for and the failure of Nixon's Family Assistance Plàn are most instructive, as brilliantly analyzed by one of its chief authors, D. P. Moynihan.[54] Far less bountiful than the plans we have already discussed, FAP would nonetheless have provided direct cash payments to the poor. Providing a maximum of $2,400, it would have eliminated only 60 percent of poverty but it would partially have covered the need of every poor child and concentrated on the working poor. The crisis to which Nixon was responding was seen in terms of welfare reform, and the issue of welfare, argues Moynihan,

is the issue of dependency. . . . Being poor is often associated in the minds of others with admirable qualities, but this is rarely the case with being dependent. . . . It is an incomplete state in life—normal in the child, abnormal in the adult. In a world where completed men and women stand on their own feet, persons who are dependent—as the buried imagery of the word denotes—hang.

It is one of the perversities of American life that only those who receive direct cash payments from government, not related to earnings from work, are considered dependent, and thus despicable; while those who receive services, benefits, and credits against costs they would otherwise pay, especially against taxes in the form of government guarantees, overruns, tax shelters, tax-free dividends, depreciation allowances, and the like, are considered independent, self-reliant embodiments of the work ethic. To add insult to injury, the welfare system has been designed and operated to ravish the family, degrade and deny the adult, and defeat the child. Thus, Moynihan admits, the system, seemingly deliberately to the victims, makes welfare recipients dependent in fact, unable to organize or utilize social resources of self-assertion or development in order to profit and progress, rather than slowly die as a result of the inadequacy of the payments in money and kind they receive. They are in a position analogous to that of the colonized and, in the words of Albert Memmi, "the colonized is not free to choose between being colonized or not being colonized."[55]

What is the source of such pernicious attitudes and practices? Perhaps it is the insistent strain of individualism in American culture. The exaltation of self-help, self-development, and rags-to-riches hopes certainly seems to play a part. Moynihan set the Family Assistance Plan against this background by asserting that its uniqueness derived from its assertion of "income by right." How odd that this concept should be unique—given the faith of the founding fathers in the "inalienable right" to "life." Life, but not the means to life? In a society where it is impossible to return to nature, and which cannot offer either enough work or enough pay for the work there is, one cannot sanely or justly assert the right to life without the right to the means for life.

These values of self-assertion and heroic individualism—each American making his own declaration of independence—are deemed to be a source not of pernicious outcomes, but of productivity. Productivity is considered perhaps the prime virtue; it defines the success of the individual and of the system; Erich Fromm takes it as the measure of virtue itself, although he charges the society that wishes to make people virtuous to make the unfolding and growth of every person the aim of all social and political activity. Instead, we have made it the prerequisite. Today productivity is preempted by technology, access to which is unequal. Virtue is assigned, then, only to those who control that access, a lessening proportion of the whole society. But people continue to live with their illusions, and thus to seek production, and the ordinary worker's growing sense of redundancy generates only vague anxieties. He will turn hardest against any initiative to distribute products to those who have lost or never gained any nexus with production at all. This outlook fits more easily with overall economic growth than with no growth. Times of growth justify a faith in the availability and even the meaningfulness of work. No growth threatens to awaken us to the prospect not simply of having less (which is not really necessary), but of *being* less, and without illusions. Opponents to the Family Assistance Program played on these confusions and fears: they riddled the plan with work requirements and "incentives" until the "costs" were made to appear prohibitive.

Another cause of the demise of FAP was racism. However much one wishes to be able to discuss the sources of the failure of efforts at social justice in the United States without invoking that abused word, one cannot in this case. American political life is marvelously consistent in these matters. In American mythology the bottom of the social heap is defined by blackness, and thus, despite the fact that a majority of the poor, even a majority of the "dependent poor" are white, welfare and dependency are thought of as "black problems." Efforts to improve the lot of the poor and of those on welfare are popularly characterized as "more for the blacks." Anathema!

Moynihan prefers to ascribe the greater responsibility for the failure of FAP to the liberals and to the blacks themselves. They failed, according to him, to appreciate that "the public wanted to help the poor but not to encourage dependency." He calls Nixon's term, "workfare," a mere public relations ploy, but the work requirements were compulsory. Moynihan seeks refuge from the sting of this fact by pointing to the work incentive program embodied in the 1967 Social Security amendments which had equally compulsory requirements that were not and presumably could not be implemented, because there weren't enough suitable jobs. But he notes that "Congressmen would rail against the measure, asking who was going to iron shirts once FAP was enacted," and it was in response to such criticisms that the work requirements were put in.

In a far less spiteful analysis of these proposals, James Welsh noted[56] that Wilbur Mills had provided the relevant defense against white Southern criticism in their first Congressional test, when he said, "Yes, a disproportionate number of welfare recipients are black, but most of the working poor are white, and live in the South."

Delaware's Senator John Williams, not National Welfare Rights Organization's George Wiley, was most responsible for killing FAP—although Wiley is considered the archvillain by more than Moynihan—for Williams knew that the work incentives he valued most would drive the "costs" of the program beyond the $4 billion limit Nixon had affixed for it.

Nixon wanted to win the respect of black Americans, but also of those other Americans whom Moynihan characterizes as "white wage earners in big cities, alarmed by the fantasies of the Black Panthers and such, hard enough pressed themselves, and focusing on welfare as a symbol of how government had abandoned the interests of the working class." Nixon's attention was apparently arrested by Peter Hamill's article, "The Revolt of the White Lower Middle Class," which argued that men, mostly Catholic, who earn their living with their hands or back and who "do not live in abject, swinish poverty, nor in safe, remote suburban comfort . . . earn between $5,000 and $10,000 a year. And they can no longer make it in New York." A lot of them and their kind supported George Wallace. "That should have been a warning, strong and clear," argued Hamill. "If the stereotyped black man is becoming the working class white man's enemy, the eventual enemy might be the democratic process itself." Moynihan thinks that the President agreed.

Precisely these elements of the lower middle class would stand to benefit in greatest numbers from the tax credit or negative income tax type redistribution plans we have already discussed, or even the demogrant plan so ill proposed by George McGovern. Nevertheless, popular attitudes of racism and individualism, and a mistaken belief in the uniqueness and purity of our good intentions concerning matters of social policy conspire to stifle any real action to eliminate poverty. Rather than accept the claims, which Moynihan records, that FAP was "uniquely American," or "the most important social legislation in history," or "unique in boldness," we should evaluate the plan and popular reaction to proposals for redistribution in the light of the observation Moynihan made when first advancing FAP, that the United States is the only advanced industrial state without a family assistance plan. As my erstwhile colleague Hugh Heclo has pointed out:

Today it is still easy to overestimate the role of U.S. national government in what are generally regarded elsewhere as standard welfare programmes. Old age pensions and unemployment insurance, initiated in 1908 and 1911 in Britain awaited national action in the U.S. until 1935; the British sickness benefit scheme of 1911 finds no American counterpart until Medicare in 1966: the family allowances instituted in Britain in 1945 have never been accepted; lagging over a generation behind Britain, U.S. benefits for the non-aged disabled began only in 1956, and for their dependents only in 1958.[57]

There are important differences in basic attitudes about welfare programs between the people of other industrial societies and Americans: they desire to spread the benefits and we to limit them; they see a sudden rise in the number of people drawing cash relief as a deficiency in their system of services while we blame the individual recipients; they seek to maximize the participation of the eligible and we to minimize it.

Conclusion

American prejudices are deeply rooted. They are not likely to be turned over by the weak commitment to the values that promote redistribution exhibited so far by prominent spokesmen for no-growth policies. For example, in the famous report of The Club of Rome Project on the Predicament of Mankind,[58] of the seven policy alternatives considered in simulating a condition of social equilibrium at "a decent living standard," only one related directly to the needs and conditions of the very poor elements of the world's population:

Since the above policies alone would result in a rather low value of food per capita, some people would still be malnourished if the traditional inequalities of distribution persist. To avoid this situation, high value is placed on producing sufficient food for all people. Capital is therefore diverted to food production even if such an investment would be considered "uneconomic."[59]

The authors did not suggest any basic tampering with the distribution system itself. It is therefore an open question whether some people would not go hungry even if sufficient aggregate food production were achieved to supply all people. That this danger is a distinct possibility is discernible from their own comments about the existing Green Revolution.

Where these conditions of economic inequality already exist, the Green Revolution tends to cause widening inequality. Large farmers generally adopt the new methods first. They have the capital to do so and can afford to take the risk. . . . On large farms, simple economic considerations lead almost inevitably to the use of labor-displacing machinery and to the purchase of still more land. The ultimate effects of this socio-economic positive feedback loop are agricultural unemployment, increased migration to the city, and perhaps even increased malnutrition, since the poor and unemployed do not have the means to buy the newly produced food.

The authors of the report did voice a concern about poverty and inequality and they devoted cogent but few words to attack "one of the most commonly accepted myths in our present society," namely, "the promise that a continuation of our present pattern of growth will lead to human equality." They demonstrated in the report that present patterns of population and capital growth are increasing the gap between rich and poor on a worldwide basis. They felt that "the ultimate result of a continued attempt to grow according to the present pattern will be a disastrous collapse."

They were most concerned about the general collapse they could foresee for industrial society, although presumably this would leave few pickings for any survivors. The compelling feature of the argument is not that it may be undesirable to continue present patterns of growth, but that it may be impossible to do so, and preserve society as we know it. The report is entitled, after all, *The Limits of Growth*. We may guess that, if the food resource limits are the first to be reached, then the developing countries would suffer first and perhaps most. If material resource limits are the first reached, the developed world would be hardest hit. But, either way, everybody would find the results disastrous. These absolute limits of growth, at least for industrial society, may well be reached in less than a century and a half. If they are real, approaching them will hurt people in tangible ways. Fuel costs will mount until present patterns of industrial activity and even home heating are disrupted, businesses close, and people discover neighborliness or freeze. Mineral resources will be coveted more by producers and users alike, exacerbating international tensions and driving the prices of finished products even further out of the range of the poorer elements of society. Substitutes and the production innovations necessary to use them will be searched out, but there is some question whether these will be available on a general basis, or reserved for the wealthy elements or countries. Some nonsubstitutable resources will be exhausted and we will have to adjust our life styles to do without them.

Such changes and the forces they set in motion will perhaps make less credible the appeal so often made to growth itself as a way to bring economic improvements to the poor. The social costs of continuing to deny the poor may then be such that those who pay them will be forced to take the question of direct redistribution of income, and perhaps of wealth, more seriously. Present indications are, however, that improvements for the poor are likely to result not from a shift in attitude to one which values no growth for itself, but rather from alliances between the very poor and the middle class. Both will have a direct interest in gaining a larger share of the economic pie, and together they would have the political power to wrest what they want and need from the superrich, who, constituting as little as 5 percent of the population, or at most 30 percent, will have to resort to direct police state tactics to deny their claims.

REFERENCES

1. Mobil Oil Corporation, "Growth Is the Only Way America Will ever Reduce Poverty," Advertisement, *New York Times,* April 13, 1972.

2. Glen C. Cain, "Issues in the Economics of a Population Policy in the United States," *American Economic Review,* 61, No. 2 (May 1971).

3. *Ibid.*

4. Paul R. Ehrlich and Anne H. Ehrlich, *Population, Resources and Environment: Issues in Human Ecology* (San Francisco: W. H. Freeman, 1972).

5. Peter Passell and Leonard Ross, "Don't Knock the $2-Trillion Economy," *New York Times Sunday Magazine,* March 5, 1972.

6. Alan B. Batchelder, *The Economics of Poverty* (New York: Wiley, 1971), pp. 25ff.

7. U.S. Department of Commerce, Bureau of the Census, *The Social and Economic Situation of the Black Population in the United States* (SESBPUS), Current Population Series, P-23, No. 42 (July 1972).

8. Herman P. Miller, "Changes in the Number and Composition of the Poor," *Inequality and Poverty,* ed. Edward C. Budd (New York: Norton, 1968), pp. 152-166.

9. *SESBPUS;* Theodore W. Schultz, "Public Approaches to Minimize Poverty," *Poverty Amid Affluence,* ed. L. Fishman (New Haven, Conn.: Yale University Press, 1966).

10. U.S. Office of Economic Opportunity, Office of Planning, Research and Evaluation, *The Poor in 1970: A Chartbook* (Washington, D.C.: U.S. Government Printing Office, 1972).

11. Schultz, "Public Approaches to Minimize Poverty."

12. Miller, "Changes in the Number and Composition of the Poor."

13. OEO, *The Poor in 1970.*

14. *SESBPUS,* p. 51.

15. *Ibid.*

16. Schultz, "Public Approaches to Minimize Poverty," pp. 165-181.

17. Lester Thurow, ed., "Analyzing the American Income Distribution," *American Economic Review,* 60, No. 2 (May 1970), 261-269.

18. *SESBPUS,* p. 68.

19. Ehrlich and Ehrlich, *Population, Resources and Environment,* p. 58.

20. Dennis L. Meadows, Donella H. Meadows, Jorgen Randers, and William W. Behrens, III, *The Limits of Growth,* A Report for the Club of Rome (New York: Universe Books, 1972), Table 4, pp. 56-57.

21. *SESBPUS,* pp. 38-39.

22. *The Boston Globe,* May 7, 1972.

23. Oscar Ornati, "The Poverty Band and the Count of the Poor," *Inequality and Poverty,* ed. Edward C. Budd, as summarized by Fishman, ed., *Poverty Amid Influence.*

24. *Ibid.*

25. L. E. Galloway, "The Foundations of the 'War on Poverty,'" *American Economic Review,* 55, No. 1 (March 1965), 122-131.

26. John Hardesty, "An Empirical Study of the Relationship Between Poverty and Economic Prosperity," *Review of Radical Political Economy,* 3, No. 4 (Winter 1971), 93; current figures from U.S. Department of Commerce Current Population Reports, Series P-60, No. 86, Table 5.

27. Herbert Gans, "The New Egalitarianism," *Saturday Review,* May 6, 1972.

28. *Ibid.*

29. *The Boston Globe,* March 20, 1972, p. 1.

30. Sidney M. Wilhelm, *Who Needs the Negro?* (Garden City, N.Y.: Doubleday, 1971), p. 163; U.S. Department of Commerce Population Report, Series P-60, No. 86, Table 37.

31. *SESBPUS,* Series P-23, No. 42, Table 16, p. 29.

32. *Ibid.*

33. Andrew F. Brimmer and Henry S. Terrell, "The Economic Potential of Black Capitalism," paper presented at the 82nd Annual Meeting of the American Economic Association (New York: December 1969) for 1947 and 1966 data; *SESBPUS,* p. 1, for 1971 data.

34. Brimmer and Terrell, "The Economic Potential of Black Capitalism."

35. *Ibid.;* Michigan Survey Research Center confirms in 1972 that the top 10% own 56% of all wealth. Cf: Michael Brower, "Some Issues of Economic Structure, Policy and Politics in Latin America and the U.S.," paper presented to the Annual Meeting of the American Political Science Association (Washington, D.C.: September 5-7, 1972).

36. Gans, "The New Egalitarianism," p. 44.

37. R. J. Lampman, *The Share of Top Wealth-Holders in National Wealth, 1922-1956* (Princeton, N.J.: Princeton University Press, 1962), p. 23.

38. R. C. Edwards, M. Reich, and T. E. Weisskopf, *The Capitalist System* (Englewood Cliffs, N.J.: Prentice-Hall, 1972), Table 4-E, p. 170.

39. The lower figure was computed by James Smith of the University of Pennsylvania, based on estate holdings net of debt, a methodology different from that used by

Lampman. The higher figure is what I understand that the Internal Revenue Service has calculated, taking into account certain actuarial estimates. Smith has calculated the concentration of wealth for 1953 as well, which is the higher figure reported for that year. His figures show no substantial change since that time, although all the intervening years have not yet been calculated.

40. *Ibid.*, Table 5-E, p. 211.

41. *Ibid.*, p. 172.

42. Lampman's 27,000 1953 dollar value millionaires would have numbered only 17,611 in terms of 1944 dollar values.

43. Edwards, *et al.*, *The Capitalist System*, p. 173.

44. Gans, "The New Egalitarianism."

45. *Ibid.*, p. 43.

46. William F. Buckley, Jr., "A Look Back: ITT Pulled In," *The Boston Globe*, Friday, July 7, 1972, p. 17.

47. Fred Harris, "The Real Populism Fights Unequal Wealth," *New York Times*, Op-Ed, May 25, 1972.

48. Passell and Ross, "Don't Knock the $2-Trillion Economy"; Thurow, *Poverty and Discrimination*, p. 151.

49. Donald Fusfeld, "Post-Post Keynes: The Shattered Synthesis," *Saturday Review*, January 22, 1972.

50. J. K. Galbraith, *The Affluent Society* (New York: New American Library, 1970), Ch. 22.

51. Excluding social security, direct public assistance, unemployment insurance, workmen's compensation and income-conditioned veterans' benefits.

52. Watts' calculations utilize Brookings Institution (Schultz) estimates for 1975. They assume a population of 214 million, total incomes of $1,046 billion, tax yield of $361 billion, less credits of $232 billion plus $18 billion in replaced public assistance programs. Total for government, $147 billion, as against present projections of $144 billion.

53. Passell and Ross, "Don't Knock the $2-Trillion Economy," p. 70.

54. Daniel P. Moynihan, *The Politics of a Guaranteed Income*, serialized in *The New Yorker*, January 13, 20 and 27, 1973.

55. Albert Memmi, *The Colonizer and the Colonized* (Boston: Beacon Press, 1965), p. 86.

56. James Welsh, "Welfare Reform: Born August 8, 1969; Died October 4, 1972—A Sad Case Study of the American Political Process," *New York Times Sunday Magazine*, January 7, 1973.

57. Hugh Heclo, "The Welfare State: The Costs of Self-Sufficiency," *Lessons from America*, ed. Richard Rose (London: Macmillan, forthcoming in 1974).

58. Meadows, *et al.*, *The Limits of Growth*.

59. *Ibid.*, p. 164.

WILLIAM ALONSO

Urban Zero Population Growth

IT IS REMARKABLE how rapidly the fashion for American states and cities has shifted from the traditional boosterism to a questioning and even an abhorrence of growth. It is common to read in the newspapers that states such as Oregon, California, Vermont, and Maryland want to stop or limit their growth, as do cities such as San Francisco, Boulder, and countless suburbs.

Undoubtedly this has much to do with the new Malthusian concern with the consequences of unlimited population growth at national and world levels. Some seem to think that the place to start controlling the nation's population growth is at the level of their city, metropolis, or state. Others hope that, as the nation moves toward zero population growth (ZPG), so will their communities. Both these views are misleading half-truths. Local policies to limit population are probably not very effective, and when they are effective they are regressive and counterproductive in terms of social well-being. They are seldom aimed at reducing local birthrates (except among those on welfare in big cities), but rather they are aimed at keeping outsiders out. Thus, what is locally perceived as a growth or no-growth policy in reality merely affects the geographic distribution of people and economic activity within some larger society such as the region or the nation.

Neither is it credible that, when and if the national rate of population growth moves toward zero, local populations will become stable. In the first place, natural increase (the excess of births over deaths) varies enormously from one area to another, so that as the national rate approached zero, many areas would fail to reproduce themselves while others would continue to grow by natural increase. In the second place, continued structural change in the economy is inevitable, with or without economic growth. Indeed, my impression is that such structural change would be deeper if conventionally defined economic growth were limited. Change in the economy would be mirrored in shifts in the location of economic activity and, accordingly, in population shifts. In short, a nationally stable population would be composed of many localities declining in population, many localities growing, and only some remaining stable.

Why should a city, a town, or a state prefer to stop its population growth? There are many conceivable reasons: growth might lower average income, or bring in poor people who do not mix comfortably with present residents; it might produce challenges to local social structure, or change life styles for the worse, or increase pollution and congestion, or overrun prized landscapes. These would be changes in the real city, which is composed of people and their relations to each other, to their institutions, and to their physical environment. But there is an unfortunate confusion which frequently overtakes the debate and which must be clarified at the outset. The word "city" is also used as the name of a municipal corporation which derives its income principally through taxation and, in exchange, provides certain services to the population. This corporate entity is only one of the elements of the real city. Yet very often debate and evaluation of advantages and disadvantages are based on the limited viewpoint of the municipal corporation, and thus miss many of the most important consequences, good and bad, for the real city.

This confusion and some of its implications may be illustrated by a recent case in a wealthy metropolitan suburb where a substantial reserve of land was probably going to be placed on the market, and many thousands of new houses built. A consulting firm was retained, and it reported, after considerable analysis, that this would be very costly for the city. It remarked that it would be cheaper for the city to buy the land itself with money raised through the sale of municipal bonds. This report met an enthusiastic reception. It not only addressed the central preoccupation of local tax groups, it also confirmed the questioning of growth among local youth and cultivated older people, and it surprised and delighted environmentalists by showing that preserving the landscape made economic sense. So well did it match the concern of many people that its conclusions were widely quoted in the national press and are often cited as proving the case against growth.

But the case as presented confused the municipal corporation for the real city. The fiscal effects on the municipal corporation can be predicted very easily, and the consultant's diligence in gathering numbers was not really necessary. On the average, a new house has associated with it about two school-age children. The taxes it pays rarely cover even one child's school costs. It also imposes the costs of providing other muncipal services, although these are small by comparison. Thus, in any such case, new houses are money losers for the muncipal corporation. In this particular case it only made matters worse that, as a result of the current residents' wealth and love of learning, local schools were excellent and costs per child especially high. All of this was in spite of a market analysis which concluded that the average price of the new houses would be higher than the price of existing houses in that town. It is more common in similar cases for the new houses to be cheaper than the existing ones, and inhabited by people not as wealthy as the present inhabitants.

If we consider the real city of present residents, they would probably still be worse off, although the matter is not as clear. Some property values would rise; some merchants and other businessmen and their employees would profit; the small proportion of poor and minority in the city would have increased job opportunities and residential choices (and indeed they were the only ones to dissent from the nearly universal approval of the consultant's recommendations); the children of the upper middle class would meet a somewhat different group in school; some local businesses would more easily find certain types of labor; shopping and entertainment facilities might become more varied and extensive; and so forth. On the other hand, a lovely landscape would be largely filled up; congestion might increase; present residents would have to rub elbows with a slightly lower class and a broader ethnic group; there might be a slight increase in deviant behavior (on the part either of the newcomers or of present residents whose conduct might be redefined according to the more standard mores of the newcomers); and, of course, residents would pay higher taxes.

It is quite likely that a full consideration of these effects would result in the same conclusion: buy the insulation. But there is yet a further consideration, which to my mind is conclusive. What is the population of this city? Is it only those living there now, or does it include those who would move in if they could? If we are speaking of a future community of which there are two alternative versions, it makes as much sense to consider the interests of all the people who would make up the expanded version, as to consider those of the original version. After all, even if growth is prevented, given the mobility of Americans, only a fraction of the future residents will consist of those living there now. The future majority will consist of newcomers, although they will be socially and economically similar to present residents. Who is choosing for whom?

If this seems abstract, the matter can be put another way. Suppose that growth is restricted. What happens to the people who would have moved in but could not? Obviously neither they nor their children cease to exist. They will find second-choice homes; their children will go to more run-of-the-mill schools and impose their costly presence on people who are less able to afford this added burden than the wealthy residents of the suburb in question. It would appear that they will be worse off, and so perhaps will the present residents of wherever they end up. The rub is that what seems from the local viewpoint an issue of growth is, in a larger framework, an issue of distribution, both in the social and in the geographic sense—not whether these people and their children shall exist, but where and how. In the abstract, the distribution problem could be solved if residents of the excluding locality made compensatory payments (a form of rent) to those whom they would exclude. But no feasible way of arranging for this suggests itself.

The point of the example is that the current balkanization of metropolitan areas into dozens and even hundreds of local governments encourages beggar-thy-neighbor strategies. Furthermore, confusing the municipal corporation for the real city leads to the meanest forms of municipal mercantilism, ones which ignore more important consequences for people. Perhaps the most hopeful recent development on this matter, in spite of set-backs, is the emergence of a number of court opinions, of which *Serrano vs. Priest* was the first, that, under the equal protection principle, rule it unconstitutional to rely on property taxes for financing schools. If these decisions stand, their logic points to their application to other services and broader geographic areas. Hopefully, too, they will lessen the influence of base motives on the formulation of local population policies.

I cannot abandon the subject of local fiscal impacts, however, without making clear the abysmal state of knowledge in this area. It is perfectly clear that an ordinary fertile family is a money loser for the local fisc. Similarly, the underprivileged create a fiscal drain through their children, their criminality, their sickliness, their morbidity, and their reliance on welfare payments. This was the basis of much of the urban renewal activity of the 1950's and 1960's, which tried to rid the central cities of such troublesome residents (where were they to go?), and bring back those who were then called "the people," the upper middle class apartment and town-house dwellers without these problems. The fiscal consequences of factories, skyscrapers, commercial developments, apartment houses, and military bases are very poorly understood, even in the direct sense of the net balance between their direct contribution in taxes and the direct cost of the services they need. Their indirect effects are even less known. Such developments always affect property values and promote or retard other developments which are difficult to predict and whose fiscal impact is also imperfectly understood, so that uncertainty is compounded in estimating their full fiscal effects. To my mind all of this makes the use of this basis for local population and development policy even worse, for it invites cruelty without certainty of advantage.

Our knowledge is no greater if we try to go beyond fiscal consequences to a more general evaluation of the impact of development upon the real city. Take the case of office buildings. They create jobs in construction, and later they provide white-collar jobs for the rising lower-middle classes and for a smaller number of professionals and administrators; they pay taxes, they increase congestion, they require new types of fire-fighting equipment, they alter the skyline and the look of the streets; they increase panoramic views for those who work in them while reducing those of residents in cities fortunate enough to have this problem, and so forth. Some of these are matters of fact which might be determined through investigation, some are matters of taste, and some are matters of conflict. Beyond these quite direct consequences, there are others, fairly closely linked, which can often be guessed at and even estimated. For instance, offices may generate nearby parking lots and eating places, which may then be used at night in association with entertainment activities; the new office space, by increasing supply, may affect rents, values, and usage of the older stock of offices; and so forth. Beyond this ring of effects there is another, vaguer but probably more significant in the long run. Offices are where information is received and processed, bargains are struck, and decisions are made. A city without offices is limited to hand functions subsidiary to another city's head functions, and its economic base will consist of branch plants and other dependencies. It will not generate the sorts of men and institutions that are in daily contact with the national and international web of information, ideas, and modes of decision. Compared to a city with offices, it will be out of touch, sluggish in its reponses, and therefore fragile in the face of continuing technological and economic change.

On the whole, I think that office development is good on social, economic, and fiscal - grounds, not too bad on ecological grounds, a matter of taste aesthetically, and often troublesome for traffic congestion. Yet, even with considerable familiarity with the professional and scholarly literature on the subject, I would be hard put to make an exhaustive list of the direct effects of office, manufacturing, or other types of development. Many of the effects that I can think of, I could not measure. Many that I could measure, I could not evaluate. And many that I could evaluate hide within their total value sharp gains for some and losses for others. The relatively few serious attempts to find out about these matters have run into grave theoretical, definitional, and data difficulties. Although some progress is being made through research, in the meantime debates and decisions are quite naturally based on shallow reasoning and spurious numerology. Some decisions will not wait.

It is an open question whether a community can effectively enforce a choice to grow or not to grow, however it arrives at this choice. Until recently virtually every city in America tried to encourage growth by a variety of local actions and by seeking state and federal preferential treatment. Although there have been some dramatic successes, there have been very few. Indeed, there is now in this country, as in many others, a national policy of establishing growth centers for depressed regions, which by a variety of federal, state, and local actions, tries to induce rapid growth in selected small cities, but these programs have had very limited success.

It might appear to be easier to limit growth than to promote it, but this is not the case according to a rich experience of national policies in Europe and the socialist countries. Moscow, Paris, London, and Warsaw are among the centers where vigorous policies have been followed to contain and even reverse growth. The means at hand have often appeared foolproof, including not only the tax incentives and disincentives, subsidies, land use regulations, and other devices familiar in American experience, but also direct command over the location of jobs and people through state control over many enterprises, location and expansion permits for industry, residence permits, and job and housing assignments for people. Even so, these centers have continued to grow, although perhaps less than without these measures. These powerful tools have failed in the face of more powerful social and economic currents. Even in totally controlled societies power is not controlled monolithically, but distributed among the agencies of the state. In setting priorities and bargaining over specific decisions, the agencies charged with territorial distribution have not been able to count as much as the sectoral ones.

A locality in America may similarly choose to discourage growth either by making it hard for people to establish residence, or by discouraging the creation of jobs which would attract people. While a small independent city might succeed in this, it appears that a metropolitan area cannot. An industry or person excluded from one municipality will find a place in another within the metropolis. Overall metropolitan levels of population and employment are set largely by economic and demographic forces at national and international levels. Local policy affects primarily the intra-metropolitan form and distribution of that development, and, if it is set by the selfish interests of the component municipalities, it does so inefficiently and unjustly. A suburb may be able to keep population or industry out, but it can do so only by directing it to other suburbs or by keeping it cooped up in the central city.

Examine the normal instruments by which a municipality keeps people out. It may restrict the use of space, either absolutely through land reserves such as parks which keep everyone out, or through zoning which keeps out those who cannot afford large lots. Other devices of varying subtlety are available. It may refuse to accept subsidized housing. Or it may set high standards through building and related codes which raise the cost of housing. Or it may set very high standards for public services, especially schools, creating high local taxes that will discourage those who cannot afford them. Or it may maintain very poor schools, so that it is unattractive to the suburbanizing lower-middle class looking for the advancement of their children through education, but acceptable to those who can send their children to private schools. Or it may refuse to provide utilities for large-scale developments, but permit low density development by allowing septic tanks and water wells. Or it may keep out the jobs that would bring in new people, primarily potential industrial workers, by zoning, or by strong regulation of pollution, or by not allowing necessary infrastructure such as highway access.

It is clear that all of these instruments aimed at keeping people out tend to keep out those of lower income. In short, local population control policies are regressive. Thus what we see today, in city after city, and often at the state level, is a three-cornered political fight among the advocates of business and development, the poor and working class and their liberal advocates, and the environmentalists in alliance with no-growth people who are usually middle-class young or upper-middle class. This situation brings about strange alliances between, for instance, business groups and minority people, or ecologists and tax leagues. These same conflicts and contradictions are mirrored within many people who, traditional liberals, find themselves unable to reconcile their environmental interests with their concern for social equity.

The difficulty of tracing and evaluating the consequences of particular developments has led many researchers to examine whether some conditions vary systematically with population size across the array of American metropolitan areas. It appears that education, pollution, and crime rise with population, while the indicators of physical and mental health are mixed. Many of these characteristics are two-edged and hard to interpret. For instance, if divorce is more common, it may be evidence of more failed marriages or of a more adaptive response to marital failure. The evidence is shallow, impressionistic, or nonexistent on some of the most vital questions such as those concerning social and economic mobility, tolerance of diversity, the rigidity and invidiousness of social hierarchy, feelings of alienation, ability to control one's fate, the situation of women, and privacy.

Many people have been concerned about the possible noxious effect of population density because of a number of etiological studies showing the ill effects of crowding in animal populations. But recent and quite thorough studies show no such effects for human populations if crowding refers to the number of people per acre. They do show ill effects if people are crowded in their housing, in terms of people per room, which is a matter of poverty and not of urban size. Furthermore, the density (people per acre) of central cities and metropolitan areas as a whole is decreasing.

The effects of city size are clearest in economic areas. In the United States and other countries wages and per capita income rise rapidly and consistently with city size, even after taking into account their occupational and industrial composition. The cost of living and public costs also rise, but very little, so that real net income per capita improves markedly from smaller to bigger cities.

This rise in income with urban size argues that bigger cities are more efficient engines of production, and this is confirmed by fragmentary data relating to value added or gross regional product. Furthermore, it seems that larger cities derive more of their products from innovative activities, from newer processes, and from generating, handling, and using information and ideas. Smaller cities tend to more established, routinized activities such as mass production manufacturing with well-established technologies. The system of cities is a dynamic one, spawning innovations and new activities at the top, which, as they mature, filter down to smaller and more provincial centers.

Furthermore, statistical analysis seems to show that the cost of living and of municipal services rises as a result not of increasing urban size as such, but of other factors, most notably high income itself. For instance, it is a popular belief that it is more costly to live in bigger cities. It comes as a surprise that, when equivalent levels of consumption in different areas are actually priced, there is very little cost increase in bigger cities. A clue to this apparent contradiction is provided by a recent poll which asked people how much money they thought a family of four would need to live modestly but comfortably in their areas. Their subjective estimates did increase rapidly with population size. It would seem that what size does is to raise levels of expectation as to what constitutes a modestly comfortable way of life. In bigger cities people expect more. This may be related to their dynamism and innovation.

Another misconception is that bigger metropoles suffer more severe income inequalities. In fact, the proportion of families below the poverty level decreases steadily as the size of the city increases, and indices of income distribution show that the general range of incomes remains about the same. It may be that, although the poor are proportionally fewer, the increase in their actual number and their concentration in certain districts make their situation both more visible and more troublesome in more populous areas, but this is a different matter.

Although they have been much discussed, general indicators of well-being or satisfaction are not available, and probably not possible. We do have, however, some social surveys of varying quality. The one that has received the widest publicity is a commercial poll which asked individuals whether they would prefer to live in farms, small towns, suburbs, or big cities. A majority, regardless of their present residence, said they would prefer to live in small towns. This finding has been used as supporting evidence for programs to disperse the national population. Yet one must be very wary of responses to such hypothetical questions when posed in the abstract, as in this case. It may well be that this expressed preference for small-town life is a romantic response, deeply rooted in traditional American imagery and more symbol than operational preference. What people say to an interviewer on the spur of the moment does not necessarily match what they would really do or what they really want.

A more interesting study asked Mexican Americans in a small Texas city whether they would stay there or move to particular large metropoles under alternative suppositions as to wages. When wages were supposed everywhere equal, most said they would choose to stay, but a significant proportion said they would go to the larger cities, presumably because they believed that richer lives were available there. Not surprisingly, the proportion who would leave increased when wages were supposed higher in the larger cities (which is actually the case). But even when wages were supposed lower in the larger cities, a considerable fraction would still go to them. There were interesting differences between young and old, men and women, and the more and the less educated, but the gist is that this group, like any other, contained those who would stay under any circumstances, those who would go to the bright lights under any circumstances, and those who would weigh in their decision both their place preference and the economic rewards available.

It would be very valuable to have comparable studies for other groups and other places, especially if they distinguished local roots from preferred urban scales, life styles, and economic rewards, and gave us a sense of the kinds and numbers of people who held different constellations of preferences. That preferences do differ there can be no question. For instance, another survey asked people across the country if they thought their areas were too big, too small, or about right. Most people thought their area about right, regardless of its size. A few more who lived in large areas thought them too big than thought them too small, and the opposite was true in small areas. But among nonwhites, many more thought that it would be good if their area grew rapidly. This is what we would expect from the data on the proportion of poor in larger cities and confirms our earlier analysis of the regressive character of local stop-growth movements. Indeed, the advantages of larger cities for minorities are such that blacks, who are already far more urban in their population distribution than whites, are migrating rapidly from small to large urban areas. In the decade from 1960 to 1970, the five largest metropolitan areas all had a net outmigration of whites, but they averaged a 26 percent inmigration of nonwhites.

The idea that urban size matters carries with it a temptation to think that there may be a best size, and that, if this size were known, the ideal pattern of urbanization would be to create centers of that size until the entire urban population were accommodated. This is dangerous nonsense for at least four reasons. First, historic, economic, resource, and demographic circumstances vary greatly from city to city, so that a given size has sharply different implications in different places. Second, because different population groups have different preferences and interests, what might best serve one group might not suit another. Third, a change from one population size to another (or a holding steady) occurs at some concrete rate of growth or decline in real time, which in turn has important social, economic, and institutional consequences that affect different groups differently. Fourth, there is considerable evidence and some passable theory that the urban areas of a country are a system of interdependent elements and relations, so that a change in the size and the economic activities of Wichita affects in part those of Los Angeles. The issue is one of finding the most satisfactory constellation of interacting sizes, not of finding a single best size. The idea of finding an ideal size to be repeated over and over is comparable to a musical theory that would find the most beautiful note and then compose a symphony by endless and exclusive repetition of that note.

The concept of a system of cities has many facets, but one of particular interest for our topic is the concept of *borrowed size,* whereby a small city or metropolitan area exhibits some of the characteristics of a larger one if it is near other population concentrations. A statistical measure called *population potential,* which measures the accessibility from a given location to other centers of population, behaves very much like population in statistical analysis. For instance, per capita income in a place is as strongly associated with this measure as with its actual population. This makes sense if one considers that the essential reason why income and population levels are associated is that population is a rough index of the number of opportunities for interaction available in that place. Similarly, population potential is an index of the opportunities for interaction with people in other places, and may be thought of as an index of borrowed size. Thus, because of their high population potential, small metropoles in megapolitan complexes, such as that on the Atlantic seaboard, have much higher incomes than independent metropoles of equivalent size. In simple terms, while they retain many of the advantages of smaller size, such as lower levels of congestion, they enjoy the advantages of larger size through their easy access to other centers. Their people can use the shopping and entertainment facilities of other cities to complement their own, their businessmen can share such facilities as warehousing and business services, and their labor markets enjoy a wider and more flexible range of demand and supply.

This phenomenon of borrowed size, with the hint that it is possible to have one's cake and eat it too, has not been sufficiently studied, in spite of the strong statistical evidence of its existence. It seems to account for the fact that in the large American megapolitan constellations, the smaller metropoles are growing more rapidly than the bigger ones. It is also quite visible, although virtually unstudied, in certain European urban patterns, such as those of Germany and the Low Countires, whose cities, quite small by our standards, apparently achieve sufficient scale for the functioning of a modern economy by borrowing size from one another. This phenomenon transforms the issue of the size and growth of a city by redefining it to include, in some degree, its neighbors.

However, by studying the attributes of a cross section of urban sizes at one moment in time, one cannot draw reliable implications about what changes in size through time will do in any particular city. Unfortunately, little can be said about the consequences on a city of population growth, decline, or stability because the subject has been little studied. A rare recent study suggests that slow-growing areas show lower crime indices than comparable fast-growing areas. Possibly they have a different industrial structure. In addition, they tend to have a lower proportion of young adults because, under the rates of natural increase which have prevailed, slow growth is based on emigration, and it is the young who leave. For those who hope for greater tranquility with the passing of growth, it may be of interest to consider that this outmigration of the young may account for the low crime indices, since it is the young who are responsible for most crimes.

The absence of studies on the consequences of growth or no growth cannot be blamed altogether on scholarly neglect. The difficulty is that the growth rates that have existed have included a substantial natural increase, so that a locality that has exhibited anything like zero population growth in the past decade has had a substantial net outmigration, of the order of 10 percent. An extreme case is McAllen-Pharr-Edinburg, Texas, which has held virtually stable in population through a natural increase of 25.8 percent and an outmigration of 25.4 percent. Since it is primarily the young who leave, this leads to a population with few young people and many old ones, and this, among other things, lowers the local birth rate and raises the death rate. Thus, Scranton, Pennsylvania, with a net outmigration of 20 percent for the past two decades, had a yearly rate of natural increase of only 0.16 percent in the 1960's.

Such large rates of net outmigration occur only in distressed local economies, for, given the high rates of natural increase in the last decade, no reasonably prosperous area failed to grow by about 10 percent. Thus we have no instances for study which combine local zero population growth with economic well-being.

But the relation of migration to natural increase is more complicated than this suggests, and makes local population growth a more complex matter than national population growth. The key point is that, demographically, the United States is quite self-contained while urban areas are highly open systems. On the surface this does not seem to be so. Currently the United States population is growing by 1.1 percent a year, and a fifth of this growth comes from abroad (much of it accounted for by returning Americans). Similarly, in the last decade, three-fourths of metropolitan growth was accounted for by natural increase and one-fourth by new arrivals.[1] But these figures for average net migration mask tremendous cross-movements of population. As a rule of thumb, it takes ten migratory moves in and out of a metropolis to leave or take away one net migrant.

The figures of the 1970 Census are not yet available, but figures for the 1955-1960 period serve to make the point. Net migration from non-

metropolitan to metropolitan areas was 1.2 million, but this was the trace
of 10.2 million moves: 5.7 million into metropolitan areas and 4.5 million
out of them.[2] There were 7.7 million moves from one metropolitan area
to another. Thus, a metropolis like Philadelphia, with a net inmigration
of 12,000 in the five-year period appears to have led a quiet life; but
this net migration represents the trace of 668,000 moves in and out. A fast
growing area, San Francisco, had a net inmigration of 56,000, but even
so 361,000 people left it. Had arrivals been 15 percent lower, there
would have been a slight outmigration. And, in Pittsburgh, the largest
metropolis near zero-growth, we find that 180,000 left and 113,000 came,
for a net outmigration of 67,000. Thus net migratory gains or losses are
only surface ripples of powerful cross-currents, and even apparent migratory
stability conceals vast exchanges of populations.

Recent studies of these flows have made surprising findings of consequence for local population policies. Rates of inmigration are higher for
prosperous places, but rates of outmigration do not appear to vary, except
perhaps marginally, with local economic conditions. Instead, they depend
primarily on the local proportion of young people. It seems that the young
leave home in about equal numbers whether their home district is prosperous or distressed.[3] Thus, a policy which increases pay levels and the number
of jobs in poor areas in an effort to retain the young may shift net migration
from negative to positive, but it will do so by attracting more newcomers
rather than by slowing down the exodus.

Conversely, if prosperous areas want to slow down arrivals, they could
do so by making themselves ugly in economic terms. Their young would
continue to leave, while inmigration would slow down or disappear, resulting in net outmigration. This, in turn, would gradually lower their
rate of natural increase because the diminishing proportion of young people
in their populations would lower the birth rate while the increasing age
of the population would raise the death rate. Eventually, there would be
few babies to grow into youth and leave, and the outmigration rate would
slow down. This is, no doubt, a fanciful scenario. It amounts to choosing
poverty, unemployment and old age. In brief, it amounts to choosing to
be Scranton, and this is a choice that few will make. The alternative way
of containing growth is by erecting barriers to migrants and this, as I
have discussed, is likely to be ineffective; and if effective, it is regressive.

This example is based on the assumption that the local net reproduction
rate would continue to be higher than a ZPG level.[4] To compensate for
this, the age distribution for local ZPG would have to include far fewer
young and far more older people than would a national ZPG situation.
Even a metropolis which, through local family planning, achieved ZPG
net reproduction rates might eventually maintain a balance of in- and
outmigrants only if it were slightly less prosperous than the average.
Otherwise, although it would have fewer births, it would also have fewer

outmigrants, and would show a positive net migration since the potential pool of migrants from other places would be proportionately bigger than its own.

There is yet another paradox. I have focused the discussion thus far on the consequences and possibilities of local policies of population limitation, since this is the usual frame of reference, and I have obviously been negative about them. But examination of current patterns and trends persuades me that, whatever the difficulties of induced zero growth, it is quite possible that we will be faced in the 1980's with about eighty metropoles (central cities and their suburbs) which have spontaneously arrived at something near zero population growth. Whether this is good or bad, we have little understanding and experience of what such metropoles will be like. They will certainly be different from anything in our present experience but we are ill prepared to anticipate their problems and opportunities. The key difference will be that these will be reasonably prosperous places, whereas today only economically distressed ones show population stability.

This forecast is a chancy one, I realize, for two reasons. The first is that demographic forecasting has had an atrocious record. The second is that local forecasts are, of statistical necessity, much more prone to error than national forecasts. Nonetheless, I make this prognosis on the following basis.

In the past decade, the birth rate fell by about one-fourth and, in consequence, since the death rate held about constant, the rate of natural increase fell by about 40 percent. Should there be another one-fourth drop in birth rates in the coming decade, which seems perfectly possible in view of such social changes as the redefinition of female roles, the rate of natural increase will be cut approximately in half to about 4 percent. Of 243 metropolitan areas, nearly 60 percent had net outmigration during the 1960's and 10 percent, mostly small ones, had actual population losses. While net outmigration and population loss are more typical of the smaller metropoles, principally because of their economic fragility, four out of the ten largest metropoles had negative net migration, and an additional three had positive net migrations of less than 1 percent in the decade. At the same time, migration from nonmetropolitan areas is decreasing, and migration from abroad promises to stay stable by congressional decision.

Meanwhile, natural increase varies surprisingly widely. Localities that have large numbers of poor, of blacks, of Mexican-Americans, of Mormons, and of some other groups tend to have much higher birth rates. Localities that have experienced sustained net outmigration have lower birth rates. The interaction of these factors yields a range from virtually no natural increase for depressed areas in the Northeast to rates of 25 to 30 percent in the South and Southwest, rates comparable to those of underdeveloped countries. Even among the twenty largest metropoles the decennial rates varied from 7 to 25 percent.

This outmigration and variation in local rates of natural increase combined with a falling national rate point to the emergence of changes in quantity which amount to changes in quality. Whereas today any area that fails to grow or grows very little is poor and underemployed, should the birth rate continue to fall, we will have a new phenomenon: relatively prosperous areas which are stable in population, or which grow so little as not to matter.

What will such areas be like? They will have fewer young than today, and thus fewer children in school and a lighter fiscal burden. Economic evolution will be more by substitution than by adding new activities to existing ones, and may therefore involve more individual transitions. The burden of dependent aged will be greater. There will not be an appreciably greater continuity of population, since there will continue to be massive exchanges of the young with other areas. Two major sectors of the economy, construction and the education of children, will probably retrench.

Beyond this it is hard to see. It is possible that economic changes will be more of a shock because they will take the form of structural shifts rather than of adding on new activities. Possibly the young, being relatively scarce, will profit from accelerated social and economic mobility; but possibly the preponderance of old people and the limits on expansion will create a gerontracy. Possibly minorities will be frustrated, since there will not be new activities for them to move into and the old activities will be preempted. Possibly, however, they will benefit from lessened competition for the older housing stock which will permit them lesser per room densities together with lower rents.

There must be other questions about such circumstances that are not yet conceived. It is to be expected that, when growth is gone, there will be those who miss it, and that the current concern for bringing about ZPG may seem as quaint then as the worries of the 1930's and 1940's about the economic implications of the stable populations they erroneously forecast do now.

Local policies for zero population growth ultimately run into the problem that ours is a highly interconnected society and economy. No state or city is an island, entire unto itself. Local policies may try to limit population by passing restrictive zoning, limiting housing permits, and the like. This is the I'm-all-right-Jack-and-bar-the-door version, much favored by suburbs, which forces out the young and is regressive. Local policies may try to curtail economic growth, but effective policies lead to unacceptable social and economic consequences. And a local policy of limiting births, which seems to me the most morally acceptable of these policies, will do little to reduce growth because the young from other places will inevitably arrive.

Because the nation is so interconnected, local population policies, whether for growth or no growth, are usually an attempt at a mercantilistic beggaring of neighbors; however, because larger forces are operating in the system, they are likely to be ineffective. A hierarchy of levels is involved, so that what is viewed as an issue of growth at a lower level is an issue of distribution at the next higher level. Thus, growth decisions for each locality within a metropolitan area should be bargained out among all the components of the metropolis to insure that their effects on the futures of the other localities will be considered. This is necessary both for fairness and efficiency. If the objectives, plans and actions of diverse localities are inconsistent, they cannot all be right, and some will fail while others triumph. Only when these various growth considerations are viewed together can it be seen whether they add up, where joint action can be more effective than unilateral action for achieving complementary objectives, and where negotiation and compensation are needed to reconcile diverging purposes and interests.

For much the same reasons the growth decisions of the various metropolitan areas and other regions should be based on state and national considerations. The task is again one of coordination and mediation, and as yet we have very little operational knowledge of how to go about it, either technically or politically. Yet this is the issue which has attracted considerable, if confused, attention under the rather misleading name of "national growth policy."

In any case it is clear that, although questions of local growth should be treated as questions of distribution at a higher level, we should avoid what is often done, setting as policy goals arbitrary demographic rates (no growth or fast growth) or particular geographic patterns of distribution (dispersal or concentration). These rates and patterns are not proper goals, although they may be important instruments for advancing the real goals of material efficiency, of equity and fairness, of ecological integrity, and of a high quality of life. They are used as goals because they are easy to grasp and they avoid the real questions which are hard. They are also used, I suspect, because they substitute what appears to be a technical objective for what is really a political matter of deciding how to balance alternative and often conflicting goals, and how to deal with costs and benefits which are very unevenly distributed.

"National growth policy" should more properly be called "national territorial distribution policy," and local growth policies within metropolitan areas should be thought of as elements in shaping the distribution of metropolitan growth. In neither case am I suggesting that the ideal would have the higher level dictate to the lower one. The interests of each collectivity and each governmental unit must be represented in the making of the higher level policy. One of the urgent and unresolved issues of our times is the need to evolve processes to give a voice in the making of important decisions to the relevant collectivities, be they corporations such as local governments, or other collectivities such as ethnic and other interest groups. But this is a larger matter than the subject of this paper.

Something like national zero population growth seems to be desirable, and we appear to be moving rapidly in that direction. But it is quite clear that even in a situation of national demographic stability, some localities will grow, some will shrink, and some will stay at about the same population. Through all this, vast cross-movements of population will continue, as will structural changes in the society and the economy. Many of today's problems will continue to exist, and some new ones will arise. We will not arrive at an eternally tranquil late afternoon.

REFERENCES

1. It is startling to most people to learn that three-fifths of this net migration into metropolitan areas came from abroad, and only two-fifths from nonmetropolitan areas. Thus, nonmetropolitan net migration accounted for only one-tenth of metropolitan growth in the decade.

2. The actual number of moves was higher. These figures report the numbers of those living in one area in 1955 and living in another in 1960. They do not count the very great numbers who went somewhere and returned home within this period, nor do they count intervening moves.

3. I must note that this is a topic of considerable scholarly debate at the moment. It is quite clear, at any rate, that local economic well-being matters far less than had been thought in determining the rate of leaving.

4. This would be a net reproduction rate of one which would mean that each generation would just replace itself if current birth and death rates were continued indefinitely in the absence of migration. Strictly speaking, however, net reproduction rates would have to be somewhat below the ZPG rate to accommodate immigrants from abroad.

ROLAND N. MCKEAN

Growth vs. No Growth: An Evaluation

"Growth" is a harmless neutral concept meaning merely "a growing" or "an increase."[1] If growth meant an increase in well-being in terms of an agreed-upon criterion of well-being, it could hardly be opposed. Objections to growth must refer to the increase of particular magnitudes—in population, GNP, or power consumption—that cause negative growth of well-being according to some criterion. What is really objected to, then, is *negative or uneconomic growth* according to certain concepts of social welfare.

Disagreement about these matters is bound to occur, because *any* kind of growth will injure some individuals, and in the real world all injured persons will not be compensated. Moreover, even if they could be compensated, some might not like the outcome: in any group decision, there is a basic value or criterion judgment about which members of the group may disagree. To discuss costs or gains from any kind of growth or from anything else, however, one must keep in mind a criterion that determines how costs and gains are to be measured. In this paper I will use the concept of "economic efficiency," according to which gains (or costs) are priced at whatever individuals would voluntarily pay, at the margin, to have (or avoid) them. This means accepting (or simulating) the values that would emerge from a voluntary exchange system. One could substitute a different criterion and, although similar phenomena would occur, the values attached to them could differ.

Throughout the paper I will use the term "economic growth," as I believe most other persons use it, to mean increases in GNP or some such indicator of aggregate final output. In a sense this is a misuse of the word "economic," for growth would hardly be economic—hardly an economical use of resources—if it entailed certain costs that were not being counted (as is the case with GNP). It is convenient, however, to use the term "economic growth" in this fashion, since this usage is widely accepted. Moreover, except where I specifically mention population growth my discussion will pertain to economic growth.

Possible Interpretations of the Case for No Growth

Let us examine alternative ways of interpreting the arguments in favor of retarded or zero growth. Critics of economic growth may mean that it constitutes two steps forward and one step back—that it has bad side effects which partly offset the good effects. In that event, it makes sense to see if reducing the bad effects can yield net gains. It would not make sense, however, simply to eliminate growth, for in these circumstances, one would sacrifice the two steps forward in order to avoid one step backward. (The use of penicillin is perhaps analogous. It makes sense to prescribe it with care and regulate its use so as to reduce the undesirable side effects, but not to eliminate it altogether.) In this situation, most indexes of growth are misleading, of course, if they are mistaken for indexes of growth in welfare, for in terms of well-being they may reflect the two steps forward but little or none of the backsliding. Also, it might be noted that the distribution of benefits and injuries is not uniform. To recipients of benefits (perhaps the young and upwardly mobile), growth may seem lovely; while to the injured (among them the elderly or long-time residents who preferred their city when it was half its present size), economic growth may appear to be an undiluted evil.

Alternatively, critics of "economic growth" may mean that expansion of the economy has so many bad side effects that it really constitutes two steps forward and three steps back. As before, it would be sensible to try to reduce the steps backward as long as the effort yielded net gain. If reducing the bad side effects were too costly to be economical, however, it would be appropriate to stop the growth—in other words, to prevent the two steps forward in order to eliminate the three steps backward. Such a policy employs a meat axe instead of a scalpel, yet it is the best one can do when using the scalpel results in too many disadvantages. An analogous situation may exist with respect to many pollution policies. In terms of economic efficiency one might think initially that households should be charged for throwing away bottles according to the costs imposed on other people. Their actions, not the production of such bottles, should be made more expensive. Because of heavy monitoring costs, however, it may be more economical to retreat to a "second-best" measure, a tax on disposable bottles, or even the prohibition of such bottles. Or, to take an extreme example, it is *conceivable,* though not likely, that prohibiting the internal combustion engine would be preferable to the alternatives, given the transaction-and-intervention costs associated with voluntary contracting, government charges for spillovers, or government regulation.

It is possible, finally, that some opponents of growth believe its effects to be solely bad ones. In that case, stopping such growth would be an unambiguous improvement. I do not believe the consequences are so simple, however, and doubt that many other persons do.

Evaluating the Costs of Growth

Personally I do not think that the most highly publicized costs of growth are by themselves so ruinous and unmanageable.[2] With the possible exception of the carbon dioxide layer around our atmosphere, which is probably no more imminently destructive than another ice age, deterioration of the physical environment is unlikely to cause cataclysmic disaster. Mainly it will bring about a declining level of material well-being.[3] The world will turn out to be less rich and sweet smelling than a few people for a few decades thought it was. To have 90 percent instead of 60 percent of individuals poor again, or to have life expectancies shorter again, would be deplorable but not unspeakably disastrous (especially since high levels of material wealth and lower death rates may not have relieved man's anguish enormously anyway).

Realistic scenarios for the future would allow for the adjustments that even stubborn, stupid *Homo sapiens* can hardly avoid. To be sure, as far as forms of pollution are concerned, they result from the kinds of interdependencies in which individual action gets one almost nowhere. As Schelling has pointed out even more vividly than most,[4] individual decisions where negotiation costs are high (as they would be if we tried to hire each other to be less noisy) can trap societies in myriad and extremely persistent "nonoptimal" situations. Nonetheless, if the costs of inaction become high enough, some private agreements (to use soundproofing, for example) will seem worth the transaction costs, and government measures will appear to be worth the intervention costs. As an example of the latter, people will even adopt decimal systems if the costs of doing nothing grow large enough. Similarly, as environmental quality deteriorates, people will, through voluntary contracts and the political process, divert their resources from material goods to environmental types of material well-being. People will have to sacrifice some of both, of course, but they can still end up with a bit of fun as well as filth—as in the lifestyle, say, of Elizabethan England, which may have been pretty awful in certain ways yet left some room for pleasure and creativity.

Admittedly, the political process, either within or among nations, does not respond in a timely or precise fashion[5]—and I have little faith, incidentally, that governments will avoid thermonuclear wars, though I put them aside here—but at least it provides gross responses to gross increases in the demand for public goods. These responses will be *truly* gross, though, if debate and adjustments are postponed until crises prompt government action. In such circumstances, it seems especially likely that people will turn to bare-hands controls and large government-operated anti-externality programs instead of making relatively wide use of price mechanisms. In other words, while economic growth will inevitably bring government adjustments to avoid disasters resulting from growth as such, these inevitable responses are likely to be clumsy and to cause unnecessarily large government.

In the private sector there will be many automatic adjustments. Prices, while they will not follow appropriate paths where resources are not owned privately, or markets do not exist, or prices are regulated, will eventually respond in a gross fashion even under these adverse conditions. (Watch the prices of fish and gas over the next decade.) These price changes will also help strike a balance between environmental quality and other forms of material wealth. Thus, I assert, along with numerous others,[6] that a sensible scenario for the future portrays declines of wealth and a series of painful adjustments, including a leveling off or decline of population, but not a sudden collapse of any kind.

The exhaustion of nonrenewable resources would bring about similar adjustments as we became poorer.[7] It would be an unlikely coincidence for technological advances to maintain per capita income indefinitely; economic growth will probably became negative someday. (This is not much of a forecast; as Singer says about the basic logic of *The Limits to Growth*, it's like a meteorologist predicting rain—sometime!) But all resources will not simultaneously and suddenly vanish without advance warning. There will be signals that this ore or that material is rapidly becoming more difficult to obtain. Prices will rise, inducing people to shift to substitutes— perhaps even buggies for automobiles or card games for television. Antic- ipating further price increases, speculators (that is, all of us) will find it profitable to store scarce materials, not for distant posterity but to ap- portion them out over a thirty- or forty-year period, and some would subsequently be kept for high-value uses over subsequent thirty- or forty- year periods. These apportionments will help make the process of getting poorer a matter of painful but not catastrophic adjustment.

These prospects raise in starkest form the question, "How much are we willing to sacrifice for posterity?" Clearly people will make enormous sacrifices for their children and grandchildren. They *may* also wish to put aside extra resources for the well-being of distant generations yet be unwilling to do so unless they are assured that others will also do so.[8] This free-rider difficulty raises the issue, "Can public policy promote economic efficiency (in terms of the wishes of the existing population) by extra conservation efforts?" Individual values on this point are difficult to discern. I don't honestly know whether I would voluntarily give up one quarter of my disposable income even if this would, with 100 percent certainty, prevent extinction of the human race 1000 years hence. I rather doubt if people do care much about what happens thousands of years from now, and doubt therefore if the free-rider problem is very significant. For most people the preferred compromise may be to profess, but not really dem- onstrate, concern about the distant future. Such a pretense lets us eat our cake yet also satisfy our need, for the sake of sanity or a greater sense of purpose, to believe that mankind has a future. If we explicitly disavowed any concern about the distant future, of course, the consumption of our minerals and durable capital stock would be nothing to worry about, but I shall not entertain this extreme possibility.

Population growth will, whenever extra persons add more to total social cost than they contribute,[9] reduce material well-being and accelerate environmental deterioration and the use of exhaustible resources. Here too, however, it is impossible for me to visualize a situation in which people, even acting individually, would fail completely to make adjustments as the negative marginal social product of people became larger and larger. Their adjustments would hardly be those which would be optimal in a hypothetical world of zero transaction costs and therefore zero free-rider difficulties, but there would be reductions in birth rates and increases in death rates as extra bodies produced less useful output and more undesirable consequences. Minor disasters might be involved in this process but not sudden unprecedented madness or famine or plague. Nonetheless, the disadvantages of deliberately limiting population growth seem relatively small and hence the case for it is comparatively strong.

Other possible side effects of growth, however, worry me as much as conventional forms of pollution and poverty. These other consequences produce or aggravate what might be called poverty of the spirit. They can be regarded as unconventional forms of pollution, since, analytically viewed, all side effects are similar to pollution:[10] they stem from overuse or suspected overuse[11] of some resource (with economic efficiency as the criterion) because the consent of the damaged parties is not bought. Thus, if our individual actions spread disease or despair, they use up people's health without purchase of their consent. The following external effects of growth, although we know little about them yet, may be as ominous as its threat to material well-being as such.

I believe that, from now on, many types of growth—in, for example, population, urban density, and material affluence—increase the probability of pervasive controls and ownership by government. So far data do not show any marked correlation between growth of GNP and proliferation of government. Indeed up to this time statistics suggest that the size of government or the pervasiveness of oppressive controls and the scale of output are inversely related, because freedom from restrictions has surely promoted economic growth. Recent "exponential" increases, however, are unprecedented, and bring into play another set of causal relationships.

For one thing it is obvious that Robinson Crusoe needed neither markets, government, nor behavioral rules to cope with interdependencies. As soon as Friday arrived, however, there arose both production and consumption interdependencies. Some of these—Crusoe's use of Friday's labor and Friday's use of Crusoe's hut—could be taken into account by voluntary exchanges. As specialization and population densities increase, however, many interdependencies arise—my use of others' air or your use of others' peace and quiet—that cannot be taken into account by bargaining because of high transaction costs. The resulting (potentially relevant) side effects multiply in number and significance as growth, which involves ever greater specialization, continues. The two extreme choices confronting people may be to accept an increasing degree of interference with each other, which is frustrating, or to vote for various majority-rule government restrictions, which are also frustrating. In certain cultures part of the behavioral discipline that continued growth will demand might be accomplished by custom instead of coercive regulation, but generating instant or appropriate traditions is difficult. In any event, to be viable, behavioral rules have to be voluntarily accepted as a result of enlightened self-interest, and free-rider and other difficulties make it unlikely that such "social contracts" will evolve.[12] I conclude that people will move in both of these directions but with much emphasis on the use of government, on coercive restrictions imposed by majority coalitions who object to particular spillovers. But majority rule, like any other political process, is a meat cleaver method of resolving conflicts. It leaves more people dissatisfied than would smoothly working markets (which are largely unavailable for resolving the conflicts under discussion because of transaction costs). Unresolved conflicts will become deeper and more numerous. The bargaining process in government will cost more and achieve less. In short, government, as we allocate more and more burdens to its decision-making process, will become a more costly and embittering process.

Affluence itself, even apart from production interdependencies, causes potentially relevant externalities. Interdependencies arise because A wishes to help B or, more likely, wishes to take something away from B. In this instance, growth increases the likelihood of pervasive government intervention to impose complex schemes and counterschemes for wealth redistribution. Economic growth may bring some conflicts over wealth distribution closer to home. Maybe the poor feel envy more keenly when many slightly wealthier persons are in their immediate vicinity than they do when a few filthily rich persons live in some remote village on Long Island. Moreover, regardless of whether attempts to resolve such conflicts produce government expansion, affluence and the resulting expansion of opportunities multiply certain types of overt conflicts to be resolved by government (though as I note later, growth eases the resolution of other conflicts). The simple increase in the number of alternatives confronting people puts them in conflict with each other more often. If transaction costs are low, conflict resolution by bargaining is comparatively easy. If such costs are high, however, the market offers little help. Thus the proliferation of conflicts *where transaction costs are high*, ulcer generating in itself, increases the probability of an expanding and increasingly unpleasant role for government.

Rising incomes will be devoted partly to government anyway—to defense, new services, and various public goods. Despite their desirable features, these all yield bigger, more discordant government and feelings of helplessness on the part of individual citizens. Voters, in deciding whether or not to vote, to inform themselves, to write their Congressmen, face a formidable free-rider situation. Why should I inform myself when the chances of my deciding an election or influencing anything, even of affecting the decisions of others to vote or inform themselves, are infinitesimal? As a consequence, government seems, from the standpoint of each voter, to have enormous arbitrary power. The disgruntled citizen cannot turn to a competitor, and, as government grows, he feels a growing sense of impotence, especially when, as inevitably happens from time to time, a particularly petulant and power-hungry person climbs to the top. Moreover, at best, the purchase and distribution of goods and services by government yield frustration, because almost no one, except the famous median voter on each issue, gets the amount or kind of defense or Medicare that he prefers for his tax dollar. Also, it should be remembered, the public goods themselves (defense or highways for example) inflict distressing external impacts without purchasing the consent of the damaged persons.[13] In general, then, while growth may be neither a necessary nor a sufficient condition for big government, I am convinced that from now on extra growth increases the probability of bigger and more conflict-ridden government.

Other more speculative impacts of population and economic growth may rob life in the future of much flavor and quality. With growth there is pervasive change and perhaps a reduction in the probability of durable nonsuperficial relationships.[14] In a large and mobile population, for example, the chances of encountering or dealing with a person a second time and the chances of frequent or persistent dealings are comparatively small. The village pub tends to become an urban cocktail bar; the department store is not conducive to regular sessions around a pot-bellied stove. New social organizations arise, of course, but *if*, on balance, the process of growth reduces the chances of having durable nonsuperficial relationships, this in itself is a considerable loss, for much of life is an almost pathetic search for such relationships.

More importantly, however, change and the impersonality of relationships may contribute to the decline of customs and behavioral rules which have, in the past, helped to reduce many external costs that people would otherwise have inflicted on each other.[15] At best there is a serious free-rider problem involved in people's decisions as to whether to be friendly or courteous, to take garbage cans to the rear of the house, to serve as witnesses, to refrain from making noise, and even to be honest. Why should I do my bit, which is just a drop in the bucket, when other people may not reciprocate? Through the centuries man developed ethical rules, and often enforced them by threats of retaliation, ostracism, and eternity in hell, to cope with various free-rider difficulties. Along with the decline of religion which threatened personal punishment and allowed no free riders, larger and more mobile societies suffer a decline in the possibilities of personal retaliation or ostracism, a decline which undermines behavioral codes and aggravates free-rider problems. In large cities, accordingly, while there are forces pushing in different directions, there appears on balance to be less warmth, courtesy, trust, and adherence to behavioral codes than in small towns. Suburban neighbors hesitate less than village neighbors to ignore nearby screams, to use chainsaws on Sunday mornings or head-lighted power mowers at night. In crowded, impersonal, yet affluent societies, it costs more and is worth less to by-standers to interfere with muggings. Witnesses step forward less often. Even a high degree of honesty, which, for the entire group, is extremely economical in social and business intercourse, may now cost more than it is worth to many individuals. One person's future dealings with any other person will be few, he feels no obligation because of personal ties, and he cannot count on others to provide reciprocal favors according to the old rules. In my judgment, increasing material wealth, specialization, and population may exacerbate all these factors. They do not change our taste for morality or a behavioral code; they simply make it more costly and less rewarding to each individual to be considerate of others and to adhere to customs or ethical rules. In other words, growth tends to undermine the "social contracts" that are so important to the enforcement of amenity rights and the functioning of capitalism.

These observations are highly speculative, for many variables and uncertain relationships are involved. Furthermore, and this deserves emphasis, I am not suggesting that things were better under Peter the Great. On balance, life was probably dreadful for most people in most earlier eras, and at present it may be getting better every day, but this is irrelevant. The relevant question is this: if growth is not, or will not in the future be, a free lunch, are there policies that could make us better off in the decades ahead than we would otherwise be?

Another force helping to generate some of the above side effects as well as others is the rising value of time, in terms of real income that can be earned per hour, which results from economic growth. Increases in personal income influence a person's choice between work and leisure and his choices among leisure activities.[16] The extra income makes him able to afford more leisure and time-consuming activities, but the higher earnings per hour make such pursuits more expensive to him. That is, he has to sacrifice more to take an hour off. This causes him to substitute relatively more productive uses of leisure time for those that yield constant results per hour (such as walking in the woods). In many cases this "substitution effect" dominates the "income effect." Hence, as Linder has pointed out,[17] one often finds capital and other inputs being used to save time or make each hour more productive, and less time devoted to uses of time that cannot be made more productive. One observes more leisure activities involving television sets, cameras, automobiles, boats, and TV dinners, and fewer leisure activities using mainly a person's time.

What concerns us here are the possible repercussions on others of these new choices by each individual. Thinking and decision making are among the uses of time that are becoming relatively expensive, so unless citizens gradually come to value these activities more, they may spend less time on them. Each of us has a stake, however, in getting other citizens to be well informed, to think about issues, and to make decisions carefully. Perhaps the impact of rising real incomes is offset by other developments, but this may be another way in which growth is aggravating the free-rider difficulties that plague the democratic process. Is growth pushing us more and more toward quick decisions, the acquisition of superficial information about numerous subjects, and centralization of effective power? If so, it may further increase the difficulty—the cost, that is—of governing ourselves.

Moreover, the costliness of time further exacerbates the problem of establishing nonsuperficial friendships. Giving genuinely concerned attention to each other is relatively expensive. It is more efficient to go to cocktail parties than to spend time with one friend at a time. Such results of individual decisions make it more costly for each of us to obtain the approval and attention we crave. Along this line too, paying attention to old people becomes prohibitively expensive so that we simultaneously struggle to prolong their lives and manage to make their lives almost unbearable.[18]

All of these effects seem as serious to me as the prospective decline in material well-being. People can apparently endure considerable poverty or physical hardship if struggling still yields slight improvements, and if they feel as though they can influence events somewhat. If struggle results in virtually no response, however, if events seem increasingly to be beyond the individual's control, then a deeper sort of poverty sets in than just the material sacrifices of having more pollution and fewer goods. Trying to deal with bureaucracy, even in a comparatively small organization like a university, or to do anything about spillovers that result from the erosion of rules and respect for individuals can make life frustrating and tasteless. Whatever happens to GNP, a sufficient decline in control over their lives can render many people hopelessly depressed or violently angry.

Also, to the extent that growth beyond some point does aggravate these spillovers, taking steps to check economic and population growth itself might be a more economical way of reducing the external costs than trying to alleviate the spillovers while reaping the desirable consequences of growth. In other words, it is conceivable that growth yields net disadvantages yet that direct attacks on the disadvantages cost more than they gain. For instance, how, at low cost, can public policy directly promote economical behavioral codes or a more thoughtful citizenry? It is also conceivable, though, that by implementing a low-growth policy, government could alleviate the erosion of behavioral rules and the other spillovers described above.

It should be stressed that the relevant magnitudes are the marginal advantages and disadvantages of growth. Clearly, up to some point population and economic growth contributed more than it cost. No man is an island; there are economies of agglomeration—a wide range of choice in shopping, for example—for which people make great sacrifices and tolerate certain diseconomies. Beyond some point, however, these forms of growth yield decreasing marginal returns, increasing marginal costs, and ultimately net marginal disadvantages. These net marginal disadvantages may climb rapidly as growth rates soar even if past growth has brought rich rewards.

To keep things in proportion, however, I must admit that attributing the above costs to economic growth is highly speculative. Other variables obviously contribute to the expanding role of government, the slump in respect for the individual, and the crumbling of useful traditions. Perhaps growth has nothing to do with these phenomena.

Past evidence is far from illuminating. Clearly, growth is neither a necessary nor a sufficient condition for the existence of such side effects. Some societies have had high population densities or high rates of economic growth without marked difficulties. Other societies have exhibited these effects without startling population or economic growth. Conflicts, externalities, powerful and pervasive government, and changing behavioral codes go back to the beginnings of man. Finally, regardless of the magnitudes of such phenomena, and even if growth would henceforth *help* produce them, everyone is free to make different value judgments about their significance. None of us gets up each morning and asks, "What can I do today for economic efficiency?" For example, some, especially those who are on top, or think they will be on top, do not feel that the average individual's frustration matters much unless it threatens revolution.

My personal feeling, however, is that something is going wrong in terms of satisfying individual demands, and that congestion, interferences, and government expansion are contributing to the malaise. In recent years, writers and artists attract unusually large audiences by portraying the frustrations and emptiness of life, and there is pervasive resentment of the constraints imposed by families, fellow citizens, firms, governments, and other organizations. Whether or not growth has played a significant role in the past, I cannot help believing that continued growth will make it harder and harder for us to avoid interfering with each other, harder and harder for us to govern ourselves.

Evaluating the Costs of No Growth

We should now examine the principal costs of stopping growth and try to make some comparisons with alternative policies. Maybe growth will appear to be like democracy: the worst possible situation one can imagine—except for the alternatives. In the case of retarding population growth, apart from the difficulties of implementation, I cannot believe that the costs could be great. The consequences of settling for no more than four billion human beings on this planet, or 250 million in the United States, could hardly be catastrophic. If additional people still yield a positive net return at all, it is a modest one, and, at worst, limiting population would sacrifice a modest amount of material well-being. In saying this, I am assuming that one or two children per couple would yield most of the value of offspring as a consumption good. If most people have an intense desire to spawn and rear large families, then growth might yield a high return to the existing population even if the adverse effects on living conditions were serious. The basic dilemma would then be more difficult. Even so, at some population level, externalities would make it economical to ask people to give up demands for large families in order to meet other intense demands.

The case is not quite so clear when one considers implementation, though here too I am comparatively optimistic regarding the retardation of population growth. One can visualize controls that would be ominous and horrible, like selective sterilization, or the selective elimination of children, perhaps along lines adopted by the Spartans. Another ancient Greek practice, forcing everyone over sixty years of age to drink poison hemlock, might not actually be so bad, except for the fact that exceptions, discretionary authority, and corruption would arise. In connection with population control, however, at least in comparison with many other kinds of government controls, I am somewhat sanguine about the prospects for nonhorrible actions.[19]

On the whole I believe working toward low or zero population growth, if it does not come about naturally, would probably be worth the cost. Maybe I am naive to trust that advocating and debating such a policy will not lead to some tyrannical form of genocide. However, while I realize that mankind reverts to bestiality at the drop of a hat, I do not believe that a proposal or precedent for population control would greatly *increase* the probability of bestial actions. A nation could try exhortation, education regarding birth control, and moderate taxes per child, though I doubt their effectiveness. When these methods fail, a certificate system could be introduced unilaterally, with immigration controls applying to those countries that fail to adopt similar systems. I don't see that this in itself would give underdeveloped nations great cause for complaint.

How would one set about stopping economic growth? Putting a legislative ceiling on the GNP would hardly affect anyone's behavior, since the GNP is merely the result of adding together various components that are determined by a host of variables. The only way to do anything would be to work on the variables that affect investment and consumption behavior. Government would have to do things to influence particular output decisions rather than just say grandly, "Let there be no growth."

Establishing ceilings and controls on each industry's output would convert a private enterprise economy into a centrally planned one, thereby losing the coordination provided by markets. The result, I assert, would be clumsily inefficient, at least in terms of conventional criteria. If detailed central planning was the only way to achieve no growth, I would chalk this up as an awesome cost of a no-growth policy.[20] Let us look, however, at other ways of reducing economic growth in a mixed economy.

Outputs could be reduced, though in a rather haphazard fashion, by measures short of detailed planning, such as limiting the work week to say thirty hours. Such a step would still require a lot of repugnant enforcement and loop-hole-plugging activities, perhaps even the monitoring of consumption and the use of leisure time. Furthermore, measures like limiting hours of work are extremely imprecise tools, which would cut back on many services that contribute little to pollution or depletion yet entail many of the disadvantages of central planning.

In my view the least unappealing type of mechanism would be to tax all output of goods for both consumption and investment, and devote the proceeds to environmental repair. With the objective of no growth, the taxes and outlays would be adjusted to hold constant some such output indicator as GNP, and one would simply hope that the outcome yielded an appropriate amount of pollution and exhaustible resource use. I am using the word "pollution" to represent all the external costs discussed earlier, since most of them, if they are functions of growth, would be held down to varying extents by the cessation of growth. For present purposes the kind of tax—sales, value added, turnover, or income—does not matter much; the pattern of output curtailment would differ under different kinds of taxes, but this whole technique of curtailing aggregate output—or, as I noted above, any known technique—is a rather clumsy way to reduce pollution and consumption of depletable resources. (I will also neglect repercussions on and from interest rates in order to concentrate on directly pertinent impacts.)

Note how imprecise the linkage is between no growth and these undesired effects. One could have no growth of the GNP and still be polluting or using up energy sources at various rates. One's conclusion depends partly on how one measures growth, but practically any index will have only a loose connection with the increase in pollution or the consumption of exhaustible resources. For example, as costs of production rise due either to pollution or to the inaccessibility of selected resources, the prices of goods might rise while the quantities produced fell, and the indicator of final output might not increase. The actual level of pollution will depend upon the composition of the output and the way it is produced —upon the extent to which pollution is cleaned up after being generated, or is prevented by shifting to new "cleaner" outputs or by producing the old outputs in more expensive ways. Also, the combination of outputs and methods of production may either increase or decrease the consumption of energy and other nonrenewable resources. Thus, simply holding GNP or any other practicable index of output constant to reduce pollution or the consumption of stored-up energy is like holding a consumer's total budget constant in order to reduce his disposal of trash along the highway or his consumption of fats. The linkage is indirect and different for different kinds of trash or fats. As for the linkage between GNP and its undesired impacts, some forms of output are associated with high rates of pollution and depletion of nonrenewable resources; others are not.

If, however, we start regulating particular outputs, we're back in the business of detailed planning in order to do something other than just stop growth. If we start taxing particular outputs, we're trying to curtail the side effects rather than growth per se (which may turn out to look very sensible but which is not the topic at hand). Keeping in mind the imprecision of these linkages, let us consider the costs or disadvantages of tax expenditure programs that would prevent any increase in, say, the cumulative measure of consumption plus investment plus government expenditures for *goods* (as opposed to goods plus services).

There are several significant disadvantages of zero economic growth, some inherently associated with a static as opposed to a dynamic economy, and some connected with the particular measures required to implement a ZEG policy. First and most obvious, the sacrificed consumption and investment would obviously have been desirable from the standpoint of existing persons. Also, some of the investment in durable facilities would have created returns for near future generations. Hence, if we stop economic growth to promote one set of objectives, we must give up the at least partially offsetting material benefits. In a free economy this would mean giving up not exactly what you and I personally visualize as frills but whatever consumers in general regarded as their least important purchases, presumably including quality and quantity in most categories of goods—food, housing, books, music, art, medical care, and so on. In a planned economy, it would mean giving up, again not what you and I think of as frills, but whatever the planning establishment regarded as marginal—education, research, or welfare programs. In other words, whether you think pollution and resource depletion constitute one or three steps backward, you have to sacrifice the two steps forward if your remedy is stopping the growth of total output. Below, I will argue that this sacrifice would be larger under a no-growth policy than under an alternative approach.

In the short run there would be transitional difficulties. The shock of taxes to prevent growth, though it would depend upon factors about which we know little, might be considerably greater than defense mobilization or demobilization, for the policy would throw most industries into readjustments. Unlike mobilization, which changes the composition of output, the no-growth policy would, in addition, stop investment and growth of total output. Accompanying this resource re-allocation would be a traumatic adjustment of attitudes as people were confronted, even gradually, with a drop in real income in comparison with their previous expectations, with the prospect of no future wage increases except perhaps for superior individual performance, and with the prospect of a relatively static society. Such a shock often has a sharp impact on one family; when it occurs simultaneously to everyone, the difficulties might be smaller, or they might be greater.

A more serious problem is that a no-growth policy would heighten distribution conflicts within the nation and among nations. (Note, however, that if my earlier arguments are correct, no growth would reduce certain other conflicts attributed to growth—interferences with each other as a result of noisy equipment, other manifestations of affluence, and crowding, wherever there were high transaction costs.) Consider distribution conflicts within a nation. People resent it less when someone else gets a promotion or a higher income if they suffer only a comparative rather than an absolute loss. It is easier to dispense rewards if one can give A a promotion or higher income without taking anything away from B, harder if one can award something to A only if it is taken from B. When industries are expanding, when the pie is growing, it is possible for Negroes or young people to move into unions or better jobs or new occupations without anyone else suffering in an absolute sense.

No growth, however, might sharpen these conflicts and make it more difficult for politicians to encourage free entry into occupations and industries or to allow freely moving prices and rates of hire, more difficult for collective bargaining and government processes to work satisfactorily. British experience suggests that lack of growth may "produce as many and as unpleasant stresses on the social and political economy as industrial growth can impose on the ecological and natural resources of the globe."[21] No growth may imply sharper distribution conflicts and the costs associated with them in terms of resources devoted to bargaining and conflict resolution and, perhaps more important, resources of the spirit squandered in anger, bitterness, and violence.

Conflicts among nations would be exacerbated for these as well as other reasons. If all nations did agree to retard economic growth, the underdeveloped nations would find it more difficult, whatever the agreed-upon formulae, to get ahead. Such countries would probably find the door forever closed to anything approaching the incomes enjoyed by the advanced countries. They would find it more difficult to bring about changes in resource allocation (and, as Beckerman points out, they may object to endless prospects of dressing up in archaic costumes and studying folkdancing to amuse the tourists.)[22]

But the conflict in interests is so sharp that it is hard to imagine world-wide agreement to limit growth. The United States, for instance, has about 6 percent of the world's population and consumes about 40 percent of the world's fossil fuel and other outputs. Suppose the U.S. pushes for an agreement to stop economic growth in order to reduce pollution and the use of exhaustible resources. It is difficult to imagine the underdeveloped nations agreeing to large sacrifices for the sake of the rest of the world, and, in view of the sensitivity of advanced nations about national security, one can hardly foresee their making large concessions. Without a world-wide agreement, however, the free-rider problem makes it hard to imagine unilateral or small-group action.

What do these conflicting interests among nations signify for the costs of a no-growth policy? They imply that it would require tremendous negotiation costs and sacrifices of "national security" and "fairness among nations" to implement a no-growth policy. An alternative way to put the point is simply to say that the chances of any nation's adopting no-growth policies are slight. Some people might even argue that no-growth postures would produce extra temptations and less deterrence and hence increase the chances of thermonuclear war. In view of the complexities, however, about all one can say, it seems to me, is that the potential provocations and probabilities for thermonuclear war are large in any case, and probably not significantly different whether there is continued growth or not.

Another speculative, yet perhaps important, consideration is the set of sacrifices entailed by having a more nearly static society. Under a no-growth policy, it would necessarily be less rewarding than before, in comparison with other activities, to search for changes in technology, to seek to identify changes in taste, or to shift resources. In short, changes, which may seem too attractive currently, would become less rewarding, relative to "housekeeping" and status-quo production, than at present. Initially there would be considerable re-allocation of resources in response to the new taxes and government programs. Investment in growth-promoting innovations would become relatively unattractive, however, since growth promotion would no longer be permitted. This might have some desirable consequences, such as reducing the adverse impacts of "future shock," but it would also have some deleterious ones. For one thing man craves variety, a degree of uncertainty, and the hope that he may find some satisfying purpose in life. One can vividly appreciate these desires by asking himself the old but illuminating question: "Would life be satisfying if it consisted merely of pushing buttons to stimulate the pleasure centers of the brain?" A static society is, to some extent, less conducive to the pursuit of varied objectives than is a growing society. With fewer possibilities of change, people might feel they had less "adventure," less hope of discovering some larger purpose in life, less hope of something better ahead.

A closely related yet less speculative cost of the reduced rewards for change would be the weakening of incentives for producing knowledge and cultural diversity.[23] It would be possible, naturally, for some discovery and cultural innovations to occur, but study, research, new knowledge, and innovation would almost certainly be less rewarding than in a growing society, and fewer resources would be devoted to them. Although wages and rewards in general would be lower than in a growing economy, those available for growth-promoting activities would be especially affected. If government officials found it rewarding to sponsor research and selected innovations, resources devoted to them could be maintained or even expanded, but it is doubtful whether, in such a context, voters and politicians would give strong support to these activities[24] or that in any case an atmosphere conducive to exploration could be maintained. Successful research depends greatly on serendipity and unforeseeable interdependencies with other types of research. All in all, I am fairly confident that no-growth policies would reduce aggregate success in research and development and diminish the chances of solving particular technological problems. This sacrifice of knowledge might be terribly important, not merely because man craves exploration and knowledge for its own sake, but also because technological developments, especially those pertaining to energy and biology, might reduce problems of pollution and exhaustible resources and contribute enormously to the well-being of posterity.

My biggest objection to a no-growth policy, however, is closely related to my principal apprehension concerning unbridled growth. I believe that measures to induce no growth would likewise produce a government role that would intensify our "spiritual poverty." The taxes imposed to stop growth of consumption and investment would yield large revenues. The spending of these revenues in ways consistent with no growth would, I have suggested, be better than detailed planning, but would nonetheless bring relatively large and discretionary government.

We cannot know for sure whether the revenues collected would exceed those involved in a more finely tuned attack on pollution and resource exhaustion. For the reasons stated below, however, I believe that direct attacks on many of the side effects (a) would yield more than they cost (in which case the blunt-instrument approach of checking growth is not the appropriate one, at least initially), and (b) would result in smaller government spending programs and less discretionary authority than a growth-reduction approach aimed at yielding the same abatements in pollution and resource depletion.

Given the variability of the input-output connections between growth and different forms of pollution, no growth would leave the economy with too much of some forms and too little of others for its efficient operation. It is a ham-handed strategy somewhat like, to take an extreme analogy, reducing a city's power supply by 10 percent in order to reduce fires, accidental electrocutions, and atrocious movies; cutting down on power usage would eliminate some unknown quantities of these phenomena, but only by chance the appropriate ones.

An Alternative Policy

In my view the more economical approach to spillover abatement is probably to launch frontal attacks on the conventional externalities with the aim of reducing each form as long as the gains promise to exceed the costs. Moreover, it would often be economical to minimize the government's role, particularly its discretionary role, by using price mechanisms: effluent charges, liability reassignments (to fasten external costs on those activities that generate them), congestion fees, external-cost taxes on commonpool resources like fish, and other spillover charges. These devices would be "fine tuning" compared to regulations or government-operated abatement programs. The levying of externality-charges and the fixing of liabilities on someone in the causal chain would probably use fewer resources and less government than would achieving the same amount of pollution abatement via growth reduction. In many instances, of course, transaction costs, such as those of collection and enforcement, would make it uneconomical to use such price mechanisms in the neat and complete manner in which they could be employed in a hypothetical zero-transaction-cost world.

Similarly the logical straightforward thing to do about nonrenewable resources, if voters do want to preserve more for posterity, would be to tax the use of those particular resources, to tax outputs of petroleum (instead of giving depletion allowances to stimulate exploration), coal, uranium, ores, and so on. The size of such taxes could be adjusted by trial and error to yield the desired degree of deterrence, and the revenues could be used to reduce other taxes. (What degree of deterrence to strive for would have to be determined by the political process; we have no other criterion concerning interference to leave more for posterity.) To be realistic, however, a more effective means of doing something for posterity is probably to attempt to develop the fusion reactor and ways of tapping geothermal energy. After all, to the extent that one is concerned about distant generations, he presumably has the average person of the future in mind. One surely cares no more about unknown people of the twenty-fifth century than about those of the thirty-fifth. The relevant "posterity" is therefore an exceedingly large number of persons. Parceling out x tons of copper or y billions of GNP among an almost infinite number of people does little for the average person. The cost of our doing *much* for the average member of posterity would be fantastic, expecially if we tried to do it through simple conservation. The cost of developing technologies to keep future energy costs down promises to be somewhat less fantastic; furthermore, success would bestow benefits on our immediate descendants for whom we have special concern.

Economic growth as conventionally measured would be retarded by a combination of finely tuned attacks on orthodox forms of pollution, plus conservation or research on energy sources, plus population control. While the benefits of growth would naturally be diminished, so would the "subtle" external costs because resulting reductions in affluence, the value of time,[25] and crowding would remove some of the pressures which may contribute to superficial relationships, the erosion of behavioral rules and ethical codes, government expansion, and other spillovers. These subtle spillovers may be important, and I don't like simply to accept whatever this policy would do to them. But the no-growth policy would also let them lie wherever no growth dropped them. All I can say is that if further reductions in these effects appeared to be worth the cost, and if no growth appeared to be the economical way to curtail them, then further reductions of growth might be considered.

Conclusions

Thus, I would expect highly undesirable effects either from untrammeled economic and population growth or from government interventions to stop economic growth. As for population growth, I can visualize steps to retard or stop it that in my judgment promise more gains than costs. I do not see any disastrous costs from having a constant population, nor do I see a high probability of ruin from the implementation of such a policy.

It is conceivable that the most economical means of conserving exhaustible resources and of relieving various forms of pollution is the meat-axe approach represented by a no-growth policy, but this seems improbable when one considers alternatives even in a crude and cursory fashion. The preferable course, it seems to me, would be to attack directly conventional forms of pollution (making use of effluent charges and price mechanisms wherever they appear to be economical), and to tax the use of nonrenewable resources. This direct and more finely tuned approach would, of course, reduce growth and final output, as conventionally measured, thereby generating some of the costs and benefits attributed to no growth. Whether it reduced the growth of the GNP to 1 percent, to zero, or to a negative 2 percent would not be highly relevant as long as its impact on pollution and the exhaustion of resources was one in which gains exceeded sacrifices. The parts of the GNP that this policy would reduce are those that produce more social cost than gain, and the parts it would preserve are those that yield more social gain than cost. The by-product reduction of economic growth, in combination with zero population growth, would also diminish most of the subtle side effects discussed above, assuming that they are related to crowding, affluence, and material outputs. (Unfortunately, just as with a no-growth policy, these side effects might not be alleviated in the appropriate amounts.)[26] Perhaps most importantly, this policy would keep government from being quite as large, pervasive, discretionary, quarrelsome, and costly as it would be under a no-growth policy. In comparison with such a direct attack on the difficulties, a zero economic growth goal seems a little like trying to eliminate the clouds in order to get better-lighted offices. It is not always an error to manipulate proxies (the best way to a man's heart and all that), but I judge that it would be inefficient to do so in this instance.

REFERENCES

1. The author is indebted, for support of research related to this subject, to NSF Grant 31400X to the Thomas Jefferson Center Foundation for studying the implications of different resource rights.

2. Many of the consequences are well portrayed by E. J. Mishan, *Technology and Growth: The Price We Pay* (New York: Praeger, 1969); Harold J. Barnett and Chandler Morse, *Scarcity and Growth*, Resources for the Future, Inc. (Baltimore: Johns Hopkins Press, 1963); and Harrison Brown, *The Challenge of Man's Future* (New York: Viking Press, 1954). Kenneth E. Boulding's work includes provocative discussions of many of these issues especially in "The Economics of the Coming Spaceship Earth," *Environmental Quality in a Growing Economy*, ed. H. Jarrett, Resources for the Future, Inc. (Baltimore: Johns Hopkins Press, 1966), pp. 3-14. Recently, such consequences have been publicized more widely by the book sponsored by the Club of Rome: D. L. Meadows, D. H. Meadows, J. Randers, and W. W. Behrens, *The Limits to Growth* (New York: Potomac Associates, 1972);

and by Barbara Ward and René Dubos, *Only One Earth: The Care and Maintenance of a Small Planet,* a report commissioned for the United Nations Conference on the Human Environment (New York: W. W. Norton, 1972). W. Beckerman has provided useful criticism of such views in "Why We Need Economic Growth," *Lloyds Bank Review* (October 1971), 1-15.

3. Fred Singer, "Environmental Quality—When Does Growth Become Too Expensive?" *Is There an Optimal Level of Population?*, ed. S. Fred Singer (New York: McGraw-Hill, 1971), pp. 156-172.

4. Thomas C. Schelling, "On the Ecology of Micromotives," *Public Interest,* No. 25 (Fall 1971), 61-98. One of his many graphic summary statements is that often "the worst things in life are free."

5. For some factors that help explain government behavior, see Roland N. McKean, "Property Rights Within Government, and Devices to Increase Governmental Efficiency," *Southern Economic Journal,* 39 (October 1972), 177-186.

6. Fred Singer, "The Predicament of the Club of Rome" [a review of *The Limits to Growth*], EOS Transactions, American Geophysical Union, 53 (July 1972), 697-700, esp. 700; Rudolph Klein, "Growth and Its Enemies," *Commentary,* 53 (June 1972), 44. On the "Club of Rome Model" see also Allen Kneese and Ronald Ridker, "Predicament of Mankind" [a review of *The Limits to Growth*], *Washington Post,* March 2, 1972, pp. B1, B9.

7. For a variety of views, see especially the papers by Preston Cloud, Harrison Brown, Joseph L. Fisher, Alvin M. Weinberg and R. Philip Hammond, and Hans H. Landsberg in *Is There an Optimal Level of Population?*; and the essays in *Energy, Economic Growth, and the Environment,* ed. Sam H. Schurr, Resources for the Future, Inc. (Baltimore: Johns Hopkins Press, 1972).

8. This would imply a different "social rate of discount" from the one that emerges when the free-rider difficulty is taken as given. Also, of course, one may attach value to conservation if he does not accept economic efficiency as a criterion.

9. This depends, of course, on the stocks of land and capital, transaction costs, tastes, and one's criterion. For an excellent discussion, see Stephen Enke, "Economic Consequences of Rapid Population Growth," *Economic Journal,* 81 (December 1971), 800-811.

10. As E. J. Mishan has pointed out, the dumping of erotica into the environment creates spillover costs to some bystanders, using up at minimum their peace of mind without their consent—generating spillovers that are fully analogous to the effects of injecting pollutants into the atmosphere. "A Modest Proposal: Cleaning up Sex Pollution," *Harper's* (July 1972), 54-56.

11. Failure to produce external benefits that it would be efficient to produce can be regarded as an external cost, because it damages persons and overuses some resources in comparison with the state that could exist.

12. Roland N. McKean, "The Economics of Altruism, Trust, and Corporate Responsibility," to appear in a volume containing papers presented at the Russell Sage Conference on Altruism in March of 1972 (ed. E. S. Phelps).

13. Roland N. McKean, "Property Rights, Appropriability, and Externalities in Government," *Perspectives of Property,* ed. G. Wunderlich and W. L. Gibson, Jr. (Pennsylvania State University, Institute for Research on Land and Water Resources, 1972), pp. 32-55.

14. These points are related to some of those made in Alvin Toffler, *Future Shock* (New York: Random House, 1970).

15. McKean, "The Economics of Altruism, Trust, and Corporate Responsibility."

16. Gary S. Becker, "A Theory of the Allocation of Time," *Economic Journal* (September 1965), 493-517.

17. Staffan B. Linder, *The Harried Leisure Class* (New York: Columbia University Press, 1970).

18. Linder suggests, however, that the increased value of time has one possibly beneficial spillover effect: sex, which is less satisfactory when encumbered with much capital equipment, becomes one of the relatively expensive activities like thinking, thus alleviating the population-growth problem (pp. 83-89): "In underdeveloped countries the birth rate reportedly falls in villages when electricity is installed."

19. If the situation looked critical, the most sensible scheme, in my view, and one that has clearcut rules which would reduce the chances of arbitrary decisions, is the marketable certificate plan described by K. Boulding in *The Meaning of the Twentieth Century* (New York: Harper Colophon, 1965), pp. 135-136. There would be some nasty enforcement problems and other drawbacks that seem repulsive to many persons, but if one considers alternative ways of allocating permission to have children, they have even more repulsive features.

20. Central planning of outputs and inputs seems to me vastly more difficult than the assignment and enforcement of new rights regarding one output that the "certificate plan" for population control implies.

21. Klein, "Growth and Its Enemies," p. 43.

22. Beckerman, "Why We Need Economic Growth," p. 11.

23. We cannot claim to know much, however, about these causal connections. As Boulding once wrote, it is puzzling that the sudden growth of knowledge in the sixteenth century took place in Europe rather than in China, which was at that time ahead of Europe ("The Economics of the Coming Spaceship Earth," pp. 8-9). But the explanation may lie in the cultural diversity and familiarity with differences that must have characterized Europe.

24. Government personnel respond to costs and rewards from their individual standpoints much as managers of firms do. For thoughts on the nature of incentives in government, see Roland N. McKean, "Property Rights Within Government."

25. The Japanese have apparently tried (for different reasons) to attack even this variable in a direct fashion: levying fines on "supervisors who insist on working holidays and their normal days off," *Time*, August 21, 1972, p. 65. Personal income taxes, of course, also reduce the value of time to individuals.

26. It doesn't help much, but one can formulate the marginal conditions for appropriate policies regarding (1) those forms of pollution that can economically be attacked directly because transaction costs are low, and (2) those forms that should be attacked with various degrees of indirectness (because of collection, information, enforcement, or other transaction and intervention costs associated with relatively direct approaches). One would like to move in any of those directions as long as the marginal gains exceeded the marginal costs.

MANCUR OLSON, HANS H. LANDSBERG,
JOSEPH L. FISHER

Epilogue

THE FOREGOING essays illustrate the extraordinary range and sometimes unexpected complexity of the issues that are raised by proposals for a no-growth society and by the long-run probability of a slow-growth or no-growth economy. Yet there are many questions great and small about a growthless society that have so far been ignored in this anthology, principally because no one was found who would attempt to deal with them. Some of these questions are relatively straightforward, and it is perhaps enough here simply to state them. What implications, for example, would a no-growth policy in the United States alone have for the relationships among the great powers? Or for whatever slight stability the international system has had since World War II? Or for international trade and foreign exchange markets? Is no growth a policy that all countries, or at least all developed countries, must undertake together if at all? And if the developed nations, or even the United States alone, ceased to grow, how could the economies of less developed countries progress without the secular increase in demand for their raw materials and other exports to which they have become accustomed? The systems analysts who pride themselves on incorporating the environment in their analyses of economic growth must encompass the international system as well if their proposals are to claim the attention of policy-makers.

Some other questions that have not yet been dealt with are far more elusive and difficult to understand let alone to answer. This is particularly the case with those that pertain to the ethical or aesthetic values, psychological states, and social relationships that are probably the ultimate source of many of the demands for a no-growth society. We shall argue here that some people oppose economic growth not only because, like almost everyone else, they want a viable and wholesome natural environment, but also, and more importantly, for other reasons which, because they are usually implicit, are far more difficult to discern.

Evidently there are many needs and desires, besides the taste for a clean environment, that modern societies fail to fulfill despite growing

229

incomes. The recent crescendo of social protest may suggest that modern society is meeting these needs even less well than other societies have. Perhaps there are demands for tranquility, for reliable patterns of social interaction, and for freedom from uncertainty and even from change which modern life fails to meet, with the result that the fundamental dynamic of all modern societies (both Western and Communist) is being questioned, sometimes by people who appear at first glance to be simply defenders of the natural environment.

The New Dismal Science

There may be a few subtle signs of these extra-environmental sources of the opposition to growth even in some of the prophecies of ecological doom. These prophecies appear to rest on environmental (even on scientific) grounds alone and in fact most of them probably do. Yet they present a puzzling parallel with the doleful prophecies of other times and places. The Old Testament prophets predicted the most complete and terrifying disaster if society did not mend its ways. The early Christians predicted the imminent end of the world. Many other cultural traditions have also had Cassandras. To say that a prediction is dismal, of course, is not to say that it is wrong. And even when it is, it may do some good, given human propensities to sloth and self-delusion. As a modern text on methodology might put it, the object of the prediction may be influenced by the prediction. At the same time, endless cries of "Wolf! Wolf!" can be harmful, even if ultimately one of them is right. Thus it would be well to look at the logic of some of the ecological Jeremiads and at their relationship to economic growth, and to be alert for the attitudes about social behavior, psychological stress, and uncertainty implicit in some of them.

The prediction that once income reaches some higher level, such as the level it would reach in a generation or two at present rates of growth, there will be an all-consuming ecological disaster (no matter what preventive or ameliorative measures are taken) has met with extraordinary journalistic success. It may seem self-evident to many people that if these predictions are true, then we ought to put a stop to growth immediately. In fact, however, the proposition is logically unsatisfactory: if a level of income that is, say, three times as great as the present level would (even with *ad hoc* efforts to protect the environment) make life impossible, it might still be a good idea to continue economic growth as long as possible. To be sure, it would be essential to stop economic growth before income reached thrice its current level, but why not try to get to the highest feasible sustainable level of income as soon as possible and stop only when it is reached? (There may, of course, be psychological or economic reasons for avoiding *any* quick stop in economic growth, but most opponents of growth do not mention them.) From the assumption that we can be only so well off, it doesn't follow that we shouldn't try to become as well off as we can; that is like telling a man that however hard he tries he cannot make more than $30,000 a year and that therefore he should stop trying to better his lot now that he is making $10,000 a year. Thus the conclusion that growth ought to be stopped now follows only if one of a number of additional and often neglected premises is added.

Ecofreaks

The additional premise, an antigrowthman might say, is altogether obvious: economic growth should be stopped now before biosuicide is at issue simply because the pollution and other assaults on our aesthetic sensibilities it brings in its wake make growth unpleasant on balance. The extra market output additional growth would bring would not be worth the resulting reduction in the quality of the natural environment.

Obvious as this rebuttal seems, it involves another often unrecognized *non sequitur*. No degree of repugnance against the environmental side effects of current patterns of economic growth would be sufficient to make the stop-growth-now argument complete. This becomes evident if, whatever our true preferences, we unstintingly accept, at least for the sake of the argument, the intense, uncompromising, and moving devotion to a lovely natural environment that characterizes the "ecofreak" (Aren't all of us ecofreaks at certain moments?).* If we choose rational policies consistent with the enormous value that, by assumption, we put upon the reduction of pollution and the like, we must insist that effective punishments or staggering effluent fees be imposed against any firm or individual who treats the environment in a way that offends our aesthetic sensibility.

The initial result of the rational ecofreak policies would be that the level of measured income would fall, or at least rise less rapidly in the normal course of things than it would otherwise have done. Since the regulatory constraints and taxes would keep firms from using nature's waste absorptive capacities in some of the ways they have found advantageous, it would raise their costs and reduce market output. A welfare economist with a special fondness for environmental amenities might say that true income or welfare had increased, because he cherishes the environmental improvement gained more than the market goods foregone. But in the Introduction to this volume it was stipulated that, for the purpose of a fair

---

* The term "freak" is defined by Webster to mean such things as whim, caprice, abnormality or monstrosity; it evokes in the older generation a picture of a bearded lady. More recently, however, it has come to denote a person giving extreme importance to one particular value, condition, thing, or preoccupation. As so used by such people as members of the counterculture and hippies, its connotations are not pejorative, but perhaps even favorable. It is in this latter sense that we are using it here, as a convenient, inoffensive shorthand word to describe a person holding extremely strong views in a particular dimension.

and meaningful argument, "growth" would be defined in terms of real per capita income as calculated from the National Income and Product Accounts. Income measured in this way would fall, or at least grow less rapidly under normal circumstances, if a sufficiently rigorous policy to protect the environment were imposed.

But it would not stay at the lower level for long. If the decrease in market output did not lead to violence or political instability, it is a good bet that it would be followed by growth in the national income and probably, for a time, even unusually rapid growth. In such a situation firms would have an extraordinarily large incentive to think of ways to produce output cheaply without damaging the environment because of the great costs imposed by the regulations and taxes protecting the environment. Any firm that developed productive patterns or processes that did not contravene the new environmental regulations or make it liable to effluent fees could make exceptional profits, which would give it an incentive to expand production. Since no firm has had much incentive in the past to do such research, probably many "easy" innovations would be discovered in the first few years after the imposition of the strong environmental protection policy. To put the same point another way, it is unlikely that firms or individuals would fully adjust to tough environmental regulations until they had been in effect for some time. It is as though a healthy child were forced to use crutches: he could never go as fast or as far with them as without them, but the rate of increase in his speed as he learned how to use them might be as great as before, or even greater.

It is accordingly very important not to confuse a proenvironment policy with a no-economic-growth policy. The former policy, at least if pushed far enough, would probably lead to a drop in measured national income followed by a rise, perhaps an unusually rapid rise. The latter, if it could be carried out, would lead to a constant level of income. These two policies need to be distinguished not only because of the greatly different steps required to bring them about, but also because many who would support the former would oppose the latter. Trading off market output for environmental quality makes sense to everyone who thinks we have been giving too little emphasis to the environment; stopping the growth of income can, when the mountain of confusion has been cleared away, be the best policy only for those who are not willing to opt for more market output even if it can be obtained without impairing the environment.

There are, as we shall argue below, some people with value judgments such that they could consistently oppose growth of measured income even when it would be as likely to lead to improvement as to degradation of the environment. These people we shall, without any disrespect, describe as sociofreaks, psychofreaks, or safety-freaks. Many ecofreaks could also be characterized by one or more of these other terms, especially that of safety-freak, and may therefore consistently oppose growth. But these terms and the value judgments they reflect are logically distinct, and there are also many ecofreaks who are not characterized by any of them. There is nothing in ecofreak values themselves, however extreme, that can consistently lead to opposition to all economic growth. As the Introduction pointed out, if the composition of output is assumed to be fixed, a sufficiently intense distaste for the environmental side effects of growth could sometimes justify opposition to economic growth. Nevertheless, the rational ecofreak would always prefer to see the mix of output change in the direction dictated by his set of values.

Sociofreaks

If a single-mindedly pro-environment ideology does not by itself entail opposition to economic growth, it becomes more important to look for the other, extra-environmental attitudes involved in the no-growth movement. Here it may be significant that current opposition to growth has been foreshadowed by comparable impulses in other periods of history, and not only those that involved prophecies of doom. The 1960's were not, of course, the first years in which significant groups of people turned against the fundamental dynamic or direction of their age. History gives us many examples of revulsion against a changing present, even several back-to-nature movements. Consider, for example, Rousseau, the Luddites, and Thoreau. Perhaps the most notable forerunners of the current antigrowth-men are the nineteenth-century European romantics, of whom Thomas Carlyle is perhaps prototypical, whose rejection of the then unprecedented growth or advance of capitalism was complete, and combined with nostalgic glorification of the middle ages with its unmeasured but probably far slower rate of change. Even Marx, explicitly recognizing Victorian capitalism's rapid rate of growth of output, proposed and predicted an unspecialized and probably unchanging utopia as its ultimate successor. In the present century, the arts, at least, provide innumerable examples of revulsion at the direction and pace of modern "progress," from Charlie Chaplin's comic confrontations with mass production to Herman Hesse's mystical rejection of prewar life.

Some of the objections to previous periods of progress stemmed from resentments against those who were rising in relative position, from concern about the victims of progress, and from an uneasiness about the social disruptions brought about by urbanization and other types of geographical mobility. The incentives and opportunities that brought about change and progress made some families *nouveaux riches*, others *nouveaux pauvres*, and tore apart still other groups, like extended families and small communities. Mobility, up and down and also over space, has always been associated with advance and indeed with all kinds of social change, and there has never been any lack of people who find the rootlessness, alienation, and uncongeniality that it may involve too great a price to pay for "progress."

Thus we have our sociofreaks—those who put stable group relationships above most other objectives. Again, to emphasize, "sociofreak," like "ecofreak," is not used here as a term of abuse, but rather as a characterization of an extreme, but not necessarily mistaken, value judgment. Almost all of us are, in some ways or on some days, sociofreaks: the nuclear family, at least, is a group within which we all like to see some measure of stability. No single idea has had such a profound influence on serious sociology in the last century as the notion, whether enunciated by Durkheim or by Parsons, that individuals, or at least some types of individuals, need extensive ties to bind them to the social order, and that these ties must have at least some degree of stability.

Rapid economic growth, whether past or present, must to some degree change or disrupt patterns of social interaction. It requires technological change—new ways of producing—and often capital accumulation as well. The new techniques and machines normally require new combinations of skills and workers, and sometimes production in new localities. To achieve what the economist calls complete or "Pareto-optimal" efficiency in the allocation of resources, a number of "marginal equalities" must be satisfied, and this means that each worker must work in that group and location in which (after making allowance for any costs of transporting him to the new work) the net value of his output is greatest. Satisfying the necessary conditions for full efficiency in a world of rapid technological change requires a constant reshuffling and even migration of workers. To illustrate the general point by means of an extreme example, note that *maximum* economic growth normally requires that husbands and wives each take the job that pays the most, even if each must live in a different part of the country to do so. The nuclear family is, however, only one of many forms of social interaction, and not the only one for which a degree of stability is desired. Friendship is another, and there is at least anecdotal evidence that "old" friends have lost some of their importance because of the exceptional mobility of modern American life.

Perhaps, then, the desire to stop economic growth sometimes owes something to the sociofreak. The rational sociofreak, unlike the rational ecofreak, can, with consistency, oppose economic growth itself, for economic growth inevitably means change and presumably requires incentives which permit some to rise while others fall and which induce others to move away from their communities, friends, and even families. The stable composition and hierarchies of social groups that the sociofreak values are indeed in conflict with economic growth. It would no doubt be possible to have *some* economic growth even subject to constraints on geographic mobility, but it is doubtful whether such growth would be possible without the opportunities that permit some to rise relative to their fellows, thereby disturbing the stability of the status system that opponents of "progress," at least those in historic times, thought important.

At least in the case of Ezra Mishan, the father of modern antigrowth-men, the sociological sources of opposition to growth seem more important than the ecological. Mishan's first significant work on this subject, his book on *The Costs of Economic Growth,* puts much more emphasis on the short-comings of social interaction in modern life than on the interactions of the ecological system. Many passages, above all those that glorify a less rapidly changing past, have much more in common with Goldsmith's "Deserted Village" than with modern biological science.

Psychofreaks

The conviction that when "wealth accumulates, men decay" can arise not only out of concern about the effect of growth on social groups, but also out of abhorrence for the motives, consciousness, and habits of mind associated with economic growth. Rationality, cool calculation, and occupational and intellectual specialization are surely associated with economic as well as scientific advance. So, perhaps, are acquisitiveness, a desire to "keep up with the Joneses," and, especially in Soviet-type societies, a readiness to carry out the dictates or meet the quotas of an organizational hierarchy. Economic growth is in short associated with a distinctive ethos. This is surely true, whether Max Weber and others were right in tracing capitalism to Calvinism and the Protestant ethic and to other aspects of the Judeo-Christian tradition, or whether this ethos represents an adjustment of the Western religious and ideological inheritance to the temptations and requirements of economic growth. It is, for example, often observed that peoples of traditional or nongrowing societies generally have the "zero-sum" attitude that what one gains, another must lose; a greater respect for elders; a readier sense of awe; a quicker acceptance of mystery or superstition; and a propensity to look at phenomena or transactions in context rather than in a specialized or impersonal way. To accept economic growth, it seems, is to accept a mentality or ethos that is probably peculiar to developed societies, or conceivably to the Western religio-cultural tradition.

Whatever its source or detailed characteristics, this is a mentality or ethos that some people find offensive or uncongenial. It is surely not accidental that rejection of economic growth has emerged simultaneously with preferences for astrology, mysticism, tarot, witchcraft, Eastern religions, and "mind-blowing" or consciousness-changing drugs. At the same time, there have been resonating changes in the literary and artistic tastes of the college generation, such as those exemplified by the recent popularity of Herman Hesse's search for life's meanings and his fascination with the "mysterious East." To some extent this new mentality—approximately what Reich called "Consciousness III"—is a product of economic growth (or of high income combined with indulgent parents and the welfare state). When affluence assures survival and even some luxuries, one comes more quickly to questions like "What else do I want?" "Who am I?" and "Where am I going?" Affluence offers the opportunity to contemplate and the freedom to choose among alternative purposes. The new generation then would not have developed its distaste for economic growth had it not been so well fed by economic growth.

Thus some of the opposition to economic growth, even some that appears to rest on ecological argument, may have its true source in the "psychofreak" consciousness. This does not, of course, make it wrong. There is nothing necessarily irrational in a value system which is uncomfortable with calculating rationality, minute and often deadening specialization, and the secular or antimystical mood, and which rejects economic growth and scientific advance because they are indubitably associated with the offensive mentality. There is no reason why we cannot speak of the "rational psychofreak," and accept the human meaning of his understandable opposition to economic growth, yet at the same time insist that he should not build his case against growth under the misleading cover of respect for ecological balance.

Safety-Freaks

The remaining source of opposition to economic growth as it is defined in the national accounts is the safety-freak: the person who will go to remarkable lengths to avoid risk of great loss. Though many safety-freaks are also ecofreaks, there is no necessary connection between the two attitudes. The timid lady who looks under her bed each night before retiring on the chance that a criminal might be hiding there is a safety-freak, but she may have no special concern for the natural environment. Conversely, a mountain climber, a white-water canoeist, or an advocate of a venturesome foreign policy might, despite his readiness to accept major risks, favor substantial sacrifices to protect and improve the natural environment.

The fact that a number of safety-freaks are also ecofreaks is probably due to the danger that abuses, and even apparently innocuous uses of the environment, can lead to disasters, and conceivably even to the destruction of the planet's capacity to support life. Naturally the safety-freak is also troubled by growth of population or per capita income, since the innovations and new activities that an increase in aggregate output involves generally entail some risk of catastrophic damage to the natural environment. The possibility that almost any major development or change could lead to unprecedented disaster should not be dismissed casually, even by those who are growing tired of ecological alarms. There are two main reasons why the dangers from population and economic growth are greater than is often supposed.

The first is the unfathomed complexity of the ecological and economic systems, and of their relationships to each other, which (as Holdren and Mishan point out in their essays) means that it is not usually possible to know for certain what will result from any major new use of the environment. Consider, for example, jet flights in the troposphere. The possible effects of such flights on ozone levels, ultraviolet radiation, and meteorological conditions are by no means adequately understood, though the many experts working on this through the Climatic Impact Assessment Program of the U. S. Department of Transportation and under other auspices may in due course provide an adequate understanding. Beyond this, moreover, are the effects of any changes in radiation levels on living organisms, notably micro-organisms and through them on ecological systems, in which almost everything is said to affect almost everything else. When one adds the possibility of simultaneous changes in average temperature (and experts disagree even about the direction of the predicted change in temperature) and thus in climate and the considerable but uncertain implications of this for agriculture and economic life, the unknown interactions of changes in radiation with those in climate, and the further ecological implications of any changes in economic activity due to these changes in radiation and temperature, the possibility that something dreadful might result becomes rather difficult to rule out. One cannot be sure that there isn't, say, a one in a million or even a one in a thousand chance of monstrous and irreversible damage to the environment. And even if we could be quite certain that heavy traffic in the troposphere would be "safe" (would the odds have to be infinitely small or just very, very small to justify use of that word?), what about the thousands of other new chemicals, technologies, and activities that continued growth of population or per capita income would require? What about the effect on the world's climate of settling and farming the Amazon basin? Or of systematically draining the swamps in which life may have begun? Or the next encounter with a new drug like Thalidomide?

The second reason why the changes required by growth of population and income can create significant risks is that their environmental side effects may be very difficult, sometimes even impossible, to reverse or undo. This irreversibility or intractability of many of the unanticipated side effects of growth has three sources. One is the substantial lag or gestation period that can occur between the adoption of a policy or technology and the manifestation of the problems it may create. A nondegradable residue, for example, may seem innocuous until it has accumulated to a toxic level, progressed up the food chain, and been identified as the source of an undiagnosed malady. The length of lag between economic choices and the the proper evaluation of their side effects is longer now than it needs to be because of the paucity of social and environmental indicators; certainly everyone should be able to agree that the hazards of growth could be somewhat reduced by better monitoring systems and research agendas. Still, it is hard to imagine a monitoring system that could insure that a society would always discover an adverse or even a disastrous consequence in time to change its course.

The intractability or irreversibility of many side effects of growth has a second source in the further lag between the recognition that a change of policy or technology is desirable and an adequate response. One of the healthier features of the no-growth movement is its concern about the danger of unresponsiveness in public institutions and political leadership, and its rejection of the facile assumption that society will deal adequately with whatever unexpected side effects or shortages the future may bring. Part of this concern may grow in the same soil as the New Left's skepticism about the leadership of governments and other large hierarchical organizations. Many antigrowthmen do not expect prompt and effective responses to environmental problems from the establishment they have come to know, distrust, and even to hate. Quite apart from this skepticism, however, there is the problem of the pressure groups which build up around whatever policy or industry emerges and which tend to resist change even when it would clearly be in the interest of the population in general. The reason for this is that lobbies tend to spring up as by-products of organizations with other initial purposes, so that most industries or groups of government contractors are in due course represented by trade associations, labor unions, or other lobbies. The protection of the environment is, however, what the economist calls a "public good," one that normally benefits a large group. It can be logically proven that rational, self-interested individuals do not make voluntary sacrifices, even through support of public interest lobbies, to provide themselves with public goods, or with a sufficient supply of them. So, characteristically, the minority that particularly benefits from a given policy or industry is organized, whereas the public at large with a significant but diffuse interest in the matter is not. As a result, we can expect that societies will sometimes persist in policies that are clearly pernicious. A policy that was initially chosen out of ignorance and innocence may be maintained by organized vested interests long after its ill effects have been recognized.

The intractability of many side effects of growth has a third source that is illuminated by the "materials balance" approach to environmental problems developed by Ayres and Kneese, Boulding, and others. If the weight of the materials taken into the economy equals the weight of ultimate residuals, after adjustment for any change in the amount of recycling, economic growth will tend to increase the amount of pollutants released into the environment. Each pollution problem can of course be dealt with, or perhaps even eliminated. A society can close down its incinerators or even stop producing a commodity whose production gives rise to problems. But the materials balance approach reminds us that *any* approach, other than reducing material throughout or increasing re-cycling, will create new, though perhaps less damaging, environmental problems. Closing the incinerator will reduce air pollution but add to solid wastes; stopping production of a commodity that entails a lot of pollution will mean, if economic growth continues, that yet more resources will go into the production of some other commodity, which will presum-ably result in more of some kind of pollution elsewhere. The materials balance considerations (and perhaps also the application of the entropy concept made by the economist Georgescu-Roegen) suggest that those who habitually assume that the adverse side effects of growth are incidental problems concentrated in a limited number of activities, each of which can be dealt with on an *ad hoc* basis, simply don't understand the matter. Pollution problems are inherent in the materials throughput and energy consumption of the economy, and it cannot be assumed that all of the anticipated or unanticipated problems of pollution that continued growth will bring can be easily and cheaply ameliorated without creating new types of residuals problems.

It therefore seems that the safety-freak should definitely oppose the growth of either population or per capita income. The poor predictability of side effects combined with their possible irreversibility or intractability would appear to leave those with a sufficiently extreme aversion to risk with no choice but to oppose growth. There is also, however, some reason for the risk averter to favor economic growth. For just as economic growth brings serious risks, so it also yields resources which offer some degree of insurance against many risks. At the individual level, it is ob-vious that a sufficient accumulation of wealth lessens or eliminates the need for insurance; at the social level, too, additional wealth and produc-tive capacity gives a society the power to solve some very costly problems which might have proved fatal to a poorer society. This is aptly illustrated by the "Southern corn leaf blight" of 1971, to which the growth-oriented "genetic engineering" or hybridization left the nation's corn crop extraordi-narily susceptible. Alarming as this type of susceptibility is, it is also important to remember that the scientific advance and capital accumula-tion associated with economic growth made it possible to produce a record crop only one year after the blight epidemic began. Thus it is not by any means certain—though it is possible—that a no-growth policy would re-duce the risks of ecological catastrophe. About all that can be said for sure is that most discussions of this matter have lacked an adequate intellectual framework, and that it is important enough to deserve serious inquiry.

Conclusion

It is possible, in short, to oppose economic growth as it is defined in the National Income and Product Accounts without being logically confused, provided that one accepts some of the special value judgments that have been described. Though a belief in prophecies of ultimate ecological doom and a love of the natural environment alone do not logically entail opposition to economic growth, an extreme concern for maintaining group relationships, for achieving psychological states that are incompatible with economic and scientific advance, or, perhaps, for avoiding the risk of new kinds of action which might have unexpected side effects, can consistently lead to a no-growth policy. These value judgments are probably rather rare, however, and we do not ourselves go all of the way toward any of the extremes we have described. Yet it is important to repeat that the eccentricity of a value judgment does not make it wrong, and that the values of those whom we have somewhat lightly called eco-, socio-, psycho- and safety-freaks deserve a respect that should not be accorded to the many arguments, on both sides of the growth debate, which are not even logically consistent.

Nor does the no-growth side have all the freaks. Given our interest here in exploring the values or psychologies that might justify opposition to growth, and the fact that all three authors are professional economists, we hope we may be pardoned for not including a section on "econofreaks" or "growth-freaks"—those who are determined to discount all catastrophes which occur after their own lifetimes, who are relatively insensitive to the social and environmental side effects of growth, and who casually assume that all environmental problems can easily be solved by *ad hoc* measures. Such freaks, among whom we do not count ourselves, have a tendency to neglect unmarketable goods and a habit of neglecting uncertainty, especially the small chance of disastrous loss. In their preoccupation with market outputs and with marginal changes in the best understood variables, they could unwittingly take society step by step over the edge. In a society in which these attitudes are so common and those with vested interests in the present pattern of growth are so powerful, opposition to economic growth clearly has its uses.

At the same time, our effort to find potential merit in no-growth proposals, and thus to encourage research into the problems behind them, does not mean we believe that the advocates of zero economic growth have posed precisely the right questions. Most research should not be devoted to the question of whether economic growth should be continued or stopped, speeded up or slowed down. That way of posing the question obscures another approach that could satisfy the aspirations of most people far better.

The other approach is to reform rather than prohibit growth—to institute effluent fees, environmental regulations, public expenditures, institutional modifications, and behavioral changes that would make the composition of output more attractive to most of its critics. This would be far better for the great majority who eschew extreme values. It would probably bring a dramatically better result for those whose poverty leaves them with an intense need for additional market goods. It would also be better for the eco-freak. Even the safety-freak may possibly be made to feel more secure with reform than with stoppage of growth; any change has risks, including a shift to a mix of output with more environmental quality, but would these be greater than those associated with the loss of productive capacity and the risks of exacerbated distributional conflict and political warfare in a no-growth society? There are, after all, no utterly risk-free options for any individual or society.

The all-out sociofreaks and the psychofreaks, it is true, should not be expected to agree, and must not be ignored just because they are out-numbered. But true or properly reformed growth can, at least potentially, promise something for them as well. With the sweeter fruits of true growth, with more of what is wanted by the many, it is possible to compensate the losers yet leave the gainers better off than they would have been without growth; the majority who enjoy the fruits of reformed growth can afford to make some policy concessions to those for whom growth is unpleasant, and still have something extra left for themselves. If this isn't possible, there hasn't been true growth or progress. To be sure, the winners may not, in practice, compensate the losers, but simply exploit their own numerical stength to get what they want for themselves. Yet the point is important, for the fruits of policies that lead to growth are frequently shared, albeit often quite unequally, and the opportunity to let the losers share in them is always there. In a society without growth or progress, by contrast, what the winners in fights over policy won, the losers, inevitably, would lose. So the fights, presumably, would be mighty rough.

Notes on Contributors

WILLIAM ALONSO, born in 1933 in Argentina, is professor of regional planning at the University of California at Berkeley. As present he is traveling on a Guggenheim Fellowship. He is the author of *Location and Land Use* (1964) and, with J. Friedmann, of *Regional Development and Planning* (1964), as well as of numerous articles. He is an advisor on urban and regional problems to French, Japanese, Cuban and United States agencies; to the Rand Corporation, the Ford Foundation, and the World Bank.

KENNETH E. BOULDING, born in 1910 in England, is professor of economics at the University of Colorado, and Director of Research on General, Social, and Economic Dynamics at the Institute of Behavioral Science. He is the author of *The Economy of Love and Fear: A Preface to Grants Economics* (1973), *A Primer on Social Dynamics* (1970), *Economics as a Science* (1970), *Beyond Economics* (1968), *The Impact of the Social Sciences* (1966), *The Meaning of the Twentieth Century* (1964), *Conflict and Defense* (1962), *The Skills of the Economist* (1958), *Principles of Economic Policy* (1958), *The Image* (1956), *The Organizational Revolution* (1953), *A Reconstruction of Economics* (1950), *There Is a Spirit* (*The Naylor Sonnets*) (1945), *Economics of Peace* (1945), and *Economic Analysis* (1945, 1965). He has taught at the University of Edinburgh, Colgate University, Fisk University, Iowa State University, McGill University, Iowa State College, University of Michigan, University College of West Indies, and International Christian University, and has served as research director of the Center for Research in Conflict Resolution.

HARVEY BROOKS, born in 1915 in Cleveland, Ohio, is Dean of Engineering and Applied Physics and Gordon McKay Professor of Applied Physics at Harvard University. He is a member of the National Science Board and has served as a member of the President's Science Advisory Committee, and as Chairman of the NAS Committee on Science and Public Policy. He is the author of *The Government of Science* (1968), and of numerous articles and reviews on solid state physics and nuclear reactor physics. He is currently the president of the American Academy of Arts and Sciences, and a member of the National Science Board.

LESTER R. BROWN, born in 1934 in Bridgeton, New Jersey, is a senior fellow at the Overseas Development Council in Washington, D. C. He is the author of *World Without Borders* (1972), *Seeds of Change: The Green Revolution and Development in the 1970s* (1970), and *Man, Land and Food* (1963). From 1966 to 1969 he served as administrator of the International Agricultural Development Service, the technical assistance arm of the United States Department of Agriculture.

KINGSLEY DAVIS, born in 1908 in Tuxedo, Texas, is Ford Professor of Sociology and Comparative Studies and Director of International Population and Urban Research at the University of California at Berkeley. He is the author of *Cities: Their Origin, Growth and Human Impact* (1973), *World Urbanization, 1950-1970* (Vol. I, 1969; Vol. II, 1972), and *The Population of India and Pakistan* (1951). He is past president of the Population Association of America and of the American Sociological

Association, and a former U.S. representative to the Population Commission of the United Nations.

JOSEPH L. FISHER, born in 1914 in Pawtucket, Rhode Island, is president of Resources for the Future, Inc. in Washington, D. C. He is the author of *World Prospects for Natural Resources* (1964), and with Leonard L. Fischman and Hans H. Landsberg, of *Resources in America's Future* (1963). Before coming to Resources for the Future in 1953, he worked for the National Resources Planning Board, the Department of State, and the Council of Economic Advisors. In 1955, he served as staff director of the Cabinet Commission on Energy Supplies and Policies.

JOHN P. HOLDREN, born in 1944 in Sewickley, Pennsylvania, is assistant professor of energy and resources at the University of California at Berkeley. He is the author, with Paul R. and Anne H. Ehrlich, of *Human Ecology: Problems and Solutions* 1973); and with Phillip Herrera, of *Energy* (1971). He has served as a senior research fellow in the Environmental Quality Laboratory of the California Institute of Technology, and as a consultant on energy technology and policy and on environmental problems for the National Academies of Science and Engineering.

WILLARD R. JOHNSON, born in 1935 in St. Louis, Missouri, is associate professor of political science at the Massachusetts Institute of Technology. He is the author of *Cameroon Federation* (1970), and of numerous articles on community development and Africanization. He is the chairman of the Circle Inc., and of the New England Community Development Corporation; and a consultant to Education Services, Inc., Institute for Services to Education in Newton, Educational Development Center, and the United States Department of State. He served as chairman of the McGovern task force on Africa.

HANS H. LANDSBERG, born in 1913 in Germany, is director of the resource appraisal program at Resources for the Future, Inc., in Washington, D.C. He is the author of *Natural Resources for U.S. Growth* (1964), and joint author with Marion Clawson and Lyle T. Alexander, of *The Agricultural Potential of the Middle East* (1971); with Sam H. Schurr, of *Energy in the United States* (1968); with Leonard L. Fischman and Joseph L. Fisher of *Resources in America's Future* (1963); with Bruce C. Netschert, of *The Future Supply of the Major Metals* (1961); with George Perazich, of *Report on Nuclear Power and Economic Development in Israel* (1957); and with Harold Barger, of *Output, Employment and Productivity in American Agriculture, 1899-1939* (1941). In 1971 and 1972, he served as Consultant to the Secretary-General at the United Nations Conference on the Human Environment.

EZRA J. MISHAN, born in 1917 in England, is a reader in economics at the London School of Economics. He is the author of *21 Popular Economic Fallacies* (1969), *Cost-Benefit Analysis* (1971), and *The Costs of Economic Growth* (1967).

ROLAND N. McKEAN, born in 1917 in Mulberry Grove, Illinois, is Commonwealth Professor of Economics at the University of Virginia. He is the author of *Public Spending* (1968), *Efficiency in Government through Systems Analysis* (1958), and with Charles J. Hitch, of *Economics of Defense in the Nuclear Age* (1960). He is a past president of the Southern Economic Association.

MANCUR OLSON, born in 1932 in Grand Forks, North Dakota, is professor of economics at the University of Maryland. He is the author of *Toward a Social Report* (1969),

The Economics of the Wartime Shortage (1963), and *The Logic of Collective Action* (1965, 1971). From 1967 to 1969 he served as Deputy Assistant Secretary of the United States Department of Health, Education and Welfare.

MARC J. ROBERTS, born in 1943 in Bayonne, New Jersey, is associate professor of economics at Harvard University. He is the author of a number of articles on economics and pollution. He has served as consultant to the Environmental Protection Agency and the Ford Foundation Energy Policy Project.

NORMAN B. RYDER, born in 1923 in Canada, is professor of sociology and a faculty research associate in the Office of Population Research at Princeton University. He is the author, with C. F. Westoff, of *Reproduction in the United States: 1965* (1971), and of some sixty articles on formal demography and fertility measurement. He has served as editor of the *American Sociological Review,* and as president of the Population Association of America.

RICHARD ZECKHAUSER, born in 1940 in Philadelphia, Pennsylvania, is professor of political economy at the Kennedy School, Harvard University. He is the author of a number of articles on economic theory and public policy problems.